The Daybreak Boys

The Daybreak Boys

Essays on the Literature

of the

Beat Generation

by

Gregory Stephenson

Southern Illinois University Press

Carbondale

Copyright © 1990 by the Board of Trustees,
Southern Illinois University

Paperback edition 2009

All rights reserved

Printed in the United States of America

12 11 10 09   4 3 2 1

The Library of Congress has cataloged the hardcover edition as follows:

Stephenson, Gregory, 1947–
    The daybreak boys : essays on the literature of the beat
generation / by Gregory Stephenson.
        p. cm.
    Bibliography: p.
    Includes index.
      1. American literature—20th century—History and criticism.
    2. Beat generation. I. Title.
    PS228.B6874 1990
    810' .9' 0054—dc19
    ISBN-13: 978-0-8093-1564-2 (cloth)   88-27095
    ISBN-10: 0-8093-1564-5 (cloth)   CIP
    ISBN-13: 978-0-8093-2949-6 (paperback : alk. paper)
    ISBN-10: 0-8093-2949-2 (paperback : alk. paper)

The paper used in this publication meets the minimum requirements of
American National Standard for Information Sciences
–Permanence of Paper for Printed Library Materials, ANSI Z39.48-1992. ♾

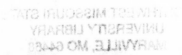

For

    my mother

    and my father

    and for Birgit

Contents

Daybreak Boys

Acknowledgments

I would like to express my gratitude to the following editors in whose publications certain of these essays first appeared:

Jim Burns of *Palantir,* V. J. Eaton of *The Literary Denim,* Rudi Horemans of *Restant,* Dave Moore of *The Kerouac Connection,* John O'Brien of *The Review of Contemporary Fiction,* Jeffery H. Weinberg of *Writers outside the Margin,* and Joy Walsh of Textile Bridge Press.

In addition, grateful acknowledgment is made to the following:

Palantir for permission to reprint "'Howl': A Reading," 23 (1983):11–18.

The Literary Denim: A Journal of Beat Literature for permission to reprint "'Howl': A Reading," 2 (1985):105–11.

Modern American Literature for permission to reprint "Infinite Resignation: Jack Kerouac's *Tristessa,*" a portion of "Circular Journey: Jack Kerouac's *Dulouz Legend,*" 7 (Winter 1983):16–17.

Restant: Review for Semiotic Theories and the Analysis of Texts for permission to reprint "The 'Spiritual Optics' of Lawrence Ferlinghetti," 13 (1985):117–29, and "Toward Organized Innocence: Richard Fariña's *Been Down So Long It Looks Like Up to Me,* 15 (1987):123–30.

The Kerouac Connection for permission to reprint "Homeward from Nowhere: Notes on the Novels of John Clellon Holmes," 15 (1988):20–27.

Gratitude is also expressed for the use of the following photographs:

The Daybreak Boys

1

Introduction

To find the Western path,
Right thro' the Gates of Wrath
I urge my way.
Sweet Mercy leads me on;
With soft repentant moan
I see the break of day.
                William Blake
                "Morning"

The title of this collection of essays on the writers of the Beat Generation is taken (respectfully and with kind permission) from John Clellon Holmes' original title for his novel *Go* (1952). Holmes has explained that the Daybreak Boys were "a river-gang on the New York waterfront of the 1840's," and that he felt it was "an appropriate title for a book about a new underground of young people, pioneering the search for what lay 'at the end of the night' (a phrase of Kerouac's)."[1] Holmes was prevented by his publishers from using the title because they had recently published a book titled *The Build-Up Boys*.

I have taken *The Daybreak Boys* as the title for this volume because I, too, found it apt and appropriate, suggestive of the essential qualities of the writings of the Beat Generation: their contraband, outlaw character, and their shared sense of a quest, of a journey through darkness to light. The phrase also resonates with images from the poetry of William Blake and William Butler Yeats. In Blake, night represents humankind's fallen state and all the forces of oppression and restraint that hold the human spirit in check, whereas "break of day," in the poem "Introduction" from *Songs of Experience*, symbolizes liberation through imagination and vision. Yeats employs the image "Daybreak and a candle-end" in "The Wild Old

Wicked Man" to express the end of one cycle (personal or historical) and the beginning of another. The themes of a journey through night to break of day, of personal and human liberation, of renewal arising out of exhaustion, and of beginning proceeding from ending are motifs that serve to link these essays.

Before proceeding to the individual essays, I think it would be useful to consider what the Beat Generation was, where they came from, and where they went.

According to Jack Kerouac, who originally named the Beat Generation (in a conversation with John Clellon Holmes in 1948) and who was its principal chronicler and representative, the Beat Generation had already begun to emerge during World War II. Kerouac recalled meeting hipsters in New York City in 1944 and feeling an affinity with them and sensing that some new consciousness was being born.

> Anyway, the hipsters, whose music was bop, they looked like criminals but they kept talking about the same things I liked, long outlines of personal experience and vision, nightlong confessions full of hope that had become illicit and repressed by war, stirrings, rumblings of a new soul (that same old human soul). And so Huncke appeared to us and said "I'm beat" with radiant light shining out of his despairing eyes . . . a word perhaps brought from some midwest carnival or junk cafeteria.[2]

Kerouac added to the word *beat* his own special understanding of it "as being to mean beatific."[3] In his novel *On the Road* (written 1951, published 1957), Kerouac uses the word in this personal sense in characterizing Dean Moriarty: "He was BEAT—the root, the soul of Beatific."[4] In the same novel, Kerouac also applies the phrase Beat Generation to the group of disaffected young men and women that his protagonist encounters and with whom he identifies: "rising from the underground, the sordid hipsters of America, a new beat generation that I was slowly joining" (*Road*, 46).[5]

The life of the Beat Generation can be divided into two distinct periods or phrases: the underground period, from 1944 to 1956; and the public period, from 1956 to 1962. These dates are, of course, approximate, but they reflect something of the changing mood and character of the Beat movement and of the gathering and the dispersal of its energies. Following Kerouac's recollection, I have taken 1944 as the point of beginning (though the roots of the phenomenon may be seen to lie even further in the past). Already in the early fifties, certain works of Beat literature, such as Kerouac's *The Town and the City* (1950), Holmes' *Go* (1952), and William S. Burroughs' *Junkie* (1953) began to appear (as well as works that dealt in part with hipsters or Beats, such as Chandler Brossard's *Who Walk In Darkness* [1951] and George Mandel's *Flee The Angry Strangers* [1952]). But it was not until after the Six Gallery reading in October 1955 and the publication of Allen Ginsberg's *Howl and Other Poems* in 1956 that the Beats began to attract public and media attention.

It is more difficult to set a precise date for the end of the Beat era since it was not marked by any particular event, but certainly by 1962 it was very much on the wane, at least in the form in which it had existed up to that time. I have chosen 1962 since that is the year in which Kerouac's *Big Sur* was published, marking an end to his personal quest and perhaps also representing an end to the Beat journey. An alternative terminal date might be the advent of the Vietnam War in 1965. Very shortly thereafter the Beats were to be succeeded by the freaks of the counterculture.

The two periods of Beat activity that I have outlined above may be seen to correspond to the two phases inherent in Kerouac's understanding of the word *beat* as being the root and soul of beatific. The first stage of this process is the Beat condition: weary, defeated, resigned, despondent, burdened with guilt and crime and sin, or caught in a blind search for understanding. This first stage was characterized by violence, desperation, confusion, and suffering among the early Beat group and their associates. During this period David Kammerer was killed; Lucien Carr, Neal Cassady, and Gregory Corso were incarcerated; Carl Solomon and Allen Ginsberg were institutionalized; Bill Cànnastra and Joan Burroughs were killed; William Burroughs was addicted to opiates and lived in exile; Michael McClure underwent his dark night of the soul; and Lawrence Ferlinghetti and Jack Kerouac pursued their separate and solitary wanderings.

The second, beatific stage of the movement is marked by the attainment of vision and by the communication of that vision to the human community. During this second period Kerouac and Ginsberg achieved, each in his own manner, their final spiritual orientations; Corso formulated and expressed his aesthetic and humanistic ideals; Burroughs rescued himself from terminal addiction and turned to active resistance against all forms of psychic parasitism; Michael McClure developed his biological mysticism; and Ferlinghetti found his voice and vision. And other Beat writers emerged from their prisons (Ray Bremser), from their private purgatories (Philip Lamantia), or from their underground obscurity (Gary Snyder, Philip Whalen, Diane DiPrima, Jack Micheline). They lifted their voices and they sang their visions. During this period the major works of the Beat Generation were printed and began to exert their transforming power on American and international art and society.

"By a generation," wrote F. Scott Fitzgerald, "I mean that reaction against the fathers which seems to occur about three times in a century. It is distinguished by a set of ideas, inherited in moderated form from the madmen and outlaws of the generation before; if it is a real generation it has its own leaders and spokesmen, and it draws into its orbit those born just before it and just after, whose ideas are less clear-cut and defiant."[6] By the terms of this definition, the Beats were, indeed, a generation as well as a movement. "One generation passeth away, and another generation cometh," says the Preacher in Ecclesiastes (1:3). And so it was with the Beat Generation, which evolved out of a confluence of influences — inheriting certain ideas from the "madmen and outlaws" of the previous generation and drawing from sources further back as well; and then, in its turn, bequeathing a legacy of ideas to be moderated by the generation that has followed it. The forebears, precursors, ancestors, and antecedents of the Beat Generation include the Lost Generation, hipsterism, bohemianism, radicalism, dadaism, and surrealism.

The Beat inheritance from the Lost Generation is less from its illustrious figures — such as Hemingway, Fitzgerald, and Dos Passos — than from the more radical wing: from Hart Crane, Harry Crosby, and Eugene Jolas; from the "Revolution of the Word" proclamation in the literary magazine *transition*; from the later Ezra Pound; and, in particular, from Henry Miller. The Lost Generation was divested of beliefs and ideals as a consequence of their participation in World War I or by the psychic shockwaves of that catastrophe. They felt themselves disillusioned, historically and culturally orphaned, and they rebelled against the manners and mores of their age. They explored and experimented; they sought new values; and they pioneered new modes of expression. In this sense, the parallels with the Beat Generation are nearly exact. The Beats were a product of the Second World War and of the cold war. They, too, rejected the social, political, religious, and artistic values of their time as outmoded and wholly inadequate; and they, too, sought new, viable ones to replace them. Interestingly, in an early article, Paul Bowles describes the future members of the Beat Generation as "the new lost generation."[7]

Lost Generation figures such as Crane, Crosby, and William Seabrook prefigured the Beats in their use of drugs, their sexual experimentation, and their pursuit of the extremes of experience. The cult of jazz was a widespread phenomenon already among the members of the Lost Generation, and it was the writers and poets of the Lost Generation from whom the Beats inherited both their attitude of social revolt and their penchant for radical literary experimentation. There is, then, a significant degree of continuity between the two generations. The principal difference between the Lost Generation and the Beats is the latter's intense interest in metaphysical issues — in mysticism and spirituality.

Another vital influence upon the Beat Generation was the phenomenon of hipsterism. The earliest hipsters seem to have appeared in the jazz clubs and teapads of Harlem in the late 1920s, though the hipster identity is perhaps as old as jazz itself. The term derives from the slang word *hip* or *hep,* meaning knowledge or awareness; thus, the hipster is one who knows or who is aware, an initiate. Hipsters originally consisted of jazz musicians and their fans and followers (black and white) who cultivated a distinctive style of dress, appearance, language, and behavior. Hipsterism represented an outlook, a code, a way of life that, in its attitudes toward sexuality and drugs, was in direct opposition to the predominant puritanical, Anglo-Saxon ethic of the society around it. Hip consciousness involved a necessary surface aloofness and imperturbability, a refusal to succumb to or to be affected by the agitations of the world, while at the same time it included a responsiveness, an openness to new and unusual experiences and ideas, together with the ability to let go, to lose oneself, to release the energies of the instincts and the spirit. It represented, in short, a sort of stoic hedonism. Hipsterism was centered upon the jazz experience, the ecstatic self-transcendence, the emotional catharsis, the exaltation and affirmation provided by creating or listening to jazz music (in something of the same manner that a tribe is centered upon a shaman or a cult upon a prophet).

Hipsterism was contemporaneous with the Lost Generation but only tangential to it. In contrast to most members of the Lost Generation who were of the middle class or the upper middle class, the hipsters were generally (though not exclusively) drawn from minority and working-class urban Americans. The hipsters sense of rebellion against and alienation from society was, as a consequence, more fundamental, more visceral and intuitive, and more sweeping than the more formulated revolt of the artists and intellectuals. The hipster milieu was socially very marginal and often bordered on and blended with that of the small-time criminal.

With the advent of bop in the early forties, hipsterism underwent certain stylistic changes; it became more hermetic and more of a mystique. Yet, it also became more widespread. Hipsterism attracted and influenced the avant-garde and bohemian coteries, while it continued to attract followers from its traditional social groups. By the middle and late forties, hipsterism constituted a sort of cultural underground throughout the United States with international affiliations. The Beats assumed the role of literary advocates for this subculture, embracing and, at the same time, interpreting and transforming it.

From bohemianism, the Beat Generation absorbed a spirit of unconventionality and of romantic egoism, an antimaterialist ethic, a sense of the inherent repressiveness and regimentation of society, and of the sterility and corruption of civilization, together with a faith in the redeeming, transforming power of art. From the radical tradition, particularly the Industrial Workers of the World, the Beats derived their general libertarian-egalitarian-populist-anarchist orientation and their strategy of forming the new society within the shell of the old. In contrast to the political radicals, though, the Beats proposed a revolt of the soul, a revolution of the spirit.

There are discernible traces, too, of a dadaist and a surrealist heritage in the Beat Generation. The Beats share with these movements several central qualities. First of all, the three movements were each artistic-social movements, groups of creative individuals protesting and rebelling against social values and institutions and against the fundamental premises of Western thought and culture. Like dadaism and surrealism, the Beats were subversive and revolutionary in a cultural-philosophical-aesthetic sense and not in an overtly political manner. In common with the dadaists and surrealists, the Beats regarded society as suffering from a collective psychosis, a madness whose symptoms manifested themselves in the form of the cold war; the threat of atomic annihilation; the consumerism, conformity, and passivity of the mass of people (with their unacknowledged secret anxieties and desires); the blandness, the aridity, and the insipidity of contemporary life; the lack of spiritual values; the erosion of human ideals and goals by self-satisfaction, indifference, compliance, and complacency; the unchallenged excesses of the bureaucracy, the military, the police, and the intelligence communities; the technology mania; and the insidious hypnotic powers of television and other mass media.

In the tradition of dadaism and surrealism, the Beat Generation cultivated extreme forms of artistic expression, employed radically experimental techniques, and broke the fetters of established taste, literary decorum, and legal censorship. Their ebullience and energy, high-spirits and wit, boisterousness and rambunctiousness, panache and zany humor are also reminiscent of the dadaists and surrealists; as is, too, their penchant for public provocation and outrage, for scandalous antics and controversy. A   of course, in the manner of dadaism and surrealism, the Beat Generation vehemently rejected traditional and conventional modes of thought and expression and sought instead to discover and explore, to reconceive and revalue, to invent new forms, and to create new visions.

The Beat Generation also has significant affinities with the transcendentalists, with Henry David Thoreau and Walt Whitman, as well as a kinship with certain poets of the English romantic movement, most notably William Blake and Percy Bysshe Shelley. Finally, though, their direct and ultimate progenitor is Shem the Penman, the archetypal rebel-writer of James Joyce's *Finnegans Wake*. The Beats are true descendants of Shem: the authentic expressions of the insurgent imagination and the embodiments of the prototypical refractory and outcast artist-hero who appears in every age and culture in opposition to the established agencies of materialism and convention. Like Shem the Penman, the Beats were outlawed, scorned, reviled, exiled, and driven to writing on their own bodies with an ink made of their excrements, recording a "broken heaventalk."

Influences and ancestors notwithstanding, the Beat Generation must be acknowledged as a distinct, original, and independent phenomenon — a native and intuitive response to the particular artistic, social, and spiritual climate of midcentury America. The character of the Beat Generation was a product of the conjunction of several maverick minds, and its spirit was a union of the individual torment and ferment of its founding figures.

7

The Beats were never (nor ever pretended or aspired to be) a homogenous or a consistent movement. They issued no manifestos, subscribed to no basic tenets, formulated no dogma, embraced no common theory, doctrine, or creed. Rather, their coherence was of another sort, one founded upon mutual sympathy and inspiration, upon affinity and a sense of kinship in personal and artistic matters. The Beat Generation may most accurately be characterized by a set of attitudes and values expressed with varying emphases and perspectives by the various writers identified with the movement. If there may be said to be an essential Beat ethos or common denominator of their writings, it would seem to be their concern with the issues of identity and vision—that is, with the knowledge of the true self and with the discovery or recovery of a true mode of perception.

Among the individual quests of the Beat writers to achieve identity and vision, there is a degree of overlap and intersection. And if the Beats are considered as a group, it is interesting to note the ways in which their writings supplement and complement each other.

In their writings the Beats share a sense that the crisis of Western civilization—as evinced by the appalling slaughter and devastation of the world wars, by the breakdown of values, the decay of ideals, and by the spiritual sterility of the modern world—is rooted in our culture's misguided faith in rationality and materialism, in the analytical faculties of the mind, in the narrow dogmatism of logical positivism and scientism, and in our identification with the conscious self, the ego. To redeem and revitalize the life of our culture and our individual lives, the Beats propose the cultivation of the energies of the body and the instincts, of the unconscious and the spirit.

Accordingly, the literature of the Beats characteristically records a descent into the darkness and the depths of the psyche—a confrontation with the baleful and the benevolent forces of these deeper strata; a struggle, sometimes prolonged or recurrent; and then ultimately, a renewal of the self and an ascending impulse toward equilibrium or transcendence.

This central and essential process of Beat consciousness—the downward quest for identity and vision, the beat-beatific movement, the journey through night to daybreak—may be seen to represent the foundation for certain common traits of the literature of the Beat Generation and for what may be termed the Beat aesthetic.

The common traits to which I refer include the treatment of the themes of criminality, obscenity, and madness in Beat writing. These qualities are aspects of the shadow or id, expressions of the dark underside of the psyche—the realm of appetite and chaos; the region of obscure, fecundating agencies and influences; the refuge of forbidden desires and repressed impulses; the abode of powers at once destructive and creative; the dominion of "the dark forces which we must obey before we can receive the light of illumination."[8]

For the Beats, the journey inward to the self inevitably means a passage through the "heart of darkness"; for it is there, strange to say, that the numinous may be discovered. Criminality, obscenity, madness, the breaking of boundaries, and the violation of taboos on the part of the Beats are not simply acts of rebellion against rationality and order; rather, these behaviors represent efforts to confront the destructiveness within and to transform it into creative energy. Like Fyodor Dostoyevsky and Graham Greene, the Beats apprehend the paradoxical affinity of the sinner and the saint; and like William Blake, they would effect a "marriage of heaven and hell" to reestablish a dialectic between the unconscious and the superconscious that we might evolve toward a true wholeness.

The treatment of these themes by Beat writers has been misconstrued by some critics as an endorsement or justification or glorification of violence and nihilism, which it most patently is not. What the Beats have given us in their writings is the record of a condition of spirit, or a state of soul that is the image of our common disease. And, more importantly, their individual, self-discovered remedies are most pertinent to the cure of our malady of mind and spirit. (Thomas Mann once wrote that "certain attainments of the soul and intellect are impossible without disease, without insanity, without spiritual crime, and the great invalids are crucified victims, sacrificed to humanity and its advancement, to the broadening of its feeling and knowledge—in short, to its more sublime health.")[9] Criminality, obscenity, and madness were, for the Beats, a necessary phase of personal, artistic, and spiritual development; and ultimately, these represented a mode of opposing the organized and collective criminality, the obscenity and madness of war, and the other social forms of human destructiveness.

It will be apparent to those familiar with the biographies of the writers of the Beat Generation that there is, in this regard, no question of a dilettantish or decadent dabbling in the forbidden, but rather, an intrepid exploration of frontiers of consciousness, often at a dire personal cost. For author and for reader alike, the writings of the Beats involve both a species of exorcism and an alchemical transmutation of the base to the precious — the dark to the bright.

In consonance with the centrality of the motif of transgression and transfiguration and with the motive power of their writing deriving from the unconscious, the individual writers of the Beat Generation evolved an aesthetic of spontaneous and untrammeled expression. Casting aside traditional literary forms and conventions as unnaturally restrictive and discarding established and hallowed notions of taste and decorum as being so many impedimenta, the Beat writers forged new forms that could accommodate the flow of energy (as imagery) from the deep regions of the psyche. Kerouac's spontaneous prose, Ginsberg's breath unit, Burroughs' cut-up method, and McClure's beast language are all radical attempts to articulate the language of the body and of the unconscious mind and to utter new and urgent truths. The Beat aesthetic proceeds from raw emotion, naked confession, and personal vision embodied in organic, intrinsic, and improvisatory forms. It attempts to clear the blockage of the conscious mind and to contact and to communicate the latent powers and potentialities of the self.

As has been the fate of virtually every radically innovative cultural movement, the Beat writers were vilified by a host of vicious, inept, and uncomprehending critics. Today we can only wonder at those supercilious, mean-spirited, hysterical, and obtuse attacks on the Beats. Perhaps, though, some of the reaction against the Beats can be attributed to the shock of their sudden and unforeseen appearance and their apparent anomalousness on the literary scene of the fifties.

Aside from the admirable and valuable work of a few novelists and poets, I do not think that it would be unfair or inaccurate to characterize the predominant mood of the generation of American writers who emerged during the early postwar period as one of caution and polite anxiety. Broadly speaking, the young writers of that time seem to group themselves into those who were carefully consolidating the advances made by the modernists of the twenties and the thirties and those were engaged in fighting a rearguard action against such advances. The general impression, in retrospect, seems to be one of faltering, of marking time, or less charitably, that of a failure of nerve. It was this sense of a prevailing lack of daring and boldness, of originality and individuality, and thus of real human relevance in midcentury American letters that Malcolm Cowley deplored in his article "Some Dangers to American Writing"[10] and that prompted Kenneth Rexroth's dismissal of the mainstream as "counterfeit" and "reactionary" and his endorsement of the Beat Generation writers (then largely unpublished or unknown) in his article "Disengagement: The Art of the Beat Generation."[11]

What distinguished the Beats from most of their American literary contemporaries was precisely their venturesomeness and their earnestness, together with their frankness and conviction. They did not seek to dissemble or disguise their personal anguish in the contrivances and artifices of technique and craft but strove to bare their hearts, to give spontaneous and honest expression to their deepest tensions and visions. Raw and unrefined, occasionally naive, even crude: there is a liberating, elemental vitality at the core of Beat writing in contrast to which much of the mainstream literature of the period seems affected, insipid, and insufficient.

The Beats were also clearly out of step with the more fashionable elements of the postwar avant-garde that so ardently embraced the sombre cerebralism of existentialism and that tendered such reverence for the work of Samuel Beckett. Despite certain apparent distinctions, the writings of the existentialists and of Beckett share a central mood of despair and futility, a sense of repugnance with the body, an atmosphere of tragic tedium, and an emphasis upon negation and emptiness. They also share an imagery of confinement and constriction, of inertia and immobility. In contrast, the literature of the Beats is informed by vigor and energy, by sensuality and by spiritual aspiration. There is in Beat writing a willingness to strive with and struggle against personal distress and adversity and to persevere in the quest for wholeness and meaning.

In this regard, I have often thought how telling is the juxtaposition of the following quintessential quotations from Samuel Beckett and Jack Kerouac:

> *Vladimir.* Well? Shall we go?
> *Estragon.* Yes, let's go.
> *They do not move.*
> CURTAIN[12]

> (*Waiting for Godot*)

"Sal, we gotta go and never stop going till we get there."
"Where we going, man?"
"I don't know but we gotta go."

(*Road,* 196)

In the first excerpt we are struck by the passivity and inertia of the characters. In the second, it is their impetus to action and movement and their essential optimism that are salient. If the characters in the second passage, Sal and Dean, seem perhaps confused or naive, they are still resolute and purposive; they believe in a goal and in a means to arrive at the goal, to "get there." Vladimir and Estragon cannot summon the will to move because they have no belief that movement will improve their lot or that things will be any better anywhere else than where they now stand. Nor do they believe that ultimately anything they do, or that anyone else does, any action or effort undertaken (other than the act of suicide, which they have just been discussing), can alter or mitigate the terrible circumstances of human existence. The ambient mood of the first quotation is one of impotence, futility, and resignation; that of the second is one of urgency, determination, and hope.

Movement, both outward and inward, physical and metaphysical, was the guiding principle of the Beats and "go!" their imperative. Kerouac wrote: "We sat and didn't know what to say; there was nothing to talk about any more. The only thing to do was go" (*Road,* 99). And, again: "We were leaving confusion and nonsense behind and performing our one noble function of the time, *move.* And we moved!" (*Road,* 111). Geographically the Beats traveled considerable distances: from coast to coast across the United States and from border to border, to the subarctic, to Mexico, to the jungles of South America, to Europe and North Africa, to India and the Orient. The real journey, though, was always inward—a passage through the arid zones and waste tracts, the wildernesses and nether regions of the self; the true course was always lightward, through night to daybreak.

"Go!" as an exhortation among the Beats (cf. *On the Road,* Holmes' *Go* and *The Horn*) denoted approval and encouragement and an incitement to the person to whom it was addressed to strive, to attempt, to put forth into action or creation. To "go" in this sense represented not an act of will but rather a relinquishing of all conscious impediments to natural energy, a surrender to the motive instinct or spirit within. There are obvious parallels here to Zen Buddhist beliefs and practices, and it was, of course, no accident that many of the Beats were attracted to Zen. To "go" was, for the Beats, to go with the flow of inspiration, to invent and discover, to bring forth and make manifest the latent powers of the deeper, truer self. To "go" far enough, long enough, and deep enough in this manner would be to become "gone" — to transcend the ego self and ultimately to transcend time and space and to attain identity with the infinite. There is a metaphysic implicit in movement; to move is an expression of faith in a final destination.

Fast-moving and far-ranging, the Beats shot like a comet across the placid cultural skies of the late fifties and the early sixties, outshining for a time many of the fixed stars and familiar constellations. Then, like a comet, they seemed to blaze away again. However, their exit was only apparent; in fact, they continued to pursue their eccentric orbit in the heavens; they had only become less visible. And cometlike too the Beats were an omen, their appearance portending the advent of a time of upheaval and change.

"We are in the vanguard of the new religion," prophesied Jack Kerouac, and he may yet be proven right.[13] What is clear, though, is that the Beats were in the vanguard of some sweeping and far-reaching changes in the arts and in the social sphere. The first phase of the impact of the Beat Generation was the creation of what may be called second generation Beats: younger men and women who, in the late fifties and early sixties, responded to and were inspired by the Beat Generation. Some notable second generation Beats would include Ed Sanders, Ken Kesey, Ted Berrigan, Emmet Grogan, Bob Dylan, Richard Brautigan, and Richard Fariña. Their writings and activities, together with those of the original Beats, helped to catalyze the second phase of the impact of the Beat Generation: the counterculture of the late sixties and the early seventies.

Beat Generation figures such as Allen Ginsberg, Neal Cassady, Michael McClure, and Gary Snyder were clearly prototypes, midwives and mentors to the freaks of the counterculture; and together with certain of the other Beats, they became cultural heroes of the new generation. The influence of the Beat Generation may be discerned in nearly every aspect of the counterculture: the rejection of commercial values and of conceptions of career and status; the interest in vision-inducing drugs as a mode of personal and spiritual exploration and the corresponding interest in Oriental and primitive religions; the centrality of rhythmic music and Dionysian ecstasy; the pacifist-anarchist political orientation (cf. Ginsberg, Ferlinghetti); the concern with ecology (cf. McClure, Snyder); the emphasis on natural and primitive models of community and the idea of tribalism (cf. Snyder); and of course, the prevalent antirational, antitechnological, visionary, and spiritual disposition of the freaks.

By the counterculture, in turn, were spawned the various forms of grass-roots activism that have since challenged and altered so many fundamental assumptions of American culture, from gender roles to foreign policy. The original impetus and the motive energy of many of these movements were already latent in the Beat Generation. And those grass-roots movements that are not directly traceable back to the Beats would in likelihood have been far less conceivable without the climate of revolt and protest created by the Beat Generation. It was the Beats who broke the crust and who ran the roadblocks, who blazed the trail, who breached the wall, and who primed the pump. At a crucial juncture of the postwar period, in a time of growing complacency and conformity, the Beats brought something untamed and disruptive onto the scene, sounding their "barbaric yawp" over the rooftops of "the tranquilized *Fifties*" (to use phrases from the poetry of Walt Whitman and Robert Lowell), and thus helping to shape the decades that followed.

The Beat Generation also contributed significantly toward the radical reorientation of American literature that took shape during the course of the postwar period. This reaction against accepted norms of poetry, drama, and the novel and against established standards of taste was given expression in journals such as *Evergreen Review, Kulchur, Black Mountain Review, Big Table,* and *Yugen,* and in anthologies such as *The New American Poetry: 1945–60, The Moderns, A Controversy of Poets, New American Story, Writers in Revolt, The New Writing in the USA, The New Naked Poetry,* and *The Poetics of the New American Poetry.*[14] Together with Charles Olson, Robert Duncan, the Black Mountain poets, and other literary mavericks, the Beats opened up postwar American literature to new modes and potentialities, to new visions and experiences.

Aside from the technical innovations of individual Beat writers, perhaps the signal contributions of the Beat Generation writers to the new American literary idiom were their aesthetic of unguarded, untrammeled expression; their emphasis on the personal-universal; their insis-

tence on feeling and emotion; and their resolutely antiformalist, antieli-
tist stance. The Beats wrote directly out of personal perception and
imagination on everyday themes and objects, on the forbidden and the
taboo, and on the sublime and the sacred; they drew upon the materials of
popular culture (radio, film, pulp magazines, comics) as a contemporary
mythology; they exploited the rhythms and imagery and emotive power
of the colloquial and the vernacular; they tapped the visions of the
unconscious mind; they explored open form and organic form; they
experimented with the relation of the written word to speech, to music,
and to sound; and they inquired into the magical properties of language
as incantation and mantra. The Beats enlarged the conceptions and
extended the boundaries of literary expression. They helped to break
down the barriers of censorship, to broaden the appeal of literature, to
reclaim the shamanistic-prophetic role for the artist in society; and they
were instrumental in transforming literary values and liberating human
vision.

Critical acceptance of the literature of the Beat Generation has been
slow in coming. After the initial savaging of the Beats by reviewers and
critics during the late fifties and the early sixties, there were years of
general neglect and dismissal. Gradually, though, one by one, serious
and sympathetic treatments of individual Beat Generation authors began
to appear in journals and as monographs, as critical studies, and as
biographies. Beginning recently, there seems at last to be a growing
recognition of the achievement of Beat writing. It is to be hoped that
finally the Beat Generation writers may be acknowledged for what,
indeed, they always were: heirs to and bearers of the essential American
traditions of advancing the boundaries of the frontier and of sustaining
the ongoing process of revolt and renewal.

The continuing appeal of the works of the Beat Generation is ascrib-
able, I believe, to their quality of authenticity. We respond to the truth of
their writings because we feel that they were created out of real pain and
hope, out of absolute personal necessity. We are excited and inspired by
them because they are informed by the very substance of life—by anguish
and anger and disgust and by sensuousness and tenderness and affirmation. The enduring value of these works lies in their particular pertinence
to the central issues of human existence, their probing of human identity,
and their quest for sacred vision. In the written records of their separate

searches, the Beats provide us with maps representing areas that we must all travel—soon or late, one way or another; it behoves us, therefore, to learn the terrain. The writings of the Beat Generation can serve to guide us on our common quest through the dark night and nightmare of our time and onward toward daybreak.

2

Circular Journey:

Jack Kerouac's Duluoz Legend

We shall not cease from exploration
And the end of all our exploring
Will be to arrive where we started
And know the place for the first time.
                              T. S. Eliot
                         "Little Gidding"

                    your goal
          is your starting place
                    Jack Kerouac
                   "113th Chorus"

*O*n the last page of his journal for 1948 to 1949 Jack Kerouac wrote, "We follow the turn of the road and it leads us on. Where? To actuality; ourselves, others and God."[1] The motif of the road and the journey is central to Kerouac's twelve-novel sequence, *The Duluoz Legend*; and the quests for identity, community, and spiritual knowledge ("ourselves, others and God") are the dominant themes of the series. *The Duluoz Legend* represents, then, a contemporary instance of the archetypal hero-quest, or the *bildungsreise*—the narrative of development, of education-into-life achieved by means of a journey.

Characteristically, the hero-quest consists of three essential movements: separation, initiation, and return.[2] It is a circular journey whose end is its own beginning. The biblical story of the prodigal son and the

Homeric epic of the wanderings of Odysseus are early instances of the archetype. In its later literary manifestations, in the form of the *bildungsroman*, the hero embarks upon a *bildungsreise* developing from an "unselfconscious adventurer in the outer world to a compulsive explorer of the world within" or from "picaro to confessor."[3] Whether as myth or as literature, the pattern of the adventure is essentially the same: the hero departs from home (where the character may already be a sort of stranger or exile) and undergoes a series of trials and ordeals in the world, often culminating in a descent to the underworld. The hero finally attains a vision or achieves atonement with God and then returns home, reintegrated into the community bringing a regenerating power or message to society and to the entire world.

My purpose in this chapter is to trace the stages of Kerouac's hero-quest or *bildungsreise* through the novels of *The Duluoz Legend*. The growth of the mind and spirit of the narrator and central figure, Jack Duluoz, may be understood most clearly by considering the component novels in order of composition rather than according to the interior chronology of the series. This is so because of the double-leveled structure of the novels by which the events of the past are described from and interpreted according to the perspective of the present. Although tension and dialectic interaction occur frequently between the levels of the narrative (between the picaro and the confessor), the particular illumination or lesson of each initiatory adventure is derived much more from the narrative present than from the narrative past of the novels.

The opening imagery of Kerouac's first novel, *The Town and the City* (written 1946–49), suggests the circular structure of *The Duluoz Legend* in its description of the course of the Merrimack River which flows placidly and turbulently seaward where it "enters an infinity of waters and is gone," and yet it is "continually fed and made to brim out of endless sources and unfathomable springs."[4] The movement of the novel is also circular: the story begins in the town of Galloway with the Martin family in a state of equilibrium and harmony (supported by images in the narrative of natural and of social order). The story then proceeds through the dislocation, dispersion, disintegration, and death of certain family members to return again to equilibrium as the remaining nucleus of the Martin family prepare to reintegrate themselves into the natural and social environment by buying a farm near Galloway. *The Town and the City* may be seen as a prelude to *The Duluoz Legend,* setting forth the essential themes and motifs of the novels that follow and prefiguring the organizational pattern of the series.

The earliest incarnation of Jack Duluoz is the character Peter Martin whose experiences are the central focus of *The Town and the City.* (The name of the protagonist-narrator varies from novel to novel because Kerouac was not permitted by his publishers "to use the same personae names in each work.")[5] Peter's *bildungsreise* takes him from his working-class home in a small mill town to an exclusive New England prep school, to an Ivy League university, across the sea on wartime voyages with the merchant marine, through the sordid world of petty criminals and junkies centered around New York's Times Square, and finally on a journey across the American continent. The nature of his acquired knowledge is largely negative—a process of disillusionment, uncertainty, self-contempt, and alienation—though he is also sustained by occasional glimpses at and glimmerings of transcendent meaning.

Peter's heroic ideals and noble aspirations are first subverted by his experiences as a high school athlete when he realizes that "to triumph was also to wreak havoc" (63). This knowledge is the inception of "a powerful disgust in his soul" (73) that culminates in a sense of himself as "some sort of impostor and stranger and scoundrel" (126). Ultimately, he renounces his athletic and educational ambitions (together with his family's expectations) and embarks on "a long journey" (498), a quest for self-definition and spiritual vision. The novel concludes with an image of Peter, alone in the night and the rain, traveling westward.

Underlying Peter's quest for an authentic identity and for new values and beliefs to replace those he has lost are fundamental metaphysical questions concerning the nature of human life and the problems of suffering and death. Death and suffering are recurrent motifs in *The Town and the City.* The theme of death is introduced in the cemetery scene in the opening paragraphs of the novel and reinforced by references to the deaths of children: "the late and beloved Julian," twin brother of Francis Martin (16), and the drowning of the Crouse boy. The theme gains increasing emphasis with the deaths of Alex Panos, the crews of the *Latham* and of the German submarine, the later sinking of the *Westminster,* and the murder of Waldo Meister and then culminates with the deaths of Charlie Martin and of the Martin father. A final summary image of death and suffering in the world occurs near the end of the book, during the fishing excursion, with the incident of "the struggling and enchained fish," torn and dying. For Peter, the doom of the fish, unexpected and terrible, is a metaphor for the human predicament. "This is what happens to all of us, this is what happens to all of us! . . . What are we going to do, where are we going to go, when do we all die like this? . . . What are we supposed to do in a suffering world . . . suffer?" (493–96). These questions provide the motive for Peter's quest, and they represent the central issues of *The Duluoz Legend.*

Despite the gravity of its themes, its preoccupation with death and suffering, *The Town and the City* is not a pessimistic book. The energy of its style and the exuberance and vitality of its characters serve to counter the more sombre qualities of the story; and although Kerouac does not pretend to be able to provide any final answers to the fundamental questions his novel proposes, he does affirm that there are answers which may be discovered. He also suggests two possible areas of enquiry or sources of meaning. The first is that of the natural order and the traditional social order described in the opening passages of the book — the rural way of life to which the Martin family returns at the end of the novel. This essentially conservative alternative represents "the forgotten medicine" alluded to in the symbolic advertisement "showing a man holding his head in despair" (343). The other possibility is represented by the urban-hipster milieu: sordid, degenerate, and cynical; yet somehow innocent, hopeful, and regenerative as well — a coterie of Dostoyevskian "sinner-saints" prophesying apocalypse and spiritual renewal.

The thematic resolution of the novel depends on both alternatives; Joe, the eldest Martin son, accepts the former, Peter the latter. Kerouac views both the deep harmonies of the rural order and the jarring dissonances of the urban frontier as viable responses to the spiritual crisis of our time, perhaps as complementary opposites. Kerouac's vision, from the outset, is inclusive rather than exclusive. In the spirit of the transcendentalists, the author seeks larger unities and affinities in apparent contradictions.

Contradictions, ambiguities, dualities, and new unities are also central to Kerouac's next novel in the Duluoz series, *On the Road* (written April 1951). The opposition and congruity, the tensions and latent attractions between such concepts, conditions, or modes of being as sensuality and spirituality, frenzy and serenity, mind and instinct, movement and stasis, the creative and the destructive, sin and grace, madness and sanity, time and eternity, and life and death provide the dynamics of the author's vision.

The Shrouded Traveler and the Protective City of the narrator's dream are key images of *On the Road*. As the narrator himself interprets the dream, the Shrouded Traveler is death, and the Protective City is heaven. We flee death and seek heaven; yet ironically, it is only through being overtaken by the Shrouded Traveler that we can hope to attain our goal; "death will overtake us before heaven." Thus our deepest terrors and our dearest wishes coincide. At the same time, according to Kerouac, our quest forward in life is motivated by our desire to return to the lost paradise of preexistence. "The one thing that we yearn for in our living days, that makes us sigh and groan and undergo sweet nauseas of all kinds, is the remembrance of some lost bliss that was probably experienced in the womb and can only be reproduced (though we hate to admit it) in death" (103).

Earthly life is an exile, then, from the paradise of spiritual existence, and each human soul is a pilgrim questing after true identity and authentic being. The portentous name of the narrator, Salvatore Paradise, suggests his pilgrim status and his quest for salvation and paradise. In this sense, *On the Road* is a sort of modern *Pilgrim's Progress* expressed not as allegory but as a picaresque narrative. The book effects a marriage between the pilgrim and the picaro.

In a contemporary version of John Bunyan's "Slough of Despond," Sal Paradise finds himself mired at the beginning of *On the Road* in a crisis of the self and of the spirit. He has recently been divorced, a "miserably weary split-up"; he is convaslescing from a "serious illness"; and he feels that "everything . . . [is] dead" (5). He realizes that a stage of his life has "reached the completion of its cycle and . . . [is] stultified." Sal is rescued from this state of mind and soul by his newly formed acquaintance with Dean Moriarty, in whom he recognizes a "long-lost brother" (10). Dean animates and inspires Sal and opens for him new vistas of experience: "I could hear a new call and see a new horizon" (11).

From the beginning, Dean is an ambiguous figure, a "holy conman," a hedonist and a mystic, an embodiment of the irrational energies of the unconscious, both destructive and regenerative (8). For Sal, Dean represents a teacher, a hero to be emulated, a man who possesses "the secret that we're all busting to find" (161). In contrast to Sal's negative, cynical, intellectual friends, Dean has a capacity for wonder and joy; he is "out of his mind with real belief" (99). In spite of Dean's less attractive aspects, his essential vision—his affirmation of life and God—is the very quality that Sal Paradise desires and requires in his own mind and spirit.

The motif of the journey and the road, already established in *The Town and the City,* becomes central in *On the Road.* The journey is a quest, the road a mode of initiation. The objects of the quest (selfhood, love, God, community) are elusive; they are grails that appear and vanish, are recovered and lost again, but toward whose final possession the quester approaches nearer and nearer.

The metaphor for the continuing quest, for the endless pursuit, is to be found in the bop improvisations to which Sal and Dean listen in reverence and rapture, receiving the sound like a sacrament. "There's always more, a little further—it never ends. They sought to find new phrases. . . . They writhed and twisted and blew. Every now and then a clear harmonic cry gave new suggestions of a tune that would someday be the only tune in the world and would raise men's souls to joy. They found it, they lost, they wrestled for it, they found it again . . ." (199). This pattern of finding, losing, and struggling to find again is germane not only to *On the Road* but to *The Duluoz Legend* as a whole.

Sal's initiation proceeds by single events and insights as he travels the road. In the beginning he is a tenderfoot, a neophyte, trying to thumb rides on untrafficked secondary highways, wearing the wrong sort of shoes for the rigors of the road. But he gains knowledge from his mistakes and setbacks, learning that his main error is in attempting to impose preconceived patterns onto experience, onto life. As his established habits of thought begin to break up, he experiences a temporary loss of identity, a sort of death and rebirth of the self, recognizing that he stands "at the dividing line" of his life between his past and his future (16).

Sal learns through his life on the road to receive and to extend kindness, and he is awakened to the beauty and mystery of landscapes and of human lives. In a vision he is told, "You're on the road to heaven" (150), but he learns too that at times it is also "the senseless nightmare road" (208). By the end of the novel Sal has reoriented himself; he has gained road savvy, and he has acquired a greater sense of inward aim and direction. The geographical distances he has traversed have had their corresponding measure in his psyche.

Two important themes are treated in *On the Road* which are extended and developed in the subsequent books of *The Duluoz Legend*: the theme of primitivism or the unconscious mind, and the beat-beatific theme.

Kerouac's variety of primitivism has affinities with D. H. Lawrence's "blood consciousness" and with the whole stream of romantic primitivism since Rousseau. It is also heir to the peculiarly American tendency to view civilization as insipid, squalid, and corrupt and to seek a refuge and a new beginning on the frontier. Kerouac's protagonists reject the materialist-rationalist assumptions of their culture, together with the concomitant imperatives of competition and acquisitiveness, and they cultivate instead the nonrational as a mode of knowledge, the unconscious as a source of wisdom and guidance.

Early in *On the Road*, Sal proclaims his preference for "the mad ones," and his friend and alter ego, Dean, most closely embodies those qualities he admires (9). Dean possesses the instincts, innocence, and energies of a modern, urban noble savage. Sal finds additional mentors, heroes, and prophets among the lowly and the outcast: the tramps and hoboes, the ragged, biblical wanderers of the road, the Chicano field-workers of the San Joaquin Valley, the bop musicians, the blacks, Mexicans, and Japanese of the Denver slums, the fellahin of Mexico. In contrast to the sterility and futility that Sal associates with the American dream at midcentury ("millions and millions hustling forever for a buck among themselves, the mad dream—grabbing, taking, giving, sighing, dying . . ." [89]), he experiences a simpler, truer, more pious, more joyous, and more meaningful way of life among the primitives and the fellahin. Sal is nourished and revitalized through contact with the energies and mysteries of primitives in the outer world and with the primitive inside himself. The revelations of the unconscious mind, the wisdom of the deepest sources of being, are of vital importance to the Duluoz hero throughout the series.

The second theme of *On the Road* which becomes a central tenet of *The Duluoz Legend* is Kerouac's conception of the beat-beatific process. At one point in the narrative Sal characterizes Dean as having become "by virtue of his enormous series of sins . . . the Idiot, the Imbecile, the Saint of the lot" (160). Sal then states, "He was BEAT—the root, the soul of Beatific" (161). For Kerouac the condition of weariness, emptiness, exhaustion, defeat, and surrender is antecedent to and causative of a state of blessedness. In being Beat the ego is diminished and in abeyance; the false, external self is temporarily weakened or circumvented, and the psyche thus becomes receptive, responsive to its deeper, more sublime aspects, the *imago Dei*—the innate spiritual wisdom of the unconscious. The structure of the story itself illustrates this process in Sal's movement from despair and stultification to new belief and affirmation and in Dean's development from manic, sensual frenzy to mystic resignation and ragged saintliness.

Despite the degree of renewal and reorientation experienced by Sal Paradise in *On the Road,* his quest, as the elegiac ending of the novel suggests, remains ultimately unfulfilled. The pursuit of "IT," of "the moment when you know all and everything is decided forever" (107), of the Protective City, and of the symbolic lost father are continuing quests that are to be chronicled and resolved in the subsequent volumes of *The Duluoz Legend.*

Although Kerouac has himself characterized his novels as picaresque narratives, the category is really far too narrow to encompass with any accuracy the sort of fiction he wrote.[6] It is true that the episodic structure of his novels and their celebration of the peripatetic life of roguish protagonists (their amorous adventures, their sensual excesses, their travels, their rascalities and thieveries) gives them certain affinities with the picaresque narrative, but the essential seriousness and universality of their concerns shows them to be misclassified within the conventions of that genre. Stylistically, structurally, and thematically, Kerouac's novels much more closely resemble the German romantic novel—intellectual autobiographies in fictional form containing the explorations of individual consciousness as epitomized by Goethe's novels *Wilhelm Meisters Lehrjahre* and *Wilhelm Meisters Wanderjahre.* Goethe was, in fact, one of Kerouac's literary idols, and repeated references are made to him and to his works, including *Wilhelm Meister,* in Kerouac's writings.[7] Kerouac may also have absorbed the German influence through his extensive and intensive reading of Melville, who was indebted to German novelistic theory and example.[8] The books of *The Duluoz Legend* are contemporary expressions of the spirit of the romantic novel, the "boundless novel," as Novalis called it—the commodious, inclusive, comprehensive novel of consciousness; the record of the growth of an individual mind and spirit integrating "transcripts of inward life," reflections, reminiscences, sentiments, dialogues, descriptions, visions, and dreams; combining styles and genres in order to embody, insofar as possible, the totality and the truth of human life.

Kerouac's third novel, *Visions of Cody* (written October 1951), is his most boldly experimental, combining stream-of-consciousness narrative, mythopoeic portraiture, realism, and surrealism. There is considerable overlap between characters and incidents in *Visions of Cody* and *On the Road,* but the effect, rather than being repetitious, is supplementary and complementary. *Visions of Cody* explores in greater detail the relationship between Sal Paradise and Dean Moriarty (here named Jack Duluoz and Cody Pomeray) providing much additional information about and many additional insights into the lives of both characters. Where the focus of *On the Road* was primarily on action and event, that of *Visions of Cody* is primarily on inner action, on thought, sentiment, memory, and imagination.

At the outset of the book, Duluoz is haunted, even obsessed, by his memories of Cody. He is reminded of him by various places and ambiences, from subway toilets to church interiors; he sees him in other people and he dreams of him. Cody is for him the ultimate referent of all data. Duluoz then relates/creates Cody's history: his boyhood and his young manhood, his adventures, his feats, his humiliations, his sufferings, and his aspirations. Traveling west, Duluoz unites again with Cody, and they exchange confessions and confidences before embarking on a final journey together; then they separate again. Their ultimate parting is for Duluoz a final resigning and relinquishing of his friend, without rancor but not without regret. He surrenders Cody to fate and to the world and submits himself to the same vicissitudes.

In mythicizing Cody, it is apparent that Duluoz is projecting his own ideal self, a lost original self that he identifies with his lost brother (whom he eulogizes later in *Visions of Gerard*). "Cody is the brother I lost," he states and repeats as a refrain.[9] He seeks in Cody deliverance from his desperation, his death-obsession and near-madness, his "emotional congestion . . . fear and self-horror" (92). In the end he learns from Cody a code of acceptance and of resignation and an optimism founded upon an awareness of the tragedy of life.

In keeping with the beat-beatific process, Duluoz ultimately attains a new spiritual perspective derived from his despondency: "My heart broke in the general despair and opened inwards to the Lord . . ." (368). He internalizes Cody's code: "I not only accept loss forever, I am made of loss" (397). In place of the elegiac tone of the ending of *On the Road,* with its imagery of gathering darkness and nightfall and loss, *Visions of Cody* concludes with the dawn of a new day, with the morning star not the evening star, with an affirmation of the daily renewal of creation and of the hopefulness of human work in the world, and with the promise of eternity: "a bird crossing the dawn in search of the mountain cross and the sea beyond the city at the end of the land" (398).

These potent, final images of bird, dawn, and cross that draw together and extend the meanings and themes of *Visions of Cody* are also important motifs in Kerouac's next novel, *Doctor Sax* (written June 1952). *Doctor Sax* is a gothic, apocalyptic novel of childhood fantasy, and at the same time, a realistic story of growing up and of sexual awakening in a small town in America during the 1930s. It is both a private myth—a rite of passage, an initiation story—and a cosmic myth: a parable of the universal struggle of light and darkness, good and evil, the divine and the demonic. Accordingly the imagery of the novel is both personal and archetypal mingling private fantasy figures, such as the eponymous Doctor Sax, Count Condu, and Amadeus Baroque, with archetypal images such as the Flood, the Great World Snake, and the Bird of Paradise.

The poles of the novel are the opposing worlds of the day and the night and those of adults and of children. The day world is safe and solid, the realm of innocent games and play, while the night world is haunted and full of evil and terror. At the same time, however, the world of the day is drab, dull, bleak, and routine, while the world of the night is glamorous, mysterious, and heroic. The former is, of course, associated with the conscious, rational mind while the latter suggests the unconscious. Similarly, the adult world is represented as a fallen world, a world of work and care, disappointment and disillusion, while the children's world is one of grace, energy, courage, and imagination. The problem for Jackie Duluoz is how to avoid the negative and destructive aspects of these conflicting realms, preserving what is worthy and of value from his childhood, while facing the biological inevitabilities and social impera-tives of growing up.

This problem is resolved through a sequence of near falls, of minor falls, of lapses, and of recoveries that occur in the course of the narrative and culminate in the final scene of the novel. The earliest of these is

Jackie's career as "the Black Thief," when knowingly and yet only half-intentionally, he terrorizes his friend Dicky Hampshire by means of a campaign of thefts, sinister notes, and alarming lies. After his discovery and confession, he wonders, "What foolish power had I discovered and been possessed by?"[10] This is Jackie's first recognition of the capacity for evil that exists within himself and of its power to overthrow and overwhelm the self. Other incidents of a similar nature occur when he inadvertently hurts his friends Ernie Malo and Cy Ladeau, and when he harms his sister, Nin. Such events demonstrate to him the corruptive nature of the external world — the fallen world which can so insidiously alter and distort our intentions and affections, transforming good to evil and love to hate.

Jackie's attraction to or unintentional support of evil and destruction reasserts itself once again during the flood. At first, perceiving the flood in purely personal terms, he sees it as a judgment and a deliverance. He heralds and applauds it: "We wanted the Flood to pierce thru and drown the world, the horrible adult routine world" (171), and he admires "the black madness, the demoniac river — it's eating away everything that ever hated us" (174). But having witnessed the carnage and catastrophe wrought by the rampaging water, he identifies the flood with the Snake and with Satan and recognizes it as "an evil monster bent on devouring everyone" (179).

Jackie's final recognition and repudiation of his own inherent destructive tendencies occur in his fantasy of the Great World Snake when he acknowledges the Snake as an aspect of himself. "I looked down to face my horror, my tormentor, my mad-face demon mirror of myself" (238). In this realization there is both ultimate terror and liberating knowledge; for if a human mind can conceive an infernal snake, it can also conceive a heavenly bird to destroy the snake. The psyche contains sufficient counterforce to overcome its own negative tendencies. This sudden reversal of action — the reestablishment of order and harmony after dire threat — may be seen as metaphoric parallel to the beat-beatific process. The technique prefigures the final crisis and resolution of *The Duluoz Legend* in the penultimate novel of the series, *Big Sur.* There, too, rescue and deliverance are achieved through the self-adjusting, restorative, redemptive powers of the unconscious mind.

The theme of victory over inherent evil in *Doctor Sax* is extended and supported by the novel's concomitant motifs of death and sexuality.

27

The image of death pervades the story and instances of death are frequent. The funerals, ghosts, and sudden deaths of relatives, neighbors, and classmates culminate in the episode titled "The Night the Man with the Watermelon Died." This dreadful and grotesque event terrifies Jackie (reanimating the trauma of his brother's death) and causes him to regress for a time to a near infantile state, seeking security in the warmth of his mother's bed. His retreat is brief, however, and he soon reemerges revitalized. "I had conquered death and stored up new life" (148).

Jackie's psychic victory over death has its parallel in his victory over lust. Sexual imagery is also recurrent throughout the story (often interwoven or in close association with the death motif): the aura of sexuality in Destouches' candy store, the masturbatory orgies with the gang, the phallic imagery of the snake and the river, the sex-crazed moron Zaza, the portentous death of Jackie's dog, Beauty, on the night that he discovers sex. Jackie's climactic confrontation with his own sexuality, with the growing libidinous impulses that threaten to overmaster him, takes the form of the symbolic encounter with the Snake. The Snake is defeated and Jackie gains a rose as his prize.

Unchecked and unchanneled, the sexual appetite can become deleterious, an impediment to psychic development. Jackie has avoided the impulse of pure animality, of imbecilic self-gratification epitomized by Zaza. Through his awareness of the potential evil and the destructiveness inherent in sexuality, he gains the ability to refine sex into love. This is the meaning of the rose: the elevation of sexuality as romantic love and the ennoblement of erotic love as a ladder to spiritual love. This sublimation of sexuality emblematized by the rose is further reinforced by the pun on "ding dong" by which the penis becomes transmuted into the sound of church bells on Easter morning (244–45). [11]

Jackie's climactic adventure, passing through a night of terror into a dawn of new hope and new life, has again, obvious affinities with the beat-beatific process. The Lenten season and the advent of Easter provide an appropriate background for Jackie's rite of passage from childhood to adolescence. He is born into the adult world but without having relinquished the imaginative, visionary gifts of childhood. These are the qualities that will make him an artist and a seeker later in life but will also make him an outsider and a stranger in the human community. Although Jackie will eventually cease to read *The Shadow* or *Star Western*, he will continue to honor and to preserve in his adult life the sense of mystery and wonder, the qualities of romance and imagination that these magazines embody. The writing of the book *Doctor Sax* by an older, grown-up Jack Duluoz is itself a fruit and a proof of this.

The changing character of Doctor Sax in the course of the story is a measure of the maturation of Jackie's psyche during this transitional period. In the beginning Sax is closely associated with death; he is "the dark figure in the corner" at funeral wakes (4). In his early lineaments he is virtually indistinguishable from Count Condu. Retaining his sinister appearance and accoutrements (his shroud, for example), Sax later becomes a benevolent figure: "my friend . . . my ghost, personal angel, private shadow, secret lover" (34) and "King of Anti Evil" (169). In the end Sax stands revealed in the plain light of day as something of an impostor, rather ridiculous and ineffectual but still stalwart and valiant in his way. (As Jackie's power grows, that of Doctor Sax diminishes.) After this, Sax reaches his ultimate refinement, a benign spirit of childhood who "only deals in glee" (245). Sax's evolution from funeral gloom to child's glee is a metaphoric counterpart to Jackie's inner development from death-obsessed childhood to life-affirming, young adulthood.

Doctor Sax is a keystone of *The Duluoz Legend* and the clearest expression of Kerouac's essential literary aesthetic: the imaginative record of his life as a mode of archetypal autobiography. The informing myth of *Doctor Sax* is both personal and cosmic in that the individual consciousness is a microcosm corresponding in its constituents and in its development to the macrocosm. As Jackie has overcome his negative and destructive tendencies, so ultimately and in the same manner will the world and the universe do likewise. *Doctor Sax* provides the essential mythic context for the other novels of *The Duluoz Legend* and represents a thematic précis of the series.

The theme of romantic love introduced in the conclusion of *Doctor Sax* becomes the central theme of the next three novels of the Duluoz series: *Maggie Cassidy, The Subterraneans,* and *Tristessa.* The first of these, *Maggie Cassidy* (written February 1953), treats Jack Duluoz' first adolescent love affair. The narrative point of view of the story (as always in the novels of *The Duluoz Legend*) is that of an unspecified time subsequent to the actual events of the novel. There is considerable tension between the rueful, woeful tone and commentary of the narrator (whose perspective is one of disillusion, despair, and sorrow) and the hopeful idealism of the younger self depicted by the narrator. To emphasize this contrast Kerouac employs a frame device, enclosing the central first-person narrative within a third-person narrative that forms the beginning and the end of the novel.

The opening pages of *Maggie Cassidy* introduce, in metaphoric terms, the three main themes of the novel: time, vanity, and love. Time is suggested by the temporal setting New Year's Eve, by memories and anticipations of the boys, and by the narrator's comments on the scene, isolating it in its poignancy, its fragility, and its transience. The theme of vanity is introduced (as we come to understand by the end of the novel) by the refrain of the song "Jack o diamonds." The theme of love begins in the anticipation in the minds of the boys as they proceed through the snow to their first dance at the Rex Ballroom.

Time (as Kerouac makes clear from the beginning of the novel) is relentless, implacable, and destructive. Only the death that time makes inevitable can free us from time. Clocks are a recurring motif in the narrative: the clock at school under which Jack has his rendezvous with Pauline Cole, the "green electric clock" of the Duluoz family, a paint-chipped reminder of loss and mortality, and the clock against which Jack races at his track meets.[12] The river, also a recurring image, marks another sort of time, that of the natural cycle. The river is lovely with "ululating lap and purl," but it is also quietly erosive: "eating night, stealing sand, sneaky" (27). In winter the river flows on in "tiny milky rivulets of icy Time" (62) indifferently reflecting the stars, and in spring the "sad tragic waters" mix the "sweet breath" of new growth with the stink of sewage and the rank odors of rot (121).

Vanity in *Maggie Cassidy* is represented in the gratification and the fulfillment of the ego at the expense of the self. The result is a corrosion of the spirit, a loss of grace and hope. Jack's vanity expresses itself in his ambitions and vainglory. He persists in wearing his thick wool football-letter sweater to school and to his party despite its discomforts. "It was huge, uncomfortable, too hot, I hung braced in its horrible corset of wool for hours on end day after day" (46). He is literally and figuratively stifled by his pride and vanity. Heedlessly and callously, Jack strives to realize his dream of becoming "a big hero of New York with rosy features and white teeth . . . incarnation of the American Super Dream Winner" (132). He dreams of achieving esteem, sophistication, and wealth and of having "a wife beautiful beyond belief, not Maggie, some gorgeous new blonde gold sexpot of starry perfection" (133). In the end he loses everything; he disappoints and betrays everyone including himself.

Only through love are time and the failings and follies of human vanity redeemable; but Jack forsakes Maggie's love in favor of the "whirlpools of new litter and glitter" of his dreams and ambitions (149). He rejects the innocence and the simplicity of hometown Maggie with "her porch . . . her river, her night" for the glamour and the meretricious enticements of the big city (149). He chooses to be Jack of Diamonds, not Jack of Hearts. The ultimate consequences of his choice are manifested in the last sections of the novel, which, taking place three years later and narrated in the third person, complete the frame and form an epilogue to the story. Jack has become "cold-hearted" as Maggie at once perceives; he has become insensitive, egotistical, predatory, and cynical (155). The prophecy of the opening page of the book, *"Jack o diamonds you'll be my downfall,"* has been fulfilled. Far from having become the "American Super Dream Winner" he wished to be, he is a spiritual pauper; he is "the garageman" as mechanical as the automobiles he repairs for a living (151–54).

Hope for a resurgence for Jack Duluoz resides in the tone of regret and remorse that characterizes the narrator of *Maggie Cassidy,* who is, of course, also Duluoz—a chastened, more mature Duluoz. Clearly, the narrator is very keenly aware of the causes and consequences of his own downfall, and in his self-examination and self-reproach there is an implicit resolve to expiate his errors and to amend his life. In this way the act of writing, of recalling, and of recording is a part of the continuing process of the death and rebirth of the self and the growth of the mind, heart, and spirit that is the central theme of *The Duluoz Legend.*

Nowhere else in *The Duluoz Legend* is the relationship between life and literature, between the ego self and the deep self, more central than in *The Subterraneans* (written October 1953). The novel is the darkest, bleakest, most desperate book of the series; its unrelieved gloom and pain are redeemed only by its unrelenting honesty. Again, the dominant theme is vanity: the obsessive pursuit of the transient and trivial, the capitulation to what is most base in the mind, the neglect and the forfeiture of that which is true and good and meaningful in life. And again, it is romantic love which provides the catalyst for struggle and self-confrontation by the Duluoz hero.

Leo Percepied, the narrator of *The Subterraneans,* describes himself as "an unself-confident man, at the same time an egomaniac" and as "nervous and many leveled and not in the least one-souled."[13] Although he is not cynical or "cold-hearted" as the garageman at the conclusion of *Maggie Cassidy* (it's fourteen years later, he is now thirty-one years old), Percepied is desperately self-divided and self-destructive. Even as he seeks solace and redemption in love, he repels and rejects love in the intensity of his wounded rage and pain. He is like a drowning person fighting off a rescuer, but both the drowning person and the rescuer are here aspects of a single, disunited, discordant psyche.

The central theme of the novel is embodied in the action of the story and is stated repeatedly in the narrative by the characters Leo and his paramour Mardou. It is during her breakdown that Mardou first understands the essential duplicity of the human condition when she suddenly sees "all the tricks people have because they want anything but serene understanding of just what there is, which is after all so much . . ." (46). Later in his pain and dejection, Leo arrives at a similar realization: "O God the whole host and foolish illusion and entire rigamarole and madness that we erect in the place of one love . . ." (125). The final statement of the theme occurs at the end of the novel when Mardou sadly reproaches Leo for his abuse of her affections: "I think you're like me— you want one love—like, men have the essence in the woman, there's an essence and the man has it in his hand, but rushes off to build big constructions" (151). Subsequently, while writing his account of their affair, Leo remembers her words and acknowledges both his failure and his betrayal. "And so having had the essence of her love now I erect big word constructions and thereby betray it really— . . . still I have to rush off and construct construct—for nothing—" (23).

Throughout *The Subterraneans* there are references to angels, to the Garden of Eden, to paradise (Mardou lives on "Heavenly Lane"), to a Reichian paradise of "lovers going to and fro beneath the boughs in the Forest of Arden of the World" (64), and to anticipations of an idyll of simple living in Mexico—all of which are images of the psyche's aspiration to a state of grace and of wholeness. In sad contrast to such heavens of hope there is the hell of actual human life as depicted in the story: a hell founded upon pettiness, selfishness, jealousy, pride, anger, fear, mistrust, suffering, and harm. Leo's "red flame" of malice and rage is the token of his personal inferno (101, 139). By his thoughts and actions in the course of the story, he feeds that flame and builds (as William Blake says) "a hell in heaven's despite," ending forsaken and ashamed and alone, wandering despondently in an internal darkness. "Suddenly the streets were so bleak, the people passing so beastly, the lights so unnecessary just to illumine this . . . this cutting world" (148). Thus, Kerouac shows us, do we evade the ultimate reality or truth of ourselves and of the world in favor of fleeting pleasures, destructive passions, and empty vanities. Hell is not, as Sartre stated, "other people"; rather, hell is ourselves.

At the very end of the novel, Leo says: "And I go home having lost her love. And write this book" (152). My understanding is not that he believes that art transcends life or that bad life can be transformed into good literature and thereby be justified. The act of writing represents for the Duluoz figure a process of refinement—a mode of confronting, learning from, and correcting his failings and mistakes. The Duluoz character is always writing retrospectively, so that all the scrupulous self-criticism and relentless self-exposure of his confessions has been assimilated, comprehended, and surpassed at the time of writing or becomes so during the act of writing. In this spirit the narrator, Leo, of *The Subterraneans* records the "truth" of his affair with Mardou (1). He is motivated not by vanity but by shame and regret: "The pain which impels me to write this even while I don't want to, the pain which won't be eased by the writing of this but heightened, but which will be redeemed . . ." (25). Such writing has the character of penance and it moves implicitly towards regeneration. Among the wreckage of his heart and his hope the writer-hero hunts such salvage as may be recovered, sifting the rubble for the materials from which new and enduring love and belief can be built.

Tristessa (written summer 1955) concludes what may be seen as a subtrilogy within *The Duluoz Legend* on the theme of romantic love. The story takes place in Mexico City at a time subsequent to the events of *The Subterraneans* (it is not specified how long afterwards, perhaps a year or two) and extends and resolves certain motifs from that book. *Tristessa* treats two parallel themes: the search for faith and the quest for human love. The two themes unite in the figure of Tristessa, the novel's main character. Tristessa, a prostitute and morphine addict who lives in the slums of Mexico City, is both the object of the narrator's religious adoration and of his romantic-erotic affections. The conflicts and tensions of the story derive from the essentially contradictory nature of his relations to her.

Tristessa embodies the beat-beatific condition. Despite the suffering and degradation of her life and the squalor of her surroundings, she maintains a "Virgin Mary resignation."[14] The narrator, Jack Duluoz, is moved by her simple piety and childlike faith, her charity and her inviolable purity. He believes that "her enlightenment is perfect" (74) and sees her as "a Madonna" (28), "an Angel" (74), "a Saint" (75), and as "holy Tristessa" (111).

As a fellahin Madonna, Tristessa is the fulfillment of earlier female figures in Kerouac's novels, such as Terri, the Chicana field-worker in *On the Road*. Mardou Fox, the Negro-Indian woman of *The Subterraneans* was admired by the narrator as "a troubled poor innocent spirit" (43) and was revered for her "spiritual suffering . . . her soul showing out radiant as an angel" (50). Despite Tristessa's dissoluteness, she is as innocent and as unself-consciously erotic as Maggie Cassidy. The Kerouac hero continually seeks more than a romantic involvement with these figures, endeavoring to assimilate the knowledge they embody. They represent manifestations of his anima, the unconscious feminine counterpart of his psyche, the force with which he must unite to achieve wholeness.

Jack Duluoz combines the instincts of a mystic with the appetites of a sensualist. In *Tristessa* he has embraced Buddhism and has renounced passion and desire in favor of compassion and celibacy. "I have sworn off lust with women—sworn off lust for lust's sake—sworn off sexuality and the inhibiting impulse" (27). His commitment to the tenets and practices of his Buddhist beliefs is, however, tenuous and problematic. His affinities with the teachings of the Buddha are largely limited to his unreserved acceptance of the first of the Four Noble Truths: All life is suffering. In consequence, he seeks oblivion rather than transcendence.

The narrator's visit to Tristessa's room on a rainy summer night is the most directly, yet naturally, allegorical part of the story. The details of the room assume a larger dimension of meaning and represent both a microcosm of the dichotomies and contradictions of existence and a projection of Duluoz' inner conflicts. The pious prostitutes; the devout thief; the bitch chihuahua in heat; the humble hen and haughty cock; the innocent, flea-afflicted, and meat-devouring kitten; the contemplative, transcendental dove; the squalor of the room and its icon of the Virgin: all are emblematic of the irreconcilable duality of the world, its disunity and its disharmony.

The two parts of *Tristessa,* "Trembling and Chaste" and "A Year Later . . . ," reflect the narrator's interior movement from metaphysical anguish and the desperation of unrequited love to his final resignation. He recognizes, by the novel's end, the ultimate incompatibility of himself and Tristessa, and he accepts his loss of her. He also resigns himself to the futility of his struggle to reconcile or transcend duality and to his continuing bewilderment in the face of the enigma of existence.

Having made such resignation—a self-surrender, a yielding up to the will of God—he is now in a position to receive grace. His blessing takes the form of a consolatory knowledge that consciousness is "a movie by God" in which humans and God are unified by their mutual suffering (125). His life is also restored to him as a continuing potential for realization and illumination. He will travel onward into the world, perhaps to find a woman to love, perhaps to find a faith by which to live.

The thematic resolution of *Tristessa* is achieved through the narrator's acceptance of an impasse, of uncertainty, and his acceptance of suffering as a way of knowledge. In this manner, the novel prefigures the ultimate thematic resolution of *The Duluoz Legend* in *Big Sur* and *Vanity of Duluoz* in which other degrees of suffering are endured, other levels of resignation made, and other stages of grace received.

According to the internal chronology of *The Duluoz Legend, Visions of Gerard* (written January 1956) is the first novel in the series, recording the very earliest recollections of Jack "Ti Jean" Duluoz. These memories are mainly of his third and fourth years of life, and they mostly concern his older brother, Gerard Duluoz, who died at the age of nine when the narrator was four. The life and death of Gerard had a profound effect upon the child Jack Duluoz, and the influence of the events of those years persists very deeply and powerfully in his later life. At the age of thirty-three, Duluoz explores his memories of Gerard in order to take a bearing on his own life, to confirm the course that he is following, and to rediscover and reaffirm the original motive power of his journey.

In *Visions of Gerard* we can clearly discern the roots of the dualism and the self-division of the Duluoz figure, perhaps because the narrator's visions of his childhood are equally in the nature of re-visions — retrospective projections of his present conflicts. The thematic division and opposition in the novel concerns the most essential issue of human life: belief in the primacy of the spiritual or of the material world. The first condition is embodied by the saintly child Gerard and the latter by Emil Duluoz, father to Gerard and Ti Jean.

Gerard is depicted as a mystic whose visions of transcendent reality are expressed in an imagery and a language that unites elements of Catholicism and Buddhism. He experiences visions of heaven and the Virgin Mary and ecstatic realizations of the infinite bliss of the Void. His brief life is characterized by piety and humility and by acts of compassion and charity. He counsels Ti Jean against anger and violence, urging kindness and forgiveness and imparting "teachings of tenderness" and "immortal *idealism*" to him.[15]

Gerard perceives the essential ephemerality of the material world, seeing its forms and events as "clouds . . . that materialize and then travel and then go, dematerialized, in one vast planet emptiness" (7) or "like the smoke that comes out of Papa's pipe" — "The pictures that the smoke makes" (25). Appalled and grieved by the cruelty and suffering attendant upon existence in the physical world, his death seems almost a conscious decision, an act of will: "He'll go to heaven . . . enough of this beastliness and compromising gluttony and compensating muck" (17). By his steadfast faith and through his suffering and death, Gerard is delivered to "that snowy somewhere and rosy nowhere" (22) beyond all pain and separation, to "that Pure Land" of eternal bright perfection. This deliverance is seen by the narrator as the "attainment, the glory of Gerard" (105).

Emil Duluoz, on the other hand, is "a citizen of the raving world," a skeptic, a fatalist, "a tragic philosopher" (68). He is a vital, complex man: energetic, hard-working, fun-loving, a dedicated provider and a loving father to his family, a genial extrovert and a sensitive, sorrowing, stoical man — his "sadness . . . held inside by a manly grace, or rather, a manly brace" (83). Though good-humored, kindly, and sympathetic himself, he sees life as "a jungle" where the only law is "eat or be eaten. We eat now, later on the worms eat us" (16). Innocent Gerard laments the cruelty of life saying, "I dont want it to be like this, me." Emil sadly replies, "Though you want or not, it is" (17). Emil is an inveterate (though reluctant) realist; he derives no solace from religion, and in his despondence and desperation at his son's suffering and imminent death, he can only rage against God for "doin business under conditions like that, we'll never win" (69). After the death of Gerard, Emil refuses to be consoled or comforted by well-meaning relatives and others who attempt to convince him that it's for the best, that Gerard is delivered from his pain and is in heaven. Instead, Emil remains bleakly, grimly fatalistic in the anguish of his grief and his bereavement, acknowledging only that, "It ends like it ends" (95). Like his son he is martyred by life, but unlike Gerard for whom death is a victory and a reward, life and death alike are a futility and a defeat for Emil.

The theme of spirituality and worldliness in *Visions of Gerard* is further sustained by the configuration of minor characters: the penitents of the St. Louis de France church at their devotions, the town roisterers at their drunken revelry, the pious nuns and priests, the irreverent jesting workers, Père Lalumière ("The Light") with his message of hope and comfort, Mr. Groscorp ("Fatbody") "eating his necessitous Samsara dinner" (102). A similar division exists in the mind of the narrator who, despite his best hagiographic intentions and mystical aspirations, cannot repress his affection for such sots and reprobates as Caribou, Manuel, and Old Bull Baloon. Their wild inebriate glee, Jack Duluoz admits, is "enough to make a man believe in Rabelais and Khayyam and throw the Bible and the Sutras and the dry Precepts away" (54).

For thirty-three year old Jack Duluoz, the novel is at its deepest level a dialogue of the self and the spirit, a symbolic encounter (through the medium of the characters in the story) between the materialist-sensualist traits of his personality and his spiritual appetites and inclinations. The result of the dialogue is not conclusive; there is no final resolution of the conflict but simply a commitment to continue the struggle, a renewed determination to strive toward regeneration and sanctification following the example of Gerard. In terms of Jack Duluoz' quest for identity, Gerard represents for him his own lost, original self. "For the first four years of my life, while he lived, I was not Ti Jean Duluoz, I was Gerard . . ." (7). He feels that if he could now recover and sustain his vision of Gerard, he would in some essential way be transformed, no longer doubting and despairing: "I would deliver no more obloquies and curse at my damned earth . . . could I resolve in me to keep his fixed-in-memory face free of running off from me—" (7). Jack Duluoz' quest is not only an outward, forward journey but also an inward, backward journey to recover his lost identity and thereby to restore his self to wholeness.

The quest continues: the journey proceeds in the next novel of the Duluoz series *The Dharma Bums* (written November 1957). The road followed by Duluoz (here named Ray Smith) in the events and adventures recorded in this narrative alters from railroad to highway to forest and mountain trails; but whatever the route, the Eightfold Path of the Buddha is the true line of travel in the story. As the title indicates, the narrator, Ray Smith, has embraced a sort of holy itinerancy (as prophesied in *On the Road*) traveling as "a religious wanderer . . . an oldtime bhiku in modern clothes wandering the world . . . in order to turn the wheel of the True Meaning, or Dharma. . . ."[16] Again, there is a tension between the narrative levels of the story: "I was very devout in those days and practising my religious devotions almost to perfection. Since then I've become a little hypocritical about my lip-service and a little tired and cynical. Because now I am grown so old and neutral . . ." (6).

In *The Dharma Bums* the narrator encounters a new mentor, Japhy Ryder, who represents the most complete and constructive hero of *The Duluoz Legend.* Unlike such figures as Dean Moriarty, Mardou Fox, or Tristessa who are beset and beleaguered with woes and worries and who are victims of society and of their own flaws and failings, Japhy Ryder is a man who has carefully formulated the nature of his revolt against society, and he accomplishes it by means of positive alternatives. He is a man who has liberated himself from convention, materialism, and ambition and who lives by his own code of virtues and values. Japhy is a sort of universal man: poet, scholar, naturalist, woodsman, mountaineer, logger, merchant seaman, a devout Buddhist, an individualist, an idealist—disciplined and independent, vigorous and self-reliant. In sum, as the narrator characterizes him, there is "something earnest and strong and humanly hopeful about him . . ." (14); he is "a great new hero of American culture" (27).

In addition to the road and the journey as continuing metaphors for the life and the quest of the Duluoz figure, in *The Dharma Bums* Kerouac employs mountains as a natural, traditional symbol for spiritual knowledge and attainment (cf., for example, *The Ascent of Mount Carmel* by St. John of the Cross and *The Seven Storey Mountain* by Thomas Merton). The image is first introduced into the novel through the poems of Han Shan (to whom the novel is dedicated). Japhy is translating the thousand-year-old *Cold Mountain* poems of this Chinese poet and he reads some verses to Ray: "Climbing up Cold Mountain path, Cold Mountain path goes on and on. . . . Who can leap the world's ties and sit with me among white clouds?" (18–19). In this way mountains become associated with transcendent vision. Soon after, while mountain climbing, Japhy and Ray agree that "a mountain is a Buddha" (54, 57). Similarly, at a later point in the narrative, the two friends consider a series of ancient Chinese devotional drawings depicting the gradual ascent of "the mountain of enlightenment" (137).

The development or interior growth of Ray Smith in the story may be measured by his ascent of two mountains: the Matterhorn in the High Sierras and Desolation Peak in the Cascades. Smith fails in his attempt to scale the Matterhorn, stopping when fear overtakes him and immobilizes him only a few hundred feet short of the summit. He learns from his failure, however, and vows to use his new knowledge to complete the climb at the next opportunity. Although he does not return to the Matterhorn, he spends the next summer as a Forest Service lookout on the summit of Desolation Peak. There, alone, "among white clouds," like Han Shan, he recognizes "the Great Truth Cloud, Dharmamega, the ultimate goal" (183). On Desolation Peak he experiences spiritual revelations and forms resolutions for a new life. At the end of his term of service as a lookout he prepares to descend and reenter the life of the world, hoping to hold in his mind "the vision of the freedom of eternity . . ." (190), the hope, and the love of God that he has gained in silence and solitude on his mountaintop.

The joyous affirmation of *The Dharma Bums* — its exuberance, zest, and humor, its wisdom and optimism — would seem to make it a fitting conclusion to *The Duluoz Legend*. With Ray Smith, having found and followed what is for him the Path of Truth, we might consider that the Duluoz quest is ended and that the character might at last cease wandering and return home. But as Wordsworth asks in *The Prelude*: "Where is that favoured being who hath held / That course unchecked, unerring and untired / In one perpetual progress smooth and bright?" (14, 133–35). More often, the poet remarks, the direction of our lives instead consists of "lapse and hesitating choice, / And backward wanderings along thorny ways." Or, as Ray Smith observes, "Trails are like that: you're floating along in a Shakespearean Arden paradise and expect to see nymphs and fluteboys, then suddenly you're struggling in a hot broiling sun of hell in dust and nettles and poison oak . . . just like life" (166). There is, as Kerouac learned from bitter experience, no final safety or sanctuary this side of heaven (or nirvana), and all that the traveler can do is to keep following the trail whether "floating along" in Arden or "struggling in . . . hell." Given, then, the uncertain nature of trails and of lives, the Duluoz character is not to be spared from errs and checks, from lapses and backward wanderings, nor from hot, dry, infernal torments.

Among contemplatives and mystics the phenomenon of acedia is a not uncommon occurrence. Acedia is an affliction of the spirit—a spiritual dryness that manifests itself as melancholia, apathy, listlessness, and a sense of disillusionment and disgust with life. Suddenly occurring without immediate cause and overwhelming in its effect, it can be a major impediment on the path of spiritual development. The condition may persist for years and then cease as suddenly and inexplicably as it began. In *Desolation Angels* (written fall 1956, summer 1961), Jack Duluoz is overtaken and overthrown by acedia, by despair and existential nausea, and only his momentum keeps him stumbling desperately forward on his quest.

The novel begins with Duluoz alone on Desolation Peak, searching his soul in the solitude of his mountain hermitage and resolving at last to imitate the infinite serenity of the Void, to "pass through everything . . . make no comments, complaints, criticisms, appraisals, avowals, sayings, shooting stars of thought, just *flow, flow,* be you all, be you what it is, it is only what it always is. . . ."[17] At first he feels liberated and renewed by this "Great Knowing," this "Awakening," but he soon discovers that he cannot sustain an attitude of tranquil nondiscrimination in the face of the thousandfold sorrows and enticements, the complexity and the ordinary boredom of life in the world.

Indeed, far from maintaining a calm, detached neutrality, as he has determined to do, Duluoz instead seems to lose all poise and equilibrium upon his return to the world and is overwhelmed by a sense of the hopeless sorrow of human endeavor on "the dark sad earth" where "I will die, and you will die, and we will all die, and even the stars will fade out one after another in time" (126–27). Burlesque shows, jazz clubs, bars, parties, and horse-racing tracks are all seen as microcosms of human futility, ephemeral distractions that cannot disguise or mitigate the ineluctable truth of our lives: "everybody reaching for the next kick and there's no next kick . . . We're all shuffling and waiting for nothing" (141–42). The descent from the mountain proves to be an irresistable, accelerating descent of the spirit, lower and lower, down to utter despair.

The frenetic movement and frantic activity of *Desolation Angels* rivals even the blurred, breakneck, transcontinental journeys of *On the Road.*

Duluoz races back and forth, to and fro, from border to border and from coast to coast, down to Mexico and back up, then back down and up again, traveling across the Atlantic to pass swiftly through North Africa and Europe, then returning in headlong haste, scurrying toward another country, another coast, another city. He is like a windup walking-toy with too much torque on its spring, spinning wildly, moving out of control. The road for him no longer represents a mode of knowledge, a means to "actuality; ourselves, others and God," but rather a mad, broken flight from terror and despair, a desperate search for a place to hide from the horror of his life. Marijuana, peyote, *majoun,* kif, opium, quantities of wine and whiskey no longer kindle his vision or afford him joy or even assuage his dread. His life road has reached "a complete turnabout" (229), a "turning from a youthful brave sense of adventure to a complete nausea concerning experience in the world at large, a *revulsion* in all the six senses" (309). From the Way, the Noble Path, Deluoz has made an unfortunate and unforeseen detour onto backroads into the badlands.

The root of Duluoz' despondency is the still unanswered, unresolved question that originally impelled his quest: the problem of pain, the question of suffering and death. For despite his Buddhism, Duluoz has not found an adequate or acceptable solution: "Every night I still ask the Lord 'Why?' and haven't heard a decent answer yet" (54). Pain and death are recurrent motifs in the story: the "murder" of the mouse in the lookout cabin, the doomed chickens and doves in their crates in China-town, the accidental devastation of an ant colony in Mexico, the squalor and sorrow and suffering of the poor, the essential pain and plight of each human life, the cruel and bloody chronicle of human history. Each of these distresses and appalls Duluoz, and each instance embodies the problem for him. "Why did God do it?" he asks bewildered and horrified (311). "What do we all do in this life?" (365). These are essentially the same questions asked by Peter Martin in *The Town and the City.* Buddhism does not really seem to have satisfied Duluoz' deepest spiritual needs; it has not provided him with a tenable, workable, liveable answer to his anguished question.

In contrast to his own crumbling belief and his acedia, Duluoz admires and envies "believing" men, and that word becomes his highest term of praise. Observing a counterman in a Seattle restaurant, he notes, "Here's a real believing man who won't let the night discourage him—

the awful brokenbottle sexless gut night—" (128). Or, looking at a stranger, he remarks wistfully, "Ah, there's a happy man, he dresses well, goes believingly down the morning street—" (129). His friend Cody still exemplifies to Duluoz the very model of "a *believing* man" who despite misfortunes and anxieties remains undiscouraged and continues to strive (152). "I see the furious and believing earnestness of his moves . . . and that's because he believes in God (God bless him)—" (214); "He is a *believer* in life and *wants* to go to Heaven . . ." (368). Other esteemed believers in *Desolation Angels* include Simon Darlovsky with his belief in love, Raphael Urso with his ideals of poetry and beauty, and David D'Angeli, the Catholic poet with his quiet, passionate faith. But notwithstanding his appreciation of and respect for such believers or his desire to be like them, to share their belief, Duluoz is increasingly immured in despair, seeing "nothing but horror and terror everywhere" (305) and lamenting that "the whole thing's hopeless in the end" (252).

Harried and haggard of spirit, Duluoz acknowledges the futility of "roaming around with your baggage from state to state each one worse deeper into the darkness of the fearful heart" (312). After a final frenzy of travel, he comes to rest at last, finding sanctuary living with his mother in a country house. He renounces the road and accepts "a peaceful sorrow at home," hoping to amend his life (372). But we may not always choose when to move and when to stand still, when to follow and when to forsake the road, and further distances remain for Duluoz to travel "deeper into the darkness of the fearful heart."

The downward momentum of *Desolation Angels* continues and culminates in *Big Sur* (written October 1961), which is, according to internal chronology, the concluding novel of the series. *Big Sur* records Duluoz' descent into hell and the final cataclysmic battle waged in his mind and spirit between the forces of darkness and the forces of light, the destructive and the creative, the demonic and the divine. The infernal experiences he undergoes transform him, enabling him to receive grace and vision, the ultimate boons of the hero-quest.

The imagery of the opening chapter defines the terms of the struggle in which Duluoz is engaged: the church bells awakening him from drunken sleep in his skid-row hotel room, the shouts of a Salvation Army preacher in the street below naming Satan as the agent of destruction and the cause of alcoholism. Alcohol, Duluoz' last refuge from and remedy against the horror and pain of life, has inevitably proven to be a treacherous trap, an insidious poison—itself a cause of misery, sickness, and fear. In a similar manner, as the story proceeds, Duluoz is progressively stripped of his ego defenses and self-deceptions, his illusions and evasions, until only the basic, naked alternatives of his psyche remain: damnation or salvation, death or life.

Although the distances traveled in *Big Sur* are not great, Duluoz' movements have the same abrupt aimlessness and rashness as those in *Desolation Angels*. He flees from the city to the forest at Big Sur, back to the city, then back again to Big Sur—always in a desperate, precipitate retreat from terror, ending finally in a compulsive nightlong walking back and forth from the cabin to the creek in "an insane revolving automatic directionless circle of anxiety" (163). The road metaphor, so central to the series, is carried through here as Duluoz acknowledges that he has "hit the end of the trail" (2). He refers to the portents of his incipient madness as "signposts" (31, 32, 54) and hitchhikes a last torturous stretch of highway, no longer an eager, young quester but a bleary, woeful bum with an "expression of horror" on his face (37). After having traveled for so long and for so many miles of bad road ("three years of drunken hopelessness which is a physical and spiritual and metaphysical hopelessness" [4]), Duluoz has arrived at a dead end. As foretold in his dream long ago, the Shrouded Traveler has overtaken him before he could reach the Protective City.

A central paradox in the evolution of the spirit, in the process of self-realization, is that outward loss often represents inward gain, that outward defeat may be inward victory. This mysterious action of the spirit is very much akin to Kerouac's concept of the beat-beatific process. Accordingly, in his most desperate hour, Duluoz receives a vision of the Cross that sustains him in his struggle; and in the end, the forces of darkness and destruction are vanquished and he is delivered and redeemed. Unwittingly and unwillingly, Duluoz has accomplished a sort of downward ascent, undergone what may be seen as a death and rebirth of the self: "I . . . let myself go into death and the Cross: as soon as that happens, I slowly sink back into life—" (169). In this sense, in leading nowhere the road has led to the very center of the world, to the very heart of being. Duluoz has reached the gates of the Protective City after all.

Duluoz' mid-life rite of passage in *Big Sur* has significant parallels with his earlier night journey in *Doctor Sax*. In both instances a night of supernatural terror ends in a morning of blessing and rescue. The fearful atmosphere of the forest at Big Sur (a projection of Duluoz' tortured mind) and his paranoic terror of witches, warlocks, monsters, ghosts, devils, and evil spirits vividly recall the spiders, monsters, gnomes, and nightmare horrors of the Castle. Jackie's encounter with the Great World Snake in *Doctor Sax* is repeated in *Big Sur* when Duluoz is confronted with "that horror of snake emptiness" (120). Jackie and Doctor Sax oppose the satanic powers of the world in the Wizard night; Duluoz struggles alone in the night against a host of demons. Both times the climax occurs by means of a sudden, unexpected reversal of circumstances involving a divine agency. In the first instance, young Jackie is rescued by the Bird of Paradise; in the second, Duluoz is rescued by his vision of the Cross. In both cases a critical threshold of the life journey is passed, a higher degree of initiation attained, and a new awareness achieved.

In retrospect, we can see that in subtle ways Duluoz' vision of the Cross in *Big Sur* is prefigured in earlier books in the series. The Cross appears as a final image in both *Visions of Cody* and in *Doctor Sax,* while Christian references and iconography are motifs in both *Tristessa* and *Visions of Gerard.* In *The Dharma Bums,* Japhy objects to Ray Smith's residual Christianity and predicts: "I can just see you on your deathbed kissing the cross like some old Karamazov or like our old friend Dwight Goddard who spent his life as a Buddhist and suddenly returned to Christianity in his last days" (159). And in *Desolation Angels,* David D'Angeli's dramatic return to Catholicism and Duluoz' wearing of the Cross around his neck for three days ("I feel strangely glad—" [163]) can be seen to suggest the final spiritual resolution that takes place in *Big Sur.*

The resolution of Duluoz' spiritual quest through his vision of the Cross leads to the resolutions of the other quests. The quest for the lost father, the lost brother, the true self, the Protective City, for community and communion are all implicitly fulfilled in finding God, in whom the father, the true self, and the Protective City are all to be found. The vision of the Cross provides Duluoz with an answer to the problem of pain, the question of suffering and death; for the Cross of Christ represents the triumph of the spirit over pain and death. In following the example of Christ, suffering becomes sanctified—an act of sacrifice and penance, a mode of refining the spirit and of attaining to God. The road, the sacred Way, the Noble Path, has in the end become for Duluoz the *Via Cruxis,* the Way of the Cross.

Vanity of Duluoz (written 1967), Kerouac's last novel, unites the beginning and the end of the saga and completes the circular journey of the narrator-protagonist. The narrative present of the book is 1967, nearly seven years after the events recorded in *Big Sur,* but the story concerns the period 1935 to 1946—essentially the same years and events of Duluoz' adolescence and young manhood treated in *The Town and the City,* the author's first novel. As in the other novels of the series, there is a dynamic tension between the nature of the episodes and the circumstances that comprise the story and the attitude and the tone of the narrator, Jack Duluoz, who recounts them. In this instance the contrasts are those of youthful idealism with middle-aged disillusionment and of naive hope and belief with mature fortitude and resolution.

As the title suggests, the central theme of the novel is vanity—a theme that has been explored in the earlier novels of the series, including *Maggie Cassidy, The Subterraneans,* and *Visions of Gerard.* Here Kerouac considers vanity as a personal and as a universal human problem encompassing pride and conceit and the worthlessness, emptiness, and futility of worldly ambition and achievement. In the context of the narrator's Christian perspective, vanity is essentially equivalent to the concept of maya, or illusion, in Buddhism. Like maya, vanity is seen by Kerouac to be the ignorant, deluded state of ego consciousness with all its myriad desires that serve to distract and to separate the self from awareness of true being, from the life of the spirit. Throughout the novel, deliberate echoes and evocations of the somber, admonitory mood of the Preacher in Ecclesiastes appear, but more often the narrator employs a special humor, a sort of merry cynicism, a spoofing, flippant tone, in exposing and ridiculing his own and the world's vanities. Beneath the facetiousness, burlesquing, and surface crankiness, though, the narrator's voice is one of compassion and genuine humility.

The heroism of athletics is the first of the vanities treated in the book. We follow the development of Duluoz as a star athlete from early sandlot games to collegiate, Ivy League playing. Eventually, disillusioned and bitter, he quits the varsity team in pursuit of other dreams. His idealized ambition of being a pipe-smoking collegian he likewise abandons, finding it empty and unsatisfying. Dreaming of adventure and glory at sea during wartime, he serves in the merchant marine, only to discover the brutal, senseless, and banal nature of war. Determined then to become a writer, he sacrifices, struggles, and strives for years, succeeds at last in having his novel published, and then realizes that this, too, is without real meaning or fulfillment—a hollow triumph, a mere vanity. Drugs, decadence, love affairs, involvement in murder, jail, various jobs, marriage, divorce, and the death of his father complete Duluoz' adventurous education in the transitory joys, the ceaseless toiling and suffering, and the vexation and vanity of human life.

Kerouac further extends the theme of vanity in the novel through vignettes of others characters' lives and vain pursuits: Franz Mueller, who finds death where he had hoped to fulfill his greatest desire; Claude de Maubris, whose search for a "New Vision" leads him ultimately to commit murder; Duluoz' father, whose hopes and dreams for his son end in bitter disappointment and whose own eager life ends in pain and lingering death. But, as in Ecclesiastes, only worldly desires and strivings are shown by the author to be futile and fruitless; like the Preacher, he concludes by affirming God and the life of faith.

Vanity of Duluoz may be seen as a direct extension of the experience of *Big Sur.* The narrator has taken the ultimate nakedness of nerve and spirit, which were the necessary requisites to his vision of the Cross, and has applied that perspective to his early life. In this sense, the book is as much about his present life as it is about his past life. We also learn a good deal about the narrator's present life and thoughts as he makes asides, comments, and digressions, weaving present and past together into a single fabric. Duluoz has returned to his hometown and has married a hometown girl, the sister of his childhood friend Sabbas Savakis (called Alexander Panos in *The Town and the City*). He is off the road (except in a metaphorical sense) and settled, living as a writer. He has embraced Catholicism, his childhood religion. In nearly every sense, he has returned to where he began.

The vital difference, of course, between Duluoz before the road and after the road resides in his inner transformation from desperate doubter to determined believer. He has attained the vision he sought; he has found an answer to the question that perplexed and tormented him. And through his writing, he can communicate his vision and insight, share his boons with his community and with the world. This is not to say that Duluoz is by any means a paragon or a saint, nor does he pretend to be a religious teacher or a spiritual guide. He is simply a man who after long seeking has found a faith by which to live. He has his weaknesses and his doubts; he falters and wavers in his faith. But he clings to his vision; he affirms his belief. He has learned to accept the duality and the ambiguity of the created world, its beauty and its cruelty, its perfections and its imperfections. Like Pascal, whom he quotes, Duluoz sees in the world the image but no more than the image, the reflection, of God. He acknowledges the mysteries of divine grace and mercy that persist in the midst of "this gnashing world": "Because we know that the brutish, the mean-hearted, the Mad Dog creation has a side of compassionate mercy in it . . . we have seen the brutal creation send us the Son of Man. . . ."[18] He recognizes the ultimate ephemerality of error and evil, comparing the fevers, travails, and sorrows of the world to "awful fogs, in which, yet, the central joyous source of the universe there still hung on, clear as a bell ever, the pearl of Heaven flaming on high" (252). His own vision may remain partially obscured by such fogs, but he seeks the light, knowing that it is there, affirming it.

The Cross of Christ is an important and unifying image in *Vanity of Duluoz*. Kerouac first mentions it in the dedication of the book to his wife, whose name, Stavroula, means "from the cross." He alludes to the Cross again near the middle of the novel (131) and near the end of the book where it is considered in its metaphysical and personal significance. The Cross serves in the book as an emblem of redemption, the sign of a dimension of being beyond vanity. It is the answer to the central question of *The Duluoz Legend* asked by Peter Martin in the first book of the series: "What are we supposed to do in a suffering world . . . suffer?" (*Town*, 496). Duluoz has long known suffering to be inevitable, inherent in existence, but he has come to know that suffering endured in a spirit of faith becomes a creative act, a process of regeneration and sanctification. And although Duluoz is not free of uncertainties and reservations, though he still wrestles with his angel, the vision of the Cross persists, permeating his life. "Yet I saw the cross just then when I closed my eyes after writing all this. I cant escape its mysterious penetration into all this brutality. I just simply SEE it all the time . . ." (276). His is a faith as unremitting and inexorable as doubt, as relentless as despair.

Vanity of Duluoz serves both as a conclusion and as a coda to *The Duluoz Legend,* bringing the quest to a final ending, returning the traveler home and recapitulating the main movement of the series in miniature. Beginning with complaint, the book ends in resignation and affirmation. At the end of the novel, Kerouac leaves the reader balanced between seemingly contradictory kinds of wisdom or paths of conduct, which, upon reflection, may be seen as complementary. "All is vanity" (279), the author quotes, concluding his story, and then advises: "Forget it. . . . Go to sleep. Tomorrow's another day" (280). The deliberate juxtaposition of these two observations, implying two views of life, two ways of living, I understand to mean that although we must recognize the ultimate futility of all our earthly endeavors which only end in death and dust, we must also strive each day and believe in the meaningfulness of our actions, hoping that our works and days may be redeemed in eternity. We must at once resign ourselves and continue to strive; we must act but renounce the fruits of our actions. (This attitude has close affinities with Hindu and Buddhist thought.) In a similar manner, the final images of the book, those of chalice and wine, suggest conflicting yet complementary meanings.

The author concludes by saying, "*Hic calix!* . . . 'Here's the chalice,' and make sure there's wine in it" (280). Again, symbolically, Kerouac indicates the balance we must attain, the fulcrum we must find in order to live whole and self-actualized lives. The chalice and wine images, given partly in Latin, allude to the act of consecration during the Roman Catholic Mass when the priest fills the monstrance with wine and, quoting the words of Christ at the Last Supper, pronounces, "Hic est enim calix sanguinis mei. . . ." ("This is the chalice of my blood. . . ."). Thus, the imagery refers to Christ's sacrifice and the establishment of the new covenant. But there is also a playful reference here to the more obvious levels of meaning of cup and wine—vinous joy or the wine of life. (Cup and wine as metaphors for life and joy are recurrent in *The Rubáiyát of Omar Khayyám,* a poem that Kerouac alludes to and quotes from elsewhere in *The Duluoz Legend.* There may be a glancing allusion to Omar Khayyám here.)

These two interpretations of the imagery may be reconciled if we recall the words of the Preacher in Ecclesiastes: "Be not righteous overmuch, neither make thyself overwise. . . . Be not wicked overmuch, neither be thou foolish" (7:16–17). In common with the Preacher, Kerouac cautions us that we must not despise joy or the life of the world though we cultivate the life of the spirit; for should we do so, our hearts will become dry and arid and our spirits will surely fail. We must remember that life is holy and that joy is also a sacrament. Finally, I also see in the image of the chalice an allusion to the Grail, symbolically the object of every quest and the symbol of divine mystery and grace. In declaring *"Hic calix!"* the author pronounces the Grail attained, the quest ended.

At the outset of his quest, anticipating the adventures ahead of him and the ultimate fulfillment of his spiritual aspirations, the narrator stated, "Somewhere along the line I knew there'd be girls, visions, everything; somewhere along the line the pearl would be handed to me" (*Road,* 11). And indeed, along the road there were girls and visions and much more, and Duluoz did at last gain possession of "the pearl." But the pearl was not handed to him. Like a natural pearl, it was formed within him, vitally, slowly, out of his living body and his pain. Layer by layer it grew, and when fully formed it proved to be "the pearl of great price" (Matthew 13:46).

Jack Kerouac's *Duluoz Legend* revives and renews vital psychological and spiritual patterns in our culture. Duluoz is a modern hero in the personal-universal tradition of myth and mythic literature. Not merely the alter ego of the author, he is a generic, representative man, a contemporary Everyman. We need not, of course, embrace the particular form of Duluoz' religious convictions in order to be enlarged and nourished by his insights and vision. He enacts our common quest and, in having undertaken the journey to selfhood, encourages us to do the same by counseling us, cautioning us, instilling in us something of his reverence, his sincerity, and his courage. In this dark and desperate era of human history, *The Duluoz Legend* represents an affirmation of the liberating, creative, redemptive forces within humankind, a prophecy of the universal heart and of the victory of the human spirit.

3

Allen Ginsberg's "Howl": A Reading

Where there is no vision, the people perish.
Proverbs 29:18

Much madness is divinest sense
To a discerning eye;
Much sense the starkest madness.
'Tis the majority
In all this, as all, prevails.
Assent, and you are sane;
Demur, —you're straightway dangerous,
And handled with a chain.
Emily Dickinson
"Much Madness"

*I*n the quarter century since its publication by City Lights Books, Allen Ginsberg's poem "Howl" has been reviled and admired but has received little serious critical attention. Reviewers and critics have generally emphasized the social or political aspects of the poem, its breakthrough use of obscenity and its allusions to homosexuality, or its long-line, free-verse, open form. For these reasons "Howl" is already being relegated to the status of a literary artifact. I want to consider "Howl" as essentially a record of psychic process and to indicate its relationship to spiritual and literary traditions and to archetypal patterns.

The concept of transcendence with the inherent problems of how to achieve it and where it leaves us afterward is central to romantic literature. This complex has its antecedents in Orphism, Pythagorean-ism, Platonism, heterodox Judaism, Gnosticism, and the mystical tradition. "Howl" expresses a contemporary confrontation with the concept of transcendence and examines the personal and social consequences of trying to achieve and return from the state of transcendence.

Transcendence and its attendant problems may be summarized in this way: the poet, for a visionary instant, transcends the realm of the actual into the realm of the ideal, and then, unable to sustain the vision, returns to the realm of the actual. Afterwards the poet feels exiled from the eternal, the numinous, the superconscious. The material world, the realm of the actual, seems empty and desolate. (Poe, in *The Fall of the House of Usher,* describes this sensation as "the bitter lapse into everyday life, the hideous dropping off of the veil.") The poet (like Keats' knight at arms) starves for heavenly manna. This theme of transcendence is treated in the work of Coleridge, Wordsworth, Keats, Shelley, Nerval, Rimbaud, and many other poets and writers. "Howl" describes and resolves the problems, using as a unifying image the archetype of the night-sea journey.

The night-sea journey (or night-sea crossing) is perhaps the earliest of the sun myths. "The ancient dwellers by the sea-shore believed that at nightfall, when the sun disappeared into the sea, it was swallowed by a monster. In the morning the monster disgorged its prey in the eastern sky."[1] Carl Jung discusses the myth in his *Contributions to Analytical Psychology* and Maud Bodkin applies it to "The Rime of the Ancient Mariner" in her book *Archetypal Patterns in Poetry.* The essential situation, in one form or another, may be found in a number of myths, legends, and folktales, and in literature.

For Jung and Bodkin the night-sea journey is a descent into the underworld, a necessary part of the path of the hero. It is "a plunge into the unconscious . . . darkness and watery depths. . . . The journey's end is expressive of resurrection and the overcoming of death."[2] The swallowing of Jonah by a great fish in the Old Testament, the *Aeneid* of Virgil, and the *Inferno* of Dante are records of night-sea journeys.

The movement of "Howl" (including "Footnote to Howl") is from protest, pain, outrage, attack, and lamentation to acceptance, affirmation, love and vision — from alienation to communion. The poet descends into an underworld of darkness, suffering, and isolation and then ascends into spiritual knowledge, blessedness, achieved vision, and a sense of union with the human community and with God. The poem is unified with and the movement carried forward by recurring images of falling and rising, destruction and regeneration, starvation and nourishment, sleeping and waking, darkness and illumination, blindness and sight, death and resurrection.

In the first section of "Howl," Ginsberg describes the desperation, the suffering, and the persecution of a group of outcasts, including himself, who are seeking transcendent reality. They are "starving" and "looking for an angry fix" in a metaphorical more than a literal sense.[3] Both metaphors suggest the intensity of the quest, the driving need. (William S. Burroughs uses the phrase "final fix" as the object of his quest at the end of his novel *Junkie*.) The metaphor of narcotics is extended by their search for "the ancient heavenly connection" (9). (Connection suggests not only a visionary experience in this context — a link to or a union with the divine — but also refers to the slang term for a source of narcotics in the 1940s and the 1950s.) These seekers are impoverished, alienated, arrested, and driven to suicide both by the hostility of the society in which they pursue their quest and by the desperate nature of the quest itself, by its inherent terrors and dangers.

Ginsberg's "angelheaded" seekers follow a sort of Rimbaudian "derangement of the senses" to arrive at spiritual clarity; they pursue a Blakean "path of excess to the Palace of Wisdom." They "purgatory" themselves in the manner of medieval flagellants with profligate and dissolute living (alcohol, sexual excess, peyote, marijuana, benzedrine). And through these means they achieve occasional epiphanous glimpses: angels on tenement roofs, "lightning in the mind" (9), illuminations, brilliant insights, vibrations of the cosmos, gleamings of "supernatural ecstasy" (11), visions, hallucinations; they are "crowned with flame" (13), tantalized when "the soul illuminated its hair for a second" (14), "crash through their minds" (15), receive "sudden flashes," and make incarnate "gaps in Time & Space"; they trap "the Archangel of the soul" and experience the consciousness of "Pater Omnipotens Aeterna Deus" (16). For such sensualized spirituality and for their frenzied pursuit of ultimate reality, they are outcast, driven mad, suicided (as Artaud says) by society, driven into exile, despised, incarcerated, institutionalized.

Ginsberg has phrased the issue in the first section of the poem as "the difficulties that nuts and poets and visionaries and seekers have. . . . The social disgrace — *dis*grace — attached to certain states of soul. The confrontation with a society . . . which is going in a different direction . . . knowing how to feel human and holy and not like a madman in a world which is rigid and materialistic and all caught up in the immediate necessities. . . . ."[4] The anguish of the visionary in exile from ultimate reality and desperately seeking reunion with it is intensified by a society which refuses to recognize the validity of the visionary experience and maintains a monopoly on reality, imposing and enforcing a single, materialist-rationalist view.

A number of the incidents in the first section are autobiographical, alluding to the poet's own experiences, such as his travels, his expulsion from Columbia University, his visions of Blake, his studies of mystical writers and Cézanne's paintings, his time in jail and in the asylum. Some of the more obscure personal allusions, such as "the brilliant Spaniard" in Houston (11), may be clarified by reading Ginsberg's *Journals*.[5] Other references are to his friends and acquaintances—Herbert Huncke, William S. Burroughs, Neal Cassady, William Cannastra, and others. (Certain characters, incidents, and places in "Howl" are also treated in Jack Kerouac's *The Town and the City*, John Clellon Holmes' *Go*, and William S. Burroughs' *Junkie*.)[6]

Ginsberg presents not only the personal tragedies and persecutions of his generation of seekers but alludes back to an earlier generation with embedded references to Vachel Lindsay "who ate fire in paint hotels" (9) and Hart Crane "who blew and were blown by those human seraphim, the sailors" (12).[7] And for the poet, the prototype of the persecuted and martyred visionary is his own mother, Naomi Ginsberg, who is twice mentioned in the poem and whose spirit provides much of the impetus for the poem. "Howl is really about my mother, in her last year at Pilgrim State Hospital—acceptance of her later inscribed in *Kaddish* detail."[8]

The personal nature of the references in "Howl" do not make it a poem *á clef* or a private communication. Nor is the poem reduced or obscured by its personal allusions. To the contrary, as images the persons, places, and events alluded to have great suggestive power. They possess a mythic, poetic clarity. We need know nothing of Ginsberg's experiences at Columbia University to understand the poetic sense of the lines

> who passed through universities with radiant cool eyes hallucinat-
> ing Arkansas and Blake-light tragedy among the scholars
> of war,

who were expelled from the academies for crazy & publishing
obscene odes on the windows of the skull. (9)

And we do not have to know that the line "who walked all night with
their shoes full of blood. . . ." refers to Herbert Huncke before we are
moved to pity and terror by the picture (13). For Ginsberg, as for
Whitman, the personal communicates the universal. The images are
ultimately autonomous and multivalent engaging our poetic understanding by their very intensity and mystery.

Ginsberg was not alone in lamenting the destruction of a generation of
frenzied, Dostoyevskian questers. In an early article on the Beats, Jack
Kerouac mourned "characters of a special spirituality . . . solitary
Bartlebies staring out the dead wall window of our civilization. The
subterranean heroes who'd finally turned from the 'freedom' machine of
the West and were taking drugs, digging bop, having flashes of insight,
experiencing the 'derangement of the senses,' talking strange, being
poor and glad, prophesying a new style for American culture . . . [but
who] . . . after 1950 vanished into jails and madhouses or were shamed
into silent conformity."9 Ken Kesey, in his novel *One Flew over the Cuckoo's
Nest,* also treats the issue of the imposition of a false, shallow, materialist-
rationalist reality on the human spirit and the consequent persecution
and oppression of those who cannot or will not accept the official reality.

Several lines near the end of the first section (from "who demanded
sanity trials" [15] to "animal soup of time—" [16]) describe the exploits
and sufferings of the dedicatee of the poem, Carl Solomon, the martyr in
whom Ginsberg symbolizes his generation of oppressed celestial pil-
grims. Ginsberg's statement of spiritual solidarity with Solomon—"ah
Carl, while you are not safe I am not safe"—presages the climactic third
section of the poem (16). This compassionate identification with a fellow
quester-victim is very similar to the Bodhisattva vow in Buddhism and
anticipates the poet's later interest in Buddhist thought.

After a statement on the technique and intention of the poem, the
section ends with strong images of ascent and rebirth and with a
suggestion that the martyrs are redemptive, sacrificial figures whose
sufferings can refine the present and the future.

The second section of the poem continues and expands the image of
pagan sacrifice with which the first section concludes. To what merciless,

cold, blind idol were the "angelheaded" of section one given in sacrifice?, Ginsberg asks. And he answers, "Moloch!" Moloch (or Molech), god of abominations, to whom children were sacrificed ("passed through the fire to Molech"), the evil deity against whom the Bible warns repeatedly, is the ruling principle of our age. To him all violence, unkindness, alienation, guilt, ignorance, greed, repression, and exploitation are attributable. The poet sees his face and body in buildings, factories, and weapons—as Fritz Lang saw his devouring maw in the furnace of *Metropolis.*

Ginsberg presents a comprehensive nightmare image of contemporary society, an inventory of terrors and afflictions that is as penetrating as Blake's "London." And like Blake in "London," Ginsberg places the source of human woe within human consciousness and perception. Moloch is a condition of the mind, a state of the soul: "Mental Moloch!"; "Moloch whose name is the Mind!" (17). We are born, according to Ginsberg, in a state of "natural ecstasy," but Moloch enters the soul early. (See Blake's "Infant Sorrow.") We can regain that celestial, ecstatic vision of life ("Heaven which exists and is everywhere about us!" [18]) by emerging from the belly of Moloch, the monster that has devoured us, who "ate up . . . [our] brains and imagination." We can "wake up in Moloch!" (17).

The remainder of the second section returns to a lament for the visionaries of section one. American society is seen as having consistently ignored, suppressed, and destroyed any manifestation of the miraculous, the ecstatic, the sacred, and the epiphanous.

In the pivotal section two of "Howl," Ginsberg names Moloch as the cause of the destruction of visionary consciousness and describes the manifestations of this antispirit, this malevolent god. Ginsberg also indicates that the Blakean "mind forg'd manacles" of Moloch can be broken and that beatific vision can be regained. In this section the poet has also made clear that transcendence is not merely of concern to poets and mystics but to every member of the social body. Ginsberg has shown the effects of a society without vision. Commercialism, militarism, sexual repression, technocracy, soulless industrialization, inhuman life, and the death of the spirit are the consequences of Mental Moloch.

The third section of the poem reaffirms and develops the sympathetic, affectionate identification of Ginsberg with the man who for him epitomizes the rebellious visionary victim. The section is a celebration of the courage and endurance of Carl Solomon, a final paean to the martyrs of the spirit, and an affirmation of human love.

The piteous and brave cry of Solomon from the Rockland Mental Hospital is the essence of the poem's statement; his is the howl of anguished and desperate conviction. "The soul is innocent and immortal it should never die ungodly in an armed madhouse" (19). The image of the "armed madhouse" is both macrocosmic and microcosmic. Each human soul inhabits the defensive, fearful "armed madhouse" of the ego personality, the social self, and the American nation has also become "an armed madhouse." (Kesey also uses the madhouse as metaphor in his novel *One Flew over the Cuckoo's Nest*.) The psychic armor that confines and isolates the individual ego selves and the nuclear armaments of the nation are mutually reflective; they mirror and create each other. At both levels, the individual and the national, the innocent and the immortal soul is starved, suffocated, murdered.

The imagery of crucifixion ("cross in the void," "fascist national Golgotha" [20]) reemphasizes Ginsberg's view of the visionary as sacrificial redeemer. Such images culminate in the poet's hope that Solomon "will split the heavens . . . and resurrect your living human Jesus from the superhuman tomb" (20). I understand this to mean that Solomon will discover the internal messiah, liberate himself from Mental Moloch ("whose ear is a smoking tomb" [17]), and attain spiritual rebirth.

The final images of "Howl" are confident and expansive, a projected apocalypse of Moloch, the Great Awakening "out of the coma" of life-in-death. Confinement, repression, alienation, and the dark night of the soul are ended. The "imaginary walls collapse" (walls of egotism, competition, materialism—all the woes and weaknesses engendered by Mental Moloch), and the human spirit emerges in victory, virtue, mercy, and freedom. The "sea-journey" of Solomon and of the human spirit is completed (20).

"Footnote to Howl," originally a section of "Howl" excised by Ginsberg on the advice of Kenneth Rexroth,[10] extends the poet's vision of Blake's phrase "the Eye altering alters all" in "The Mental Traveller." The poem is a rhapsodic, Blakean, Whitmanesque illumination of the realm of the actual, the material world. If we accept and observe attentively, if we see, Ginsberg tells us, then all is reconciled and all is recognized for what it in essence truly is: holy, divine.

The eye can become discerning in the deepest sense. Perceiving the inscape of each object, each event and life, we can perceive the divine presence. We can see the angel in every human form; we can see "eternity in time"; we can even see "the Angel in Moloch" (21). Perception is a reciprocal process. You are what you behold; what you behold is what you are. ("Who digs Los Angeles IS Los Angeles" — i.e., we can see either the dirty, lonely city of woe and weakness or the City of the Angels [21].) The essence of everything, of every being, is holy; only the form may be foul or corrupted; therefore, "holy the visions . . . holy the eyeball" (22). In this way Ginsberg's earlier assertion that "Heaven . . . exists and is everywhere about us" is extended and fulfilled. If we can wake up in Moloch, we can awake out of Moloch.

The acceptance of the body is essential for Ginsberg, for the senses can be a way to illumination. The body is where we must begin. Throughout "Howl" sexual repression or disgust with the body or denial of the senses have been seen as forms of Mental Moloch: "Moloch in whom I am a consciousness without a body!" (17); "where the faculties of the skull no longer admit the worms of the senses" (19). That is why the "Footnote" proclaims: "The soul is holy! The skin is holy! The nose is holy! The tongue and cock and hand and asshole holy!" (21). Body and spirit are affirmed and reconciled.

Heracleitus taught that "the way up and the way down are the same way." For Ginsberg, in his night-sea journey, the path of descent described in the first two sections of "Howl" has become the path of ascent, of victory and vision, as presented in section three and in "Footnote to Howl." "Howl" records a solstice of the soul, a nadir of darkness, and then a growth again towards light. The poem exemplifies Jack Kerouac's understanding that to be Beat was "the root, the soul of Beatific."

For many of the romantic writers the loss of vision and the return to the actual was a permanent defeat: their lives and their art became sorrowful and passive; they languished and mourned; their behavior became self-destructive, even suicidal. Ginsberg transforms his season in hell into new resolve and purpose. Like Coleridge's ancient mariner, he has returned from a journey of splendors and wonders and terrors and intense suffering with a new vision of human community, a new reverence for life. Like Blake's Bard, his is a voice of prophetic anger, compassion, and hope. Implicit in Ginsberg's vision in "Howl" of human solidarity and ultimate victory is the Blakean vow as expressed in "A New Jerusalem": "I shall not cease from mental fight . . . till we have built Jerusalem. . . ."

Ginsberg's sense of our common human necessity to redeem light from darkness, to seek vision and to practice virtue, is communicated in verse by the breath-measured, long-line, chant rhythm of "Howl." Andrew Welch observes that:

> The chant rhythm is a basic use of language that both reflects and directs social action toward community goals, a force that seems never to be far away when this rhythm enters poetry. In the Eskimo dance song, in the Navaho and Australian chants, in the prophecies of the Ghost Dance and of the Maya poet Chilam Balam, and in the poems of Ginsberg and Baraka, there is rhythmically and thematically a strong sense of movement and action, a communal rhythm enforcing communal participation and communal identity.[11]

In this way, "Howl" is linked not only to the romantic tradition but also to the preliterary, oral, magic incantations of the universal shamanist tradition.

"Howl" not only invokes and participates in the tradition of vatic poetry but significantly contributes to and furthers that tradition. The poem's considerable achievements, by Ginsberg's use of myth, rhythm, and prophetic vision, are the resolution of the problems associated with transcendence and the embodiment in verse of a new syncretic mode of spiritual awareness, a new social consciousness. A quarter of a century later, "Howl" is still on point, still vital and still pertinent. Rather than a literary artifact, the poem is likely to become a classic.

4

The Gnostic Vision of
William S. Burroughs

Mental Things are alone Real
what is Calld Corporeal Nobody knows
its dwelling Place it is in Fallacy
& its Existence an Imposture.
William Blake
"A Vision of the Last Judgment"

*I*n the following I want to consider what I call the Gnostic vision
of William S. Burroughs and to trace its development in his work with
particular attention to his key novel *The Soft Machine.* I do not mean to
suggest that William Burroughs is an adherent of Gnosticism or even
that he would endorse or concur with its tenets and practices. I do,
however, find that there are significant parallels and points of contact
between Burroughs' writing and Gnostic thought, and that these provide
a framework in which aspects of his work may be clarified.

Fundamental to religion, philosophy, and other modes of human
enquiry is the problem of the relationship of the self to the physical body,
of spirit to matter. The spectrum of opinion with regard to this problem
varies from the absolute materialist position at one extreme, through the
immanentist position in the center, to the position of the absolute
transcendentalist at the other extreme. The ideas of the Gnostics and of
William Burroughs are situated at this latter extreme. Both view the
material world as illusory, the body as the primary impediment to true
being and identity, and escape from the body and the world of the senses

as humankind's paramount concern. The terms in which they characterize their beliefs and the proposals they advance to further their goals have much in common. To this extent they share a vision of the universe and of the human situation.

Gnosticism was a religious movement that flourished in the Middle East and in the Roman world approximately during A.D. 80–200. Gnosticism incorporated elements of Hellenistic philosophy, Oriental religion, Judaism, and Christianity together with magical practices and mystical traditions from diverse cultures including Babylon, Persia, and India. Orthodox Christians considered it heretical and blasphemous, and they persecuted and finally suppressed the movement.

There were a number of different sects and systems of Gnosticism: the Simonian, Saturnian, Ophite, Naasene, Valentinian, Basilidian, Marcionite, Peratikite, Encratite, Docetist, Haimatitite, Cainite, Entychite, Carpocratian, and others. These systems had varied emphases and approaches, different terminologies and mythologies to the extent that, as one scholar has stated, "There is no one uniform set of ideas that may be singled out as gnostic; rather it is a matter of a type of thought that manifests itself in different ways in different groups."[1]

Essentially though, the attitude that characterizes all the Gnostic systems is that the world, the body, and matter are unreal and evil. They are illusions that are the products of malevolent powers called Archons, chief among whom is Sammael (the god of the blind or the blind god), also called Ialdabaoth or the Demiurge. These creator-gods are not the Deity or the Supreme Being, though they make claim to being so. The Deity is completely transcendent—absolutely distinct, apart, and remote from the created universe. However, a portion of the divine substance, called the pneuma, is enclosed in the human body—within the human passions and the human appetites where it is "unconscious of itself, benumbed, asleep, or intoxicated by the poison of the world."[2] The aim of Gnosticism is to liberate the pneuma from its material, delusional prison and to reunite it with the Deity. The Archons seek to obstruct this liberation and to maintain their dominion.

The tyrannical rule of the Archons is called *heimarmene,* which manifests itself through natural law, through human governments, institutions, laws, and conventions. It even extends to the afterlife where the escape of the soul and its return to God is prevented. In the Gnostic cosmology the universe is a closed domain, ruled by forces hostile to man, where ordinary life is spiritual death.

The situation would be entirely without hope were it not for "a messenger from the world of light who penetrates the barriers of the spheres, outwits the Archons, awakens the spirit . . . and imparts to it the saving knowledge. . . ."[3] This saving knowledge is gnosis, which means knowledge or insight. Gnosis is distinct from rational, philosophical, or scientific knowledge. It is an ecstatic, transcendent knowledge of the nature of the self and of reality, an enlightenment that redeems the pneuma from the body and from the realm of matter and allows it to escape the control of the Archons.

Gnosis may be achieved in many ways. A knowledge of the nature of the Archons, their spheres and their powers, and a ritual renunciation of their dominion is basic to the quest for gnosis. Gnosis may be the result of a long process of self-knowledge or of the correct understanding of spiritual texts, or the receipt of knowledge may be swift and revelatory. The knowledge may be attained through ascetic descipline or by means of a systematic licentiousness. Whatever means break the illusion of the body-self and the material world, whatever acts repudiate the authority of the Archons and affirm the pneuma, are paths to gnosis.

The Gnostics were strictly antihierarchical in their approach to their religion and to the social and political situation of their time. They viewed all rulers and powers on the earth as servants of the Demiurge. The distinctions between clergy and laity and the relationships of superiors and subordinates were seen as reflections of the principles of the Archons from which the Gnostic was redeemed. Elaine Pagels notes that "instead of ranking their members into superior and inferior orders within a hierarchy, they followed the principle of strict equality. All initiates, men and women alike, participated equally in the drawing; anyone might be selected to serve as priest, bishop or prophet. Furthermore they cast lots at each meeting, even the distinctions established by lot could never become permanent ranks."[4] In this way, resistance to the blind god and his minions was total, and each human was an agent of either the Deity or the Demiurge.

In a similar manner, the universe of William Burroughs' writing is also dualistic, a universe of warring powers and their agents on earth. At the highest level of abstraction, Burroughs exhibits in his novels a struggle between freedom and control, whose representatives in the universe are often portrayed as the Nova Police and the Nova Mob. The Nova Mob, also called the Board, enforces limit, authority, and single vision, while the regulatory, redemptive Nova Police have as their goal the restoration of multitudinousness, the liberation of consciousness from matter.

The head of the Nova Mob, which has occupied earth for thousands of years, is Mr. Bradly Mr. Martin, also caled Mr. & Mrs. D or the Ugly Spirit. Of him Burroughs writes:

> Mr Bradly-Mr Martin, in my mythology, is a God that failed, a God of conflict in two parts, so created to keep a tired old show on the road, The God of Arbitrary Power and Restraint, Of Prison and Pressure, who needs subordinates, who needs what he calls his "human dogs" while treating them with the contempt a con man feels for his victims — But remember the con man needs the mark — The mark does not need the con man — Mr Bradly-Mr Martin needs his "dogs" his "errandboys" his "human animals." He needs them because he is literally blind. They do not need him. In my mythological system he is overthrown in a revolution of his "dogs."[5]

Burroughs' blind god, like the Gnostic Demiurge, enforces his dominion over man through the human body and brain. By means of manipulation and control he keeps human consciousness confined to the body and reduced to the body consciousness of the ego self. His Archons include: "Sammy the Butcher," "Green Tony," "the Brown Artist," "Jacky Blue Note," "Limestone John," "Izzy the Push," "Iron Claws," "Hamburger Mary," "Paddy the Sting," "the Subliminal Kid," and "the Blue Dinosaur." The agents of Mr. Bradly Mr. Martin on earth are all the authorities and all the establishments and all the systems — the military, the police, business and advertising, religion, and such individuals as customs inspectors, con artists, politicians, pushers, all those who coerce and con, anyone in a position to impose and enforce a reality on another.

The key technique of the Nova Mob's control is image, especially as it is communicated through language. Through the manipulation of word and image an illusory reality is created and maintained. This is what Burroughs refers to as "the Reality Film."[6] It is scripted and directed by the Nova Mob and we are the unconscious, involuntary actors. The script, "the Board Books," calls for the deliberate creation and aggravation of insoluable conflicts, which serve both to keep the actors unaware of their position and to move the planet slowly, inexorably toward the Nova State that is the climax of the entertainment for the Nova Mob (*Soft,* 144). "The angle on planet earth was birth and death—pain and pleasure—the tough cop and the con cop. . . ." By these means the earth is kept as a sealed colony, exploited viciously and controlled totally by Bradly Martin and the Board.[7]

As in Gnosticism, it is "a messenger from the world of light who penetrates the barriers of the spheres" to bring the message of liberation. The Nova Police break through the blockade around the earth, infiltrate Nova Mob operations, and with the help of local partisans, eventually overthrow the rule of Mr. Bradly Mr. Martin.

The message of the Nova Police is, "This is war to extermination— Fight cell by cell through bodies and mind screens of the earth . . . Storm the Reality Studio and retake the universe." Their plan calls for "total exposure—Wise up all the marks everywhere Show them the rigged wheel" (*Soft,* 142). And their strategy is to "cut the word lines— smash the control images" (*Soft,* 76).

This program of the Nova Police is equivalent to gnosis, for it provides a way of breaking through the illusion of the material world and escaping from the body and the limits of ego consciousness. The specific method to implement the strategy is the cut-up.

The cut-up is quite simply the cutting up and rearranging of written material. There are variations such as the fold-in method or the use of tape recordings, but the intention and the effect is the same: to decondition perception, to destructure and restructure reality.

Burroughs' premises for his theory of the cut-up are these: language is a system that carries implicit patterns of perception and thought that are largely unconscious in the user of the language; these patterns are the assumptions of the system; and all patterns, all systems are reductive. We experience ourselves and the world through language, but language limits our experience to its implicit patterns. Our life within the limits of our language is our reality. If we wish to discover what other realities may exist outside of the patterns of our language reality, then we must break out of our language.

For Burroughs the cut-up method is a tool of escape from language reality into a multiverse. The cut-up can release us from the discreteness, the exclusiveness of an either/or universe into a multivalent infinity where all sets intersect. By cutting the word lines we can restructure our reality, our consciousness.

Colin Wilson has distinguished between two planes of consciousness that he names the horizontal and the vertical. "The plane of everyday experience is horizontal, static," he writes, "and my ordinary thinking moves on this plane. On the other hand, experiences of intensity tend to penetrate vertically into consciousness, and make us aware of consciousness *as freedom* instead of as passive perception."[8] This is precisely Burroughs' direction with the cut-up—from the horizontal to the vertical plane. His concern is the liberation of consciousness and its extension beyond language.

For Burroughs the cut-up is not primarily an act of destruction but an act of creation. The cut-up creates by permitting multiple connections and by unifying. Specifically, the cut-up unifies time, identity, and perception. In the multiverse of the cut-up all time is simultaneous. The past, present, and future are exploded as arbitrary and artificial distinctions. Events occur in what scientists call Absolute Elsewhere. The ego identity is likewise discovered to be an arbitrary and nonexistent limit. Self and other and *it* melt and merge in the cut-up. The modes of sense perception overlap and fuse into synaesthesia. Thus, the cut-up provides access to a new clarity, a new lucidity.

In this regard, there is an affinity between Burroughs' ideas and Aldous Huxley's view (based on the ideas of C. D. Broad and Henri Bergson) of the human central nervous system as a "reducing valve" that processes information according to its pertinence to physical survival, restricting "Mind At Large" to ego identity.[9]

Clearly though, there is a more direct line from Burroughs back to Rimbaud. Burroughs has acknowledged the relationship of his cut-ups to Rimbaud. "Images shift sense under the scissors smell images to sound sight to sound sound to kinesthetic. This is where Rimbaud was going with his color of vowels. And his 'systematic derangement of the senses. . . .'"[10]

Burroughs refers, in the above quote, to Rimbaud's poem "Voyelles," in which the poet explores the correspondences between color and sound. The same correspondence is referred to again in the "Alchemie Du Verbe" section of *Une Saison En Enfer.*[11] Like Burroughs, Rimbaud felt that true being and true identity were elsewhere and other than ego identity. ("Je est un autre." "La vraie vie est absente.")[12] And he believed that in order to attain experience of the unknown, visionary self, the ego identity and its perceptions must be destructured. ("Il s'agit d'arriver à l'inconnu par le dérèglement de tous les sens." "Le poète se fait voyant par un long, immense et raisonné dérèglement de tous les sens.")[13]

The cut-up for Burroughs is a way of knowledge, a method of resistance, and a tool of escape readily available to everyone.

The extent to which Burroughs became convinced that cut-ups represented a radical and effective solution to the human predicament is evidenced in his letter of 21 June 1960 to Allen Ginsberg. Ginsberg had written to Burroughs on 10 June 1960 from Pucallpa, Peru, describing a terrifying experience with the drug ayahuasca and its disorienting aftermath. Fearing madness, Ginsberg appealed to Burroughs for aid and advice. Burroughs replied, instructing his friend to cut-up the enclosed copy of the letter, cut-up his own poems, cut-up "any poems any prose." His message is unequivocal and is striking in its resemblance to the Gnostic vision.

> WHAT SCARED YOU INTO TIME? INTO BODY? INTO SHIT?
> I WILL TELL YOU. THE WORD. THE–THEE WORD. IN THEE
> BEGINNING WAS THE WORD. SCARED YOU ALL INTO
> SHIT FOREVER! COME OUT FOREVER. COME OUT OF THE
> TIME WORD THE FOREVER. COME OUT OF THE BODY
> WORD THEE FOREVER. COME OUT OF THE SHIT WORD
> THE FOREVER. ALL OUT OF TIME AND INTO SPACE.[14]

Apart from its insistence on language as the principal device of control, Burroughs' statement is very close in tone and sentiment to a phrase in a Gnostic text: "Why did ye carry me away from my abode into captivity and cast me into the stinking body?"[15]

Beyond the cut-up, beyond language and image, is silence, which Burroughs describes as "the most desireable state" because it leads to "non-body experience."[16] In Burroughs' view man must move from speech to silence, from image to awareness, from body identity to disembodied self, from time to space. This is the direction of human evolution as he assesses it, and these ideas are the central themes of Burroughs' middle and late work, beginning with his novel *The Soft Machine.*

The Soft Machine is a pivotal work in Burroughs' oeuvre and as distinct from *Naked Lunch* as was that book from *Junkie.* In *The Soft Machine* all that has preceded in Burroughs' work is summarized and extended, and all that is to come is forespoken. In *The Soft Machine* Burroughs introduces his new technique, the cut-up; employs a new central image, parasitism; and outlines his cosmic myth, the Nova Police versus the Nova Mob. And in contrast to his earlier works in which he restricted himself to description and detached observation, in *The Soft Machine* the author himself becomes a prescriptive and an active agent, a partisan saboteur working against the occupying forces of the enemy.

The Soft Machine was printed in three different versions, the first of which was published in Paris by the Olympia Press in 1961. The second rearranged, recombined, altered text, with deletions and additions, was published in New York in 1966 by Grove Press. Apparently, as correspondence in the Grove Press collection indicates, the author was not satisfied with this edition even at the time that it was typeset for publication and wished to make further revisions. However, the editor insisted on a cutoff date for revisions, and the book was published without incorporating Burroughs' final revisions.[17] The third version of *The Soft Machine,* the final and definitive text, was published by Calder & Boyars in London in 1968 and is still unavailable in the United States. This version contains about thirty pages of new text plus an appendix and additional material following the text.

The new technique, new imagery, and new vision of *The Soft Machine* may already be discerned in Burroughs' contributions to *Minutes to Go.* In these short pieces, the author's first cut-ups, he discovers his central metaphor, that of parasite and host; some of his most important characters, including Mr. Bradly Mr. Martin; and the dominant themes of *The Soft Machine* and his subsequent novels.

Burroughs' collaborators in *Minutes to Go,* Brion Gysin, Gregory Corso, and Sinclair Beiles, use literary, religious, or political material for their cut-ups, while Burroughs uses medical articles, especially those concerning virus. "These individuals are marked foe," pronounces one text referring to the medical profession.[18] Other texts disclose diseases and viruses as "deals" (13, 15), while another ominously reveals the "agent at work" behind cancer (18). Burroughs' final contribution to the volume presents a comprehensive delineation of the theories that inform *The Soft Machine*: "The word was a virus . . . virus made man . . . man is virus . . ." (59). The addictions to language, body, ego identity, sex, religion, and drugs are exposed as one addiction: image addiction, a virus parasitism. The Native Guide, who becomes a recurrent figure in Burroughs' mythology, is introduced as is Hassan i Sabbah and his maxim, "Nothing is true—everything is permitted" (61). And finally, Burroughs presents his countermeasure to the agents, the deals, the addictions, and the parasites that infest human consciousness: "Rub Out The Word" (62).

The Soft Machine is a full-length treatment of the ideas, images, and characters introduced in the pieces in *Minutes to Go*. Burroughs has described the book as "an obstacle course. Basic training for space."[19] The episodic structure, together with the use of cut-ups, effects a spatial and temporal dislocation, a breakdown of sequential, linear perception, inducing a sort of dream state in the reader. The recurrence of words, phrases, places, images, situations, and characters without forward narrative movement contributes further to a sense of an utter otherness that is almost familiar, almost recalled. In this manner the book fulfills its intended "training" function.

The first version of *The Soft Machine* was divided into four large sections or Color Units: Unit I, Red; Unit II, Green; Unit III, Blue; Unit IV, White. This structure was abandoned in the second and third versions of the book but it remains embedded in the text. The reference is to Rimbaud's color vowels (alluded to in the text) and the intention is, again, that of an "obstacle course." Color imagery dominates in *The Soft Machine* and is used most frequently to produce the effect of synaesthesia. Burroughs hopes to train the reader to perceive and to conceive in larger terms than the discreteness permitted by the five senses. The program, which is Burroughs' systematic derangement of the senses, is aimed at deconditioning and reconditioning consciousness to permit nonbody experience.

The Soft Machine portrays a world of violence, viciousness, mendacity, and manipulation. The earth is a planet approaching nova state as a result of the deliberate design of the Nova Mob. The first section, "Dead on Arrival," depicts the hopelessness of the human condition in images of junk, parasitism, and death. Desperate junkies wait in downtown cafeterias for "the Man," and in the suburbs "antennae of TV suck the sky" in images of addiction. Man is at the mercy of biology ("running out of veins") and of the authorities (pushers, croakers, the heat) and is receiving a short count of junk and of time (7). Parasitism is the principle of survival; the hosts attach themselves to other hosts; the junkie becomes pusher or turns stool pigeon. The strategy of parasitism is "INVADE. DAMAGE. OCCUPY.," and the pusher, promising "freedom," moves into his host with the junk (8). Death by overdose, by drowning, by hanging, by murder, by accident, by one's own hand, or at the hand of another, physical death and psychic death: we are all, by the nature of the setup, "Dead on Arrival."

Human history is a "penny arcade peepshow long process in different forms" for Mr. Bradly Mr. Martin and the Board, and they are preparing to bring it to the Grand Finale of nova when the Nova Police arrive (168). Arrests are made, and one Board member "Willy the Rat" turns stool pigeon. Partisans undertake sabotage, and agents infiltrate and destroy Board operations past and present (the Mayan control system and Trak News Agency). As the total control of the Nova Mob begins to crumble, the situation report of the conflict is, "Word falling—photo falling—breakthrough in grey room." The tyranny of image is being subverted. The Reality Studio, the "grey room," is under seige (145).

A final apocalyptic overthrow of Mr. Bradly Mr. Martin is presented in the section titled "Gongs of Violence."

> Police files of the world spurt out in a blast of bone meal . . . — Wind through dusty offices and archives—Board Books scattered to rubbish heaps of the earth—Symbol books of the all-powerful board that had controlled thought feeling and movement of a planet from birth to death with iron claws of pain and pleasure—The whole structure of reality went up in silent explosions—Paper moon and muslin trees and in a black silver sky great rents as the cover of the world rained down—Biologic film went up. (152–53)

Having shown us the end, Burroughs then shows us the beginning in the final section of *The Soft Machine*, "Cross the Wounded Galaxies." We are presented with the moment in prehistory when herbivore apes were first invaded by the parasitic consciousness of the Nova Mob. Migrating during a period of glacial advance, a band of apes is suddenly afflicted with "the talk sickness," which causes both interior and exterior transformations (168).

Whereas previously the apes had no sense of individual identity, no "me" but only "we," the "talk sickness" precipitates a radical change in consciousness, creating ego identity. (It may be, as Eric Mottram has suggested, that this passage owes something to William Golding's *The*

Inheritors [1955], but it is not a cut-up of Golding's book.)[20] This alteration of consciousness is accompanied by a physical metamorphosis: "hair and ape flesh off in screaming strips. stood naked human bodies . . ." (168).

The parasite invasion of consciousness also manifests itself in the awareness of "the white worm-thing inside" that feeds off the fear and the pain of others and that changes the dietary practices of the ape-men to carnivorousness and cannibalism (169). The ape-men become hunter-killers, practicing ritual hunting magic. This first tribal religion quickly evolves into social hierarchy and monotheism when one of the creatures tells another, "I am Allah. I made you" (170). Thus, in Burroughs' view, human religion and class structures are the extensions of psychic parasitism.

The Soft Machine ends with a coda in which the events of the myth are condensed and fragmented. Bradly Martin's arrival on earth, his long reign, his pursuit by the Nova Police, and his final overthrow are presented in twenty-two lines of cut-up prose-poetry.

The incidents and essential situations of *The Soft Machine* are repeated, developed, and further clarified in the author's next two novels, *The Ticket That Exploded* (1962, rev. ed. 1967) and *Nova Express* (1964). Subsequent novels such as *The Wild Boys* (1971), *Exterminator!* (1973), and *Port of Saints* (1970, rev. ed. 1980) also treat aspects of Burroughs' Gnostic vision but do so using different characters and situations. The problem of image and body is resolved most conclusively in *The Wild Boys,* in which all existing institutions, systems, and cultural and biological patterns are overthrown, and there is a return to a preverbal tribalism as an evolutionary medium to a nonmaterial state of being.

As the central work of Burroughs' oeuvre, *The Soft Machine* is itself centered around Mr. Bradly Mr. Martin. His phantom and elusive presence, his dual nature (as his name suggests), is the informing principle of the story.

Mr. Bradly Mr. Martin may be related to the figure of "Bradly the Buyer" in *Naked Lunch,* but he first appears under his own name in *Minutes to Go* in a piece titled "Reactive Agent Tape Cut by Lee the Agent in Interzone" (26–29). The context of his appearance is a précis of his history and his ultimate fate in Burroughs' mythology. "He had to use junk somewhere. Mr Bradly Mr Martin—slotless fade out in sick streets of cry—" (*Minutes,* 26).

Bradly Martin, the god of image and of reality, is himself addicted to image. He is junk in all its manifestations. Without his human hosts he is literally nowhere. He cannot exist without a medium. So he has to use junk somewhere. (We learn later that earth is not the first host planet for Bradly Martin. He has left a trail of novas behind him in space, across "the wounded galaxies" [*Soft*, 171]). The fade-out image foretells his ultimate disappearance following his overthrow on earth.

Bradly Martin is also in *Minutes to Go* associated with Yves Martin, a member of an actual expedition composed of four scientists and a guide that met with disaster in the Egyptian desert. The bodies of four of the members were recovered; one person remained missing. Positive identification of the bodies proved impossible due to their decomposition and due to the sharing and exchange of clothing, documents, and diaries by members of the expedition. This curious event intrigued Burroughs and contributed to his conception of Bradly Martin as a ruthless survivor of an interplanetary spaceflight, who, after a forced landing on the planet earth, assimilated and subsumed the other crew members. Burroughs refers to the Yves Martin expedition in *The Soft Machine* and again in *Nova Express*. Bradly Martin describes his arrival on earth in "The Beginning Is Also the End."[21]

In developing Bradly Martin ("God of Conflict . . . God of Arbitrary Power and Restraint, of Prison and Pressure"), Burroughs also drew on other sources. He has stated, "My conception of Mr Bradly-Mr Martin is similar to the conception developed by William Golding in *Pincher Martin*."[22]

The similarity between the two figures, Christopher Hadley "Pincher" Martin and Mr. Bradly Mr. Martin, extends beyond the obvious resemblance of their names. Their situations are essentially the same, for they are both godlike creators of a reality, the product of their remorseless will to survive. Both are eaters—viciously self-assertive, parasitic, aggressive, greedy, without scruples, and ready to survive at all costs. Pincher Martin is an actor by profession; Bradly Martin repeatedly refers to himself in the narratives as "just an old showman." Both are marooned: Pincher Martin on his island and Bradly Martin on earth. And both are erased finally, unable to completely control and thus maintain the reality that they have created.

As an avid reader of science fiction, Burroughs may also have been influenced in the construction of his cosmic myth by J. B. Priestley's short story "The Grey Ones" (1953) or by Jack Finney's *The Body Snatchers* (1955), in both of which the takeover of human consciousness by alien intelligence is depicted; by Kurt Vonnegut's *The Sirens of Titan* (1959) in which all of human history is the product of alien control; and by Brian W. Aldiss' novelette *Hothouse,* which first appeared in the early sixties, in which the human brain and intelligence are presented as being derived from and susceptible to parasitic invasion. It is also interesting to note that Colin Wilson adopted Burroughs' metaphor for his philosophic science fiction novel *The Mind Parasites* (1967), and that Lawrence Durrell's latest series of novels, of which the first two constituents are *Monsieur* (1974) and *Livia* (1978), is centered on Gnosticism.

In the second century Tertullian wrote contemptuously of the Gnostics: "They meet together to storm the center of the one only truth. . . ."[23] In 1960 William Burroughs wrote on a New Year's card to his friend Brion Gysin, "Blitzkrieg the citadel of enlightenment!"[24] This sense of urgency, of impatience with anything less than direct and immediate action, characterizes, at the deepest level, the vision of the Gnostics and of William Burroughs. In addition, as we have seen, they share an essentially pessimistic view of the material world, a radical dualism, a sense of alienated existence, a principle of the negation of physical experience, an antihierarchical approach to human organization, an urge to transcendence by means of saving knowledge, a willingness to pursue extreme measures to achieve such saving knowledge, and the predisposition to express their vision through a mythology rather than an ordered theology.

The recurrence in a twentieth-century American writer of the essential ideas and attitudes of a long vanished religion is not as surprising nor as unlikely as it may at first seem. Scholars have long recognized that art and religion share a good deal of common ground, and the problem with which the Gnostics and Burroughs have dealt may be seen as "the basic problem of the universe, the relationship between good and evil, between man and this seemingly evil cosmos."[25] Furthermore, the type of thought or vision that may be called Gnostic is not an isolated phenomenon; but rather, it is a universal and recurrent tendency. "Manichaeism among the Persians, hermeticism among the Greeks, the Ismaelites in Islam, the Jewish Kabbala, medieval alchemy, the theosophy of the Romantics, modern occultism and contemporary surrealism" have all been seen as descendants of the Gnostics. Although there is no direct continuity from one movement to the next, Gnostic thought has been seen as "a religious ideology which always tends to reappear . . . in times of social and political crisis."[26]

Although we must recognize that the political and social climate in which Burroughs writes is one of crisis, we need not accept the implication that Gnostic thought is therefore a hysterical and desperate psychological reaction to unstable historical conditions. The periodical recurrence of Gnostic thought may well be due to its relevance to the human situation or due to its not having truly been addressed and considered but only repressed and anathematized by the dominant orthodoxy.

In his essays "Passage to More Than India" and "Why Tribe," the poet Gary Snyder posits the existence of what he calls the "Great Subculture"—a tradition of thought extending back to the late Paleolithic era and resurfacing at various times in various guises. "In China it manifested as Taoism, not only Lao-tzu but the later Yellow Turban revolt and medieval Taoist societies, and the Zen Buddhists up till early Sung. Within Islam the Sufis; in India the various threads converged to produce Tantrism. In the West it has been represented largely by a string of heresies starting with the Gnostics. . . ."[27]

I believe that Burroughs' work can most properly be understood and appreciated in the context of this tradition—in the esoteric, heretical modes of thought that constitute a suppressed and subversive unconscious beneath the accepted and orthodox social, philosophical, and religious structures of civilization.

Within this tradition of Snyder's "Great Subculture" Burroughs' work serves two key functions, both essentially shamanistic in nature.

First, it exorcizes "the negative and demonic potentials of the unconscious" by presenting them in symbolic form ("Why Tribe," *Earth*, 115). Thus, the violence, obsessive sexuality, and nightmare horror that are so often characteristic of Burroughs' work represent an attempt to purge the psyche of these influences by means of their symbolic enactment. The Hungarian psychoanalyst Géza Róheim has observed: "The shaman makes public the systems of symbolic fantasy that are present in the psyche of every adult member of society. They are . . . the lightning conductors of common anxiety. They fight the demons. . . ."[28] Or, as the *Gnostic Gospel* of Thomas states: "If you bring forth what is within you, what you bring forth will save you. If you do not bring forth what is within you, what you do not bring forth will destroy you."[29]

The second function of Burroughs' writing is to provide a new cosmology. The author's space-age mythology, together with his experimental prose technique, introduces a new view of time, space, and identity, a new map of the cosmos and of our psychic geography. "In my writing," Burroughs has stated, "I am acting as a map maker, an explorer of psychic areas . . . as a cosmonaut of inner space. . . ."[30]

Both functions of Burroughs' writing, expressed in a manner similar to that of the ritual practices and mythological systems of the Gnostics, serve to effect self-knowledge, internal transformation, and transcendence. In this sense his work occupies a position in that zone of contemporary culture that is still being defined—where anthropology, philosophy, religion, psychology, and literature overlap and merge into a single discipline: human liberation.

5

"The Arcadian Map": Notes on the Poetry of Gregory Corso

> the Arcadian map
> our only anthem'd direction
> Gregory Corso
> "Ode to Sura"

> The songs of one who strove to play
> the broken flutes of Arcady.
> Edwin Arlington Robinson
> "Ballade of Broken Flutes"

"*I* contradict the real with the unreal," declares Gregory Corso in his poem "Power," and some lines farther in the same poem, he announces, "I am the ambassador of Power."[1] Correctly understood, these two short statements represent a concise formulation of Corso's poetics and of his conception of the role of the poet, and of poetry, in human society and in the universe. In the following I want to explore the significance and implications of these statements and to consider how they are related to theme and technique in the poet's work.

Corso's poetic vision may well have originated in an incident from his childhood. An orphan, repeatedly institutionalized, Corso was, at the age of twelve, incarcerated in the New York City jail, the infamous Tombs, where he was beaten and abused by the other prisoners. Out of the loneliness and terror of this experience, however, he discovered an interior world of beauty and vision. "When they stole my food and beat me up and threw pee in my cell, I, the next day would come out and tell them my beautiful dream about a floating girl who landed before a deep pit and just stared."[2] This incident represents what may be Corso's earliest instance of contradicting the real with the unreal, the true inception of his vocation as a poet. This pivotal experience prepared Corso to receive and understand the "books of illumination" (see dedication to *Gasoline*), which he read some years later while serving a sentence at Clinton Prison.[3]

Corso's poetic imagination is, then, essentially a rejection of the tyranny of the real. It is an assertion of freedom from limitation and from causality, a mode of refashioning, reinterpreting, recreating the phenomenological universe, of imposing inner desire on the external world, and by these means a way of contradicting, counteracting, and countermanding the real. Corso's poetics, though he devised them independently out of his personal perceptions and necessities, are thus very much in the romantic tradition (ultimately the Platonic, vatic tradition). The poetic imagination for Corso, as for Coleridge and for Shelley, partakes of divinity as "a repetition in the finite mind of the eternal act of creation in the infinite I AM,"[4] and as an agency that "marks the before unapprehended relations of things and perpetuates their apprehension . . . and . . . redeems from decay the visitations of the divinity in man. . . ."[5] In this manner the poet, through the act of imaginative creation, discovers and reveals the eternal, divine structures and principles underlying the "real" world, and he or she functions as prophet, messenger, or "ambassador of Power."

Principal among the "books of illumination" from which Corso gained knowledge of the world and self-knowledge during his three-year sentence at Clinton Prison was "the 1905 Standard Dictionary . . . with all the archaic and obsolete words."[6] Words, language, became the vehicle of his imagination, the weapon to assault the prison of the real, and the instrument by which to discover and inhabit the deeper, truer realm of beauty and desire. For Corso words are not passive and inert but alive and potent. They possess mystery, associative richness, and revelatory power.

They are capable of marriages and metamorphoses. Their properties are transmutative "like chemistry. You put iron and another element together and you get a third."[7]

Language for Corso is plastic, animate beyond its syntax and grammar. It is not a fixed system but a process. The poetic use of langauge is for him a discovery of correspondences and conjunctions, a reconciliation of opposites. Corso's poetry, by joining incongruous, disparate elements and by generating new combinations breaks down traditional habits of perception, repudiates ontological clichés, and celebrates the unlimited possibilities of the eternal imagination. ("Nothing is so unjust as impossibility," asserts Corso in "Power" [*Birthday*, 15].) The remarks of Gaston Bachelard concerning the process of the poetic imagination are particularly appropriate to the verbal transformation and recreation of the world as it occurs in Corso's poetry. "Imagination is always considered to be the faculty of *forming* images. But it is rather the faculty of *deforming* the images offered by perception, of freeing ourselves from the immediate images; it is especially the faculty of *changing* images. If there is not a changing of images, an unexpected union of images, there is no imagination, no *imaginative action*."[8]

Another of the "books of illumination" read by Corso in Clinton Prison was a volume of the poems of Percy Bysshe Shelley, whose life and work have influenced Corso's poetry and whom Corso reveres as "the first revolutionary of the spirit."[9] Corso shares with Shelley a zeal for liberty and a passionate faith in humankind. An outlook very similar to Shelley's "mixture of Platonism and pantheism"[10] can be discerned in Corso's work, as well as a Shelleyan aversion to "cruelty, tyranny, authority, institutional religion, custom and the formal shams of respectable society."[11] Corso also shares with Shelley a "deep interest in the ancient Greeks" and "a radical egalitarian approach to social and political questions."[12]

I do not mean to suggest that Corso's thought and poetry are directly derivative of those of Shelley. Indeed, I am convinced that the impact of Shelley's thought on the young Corso involved to a high degree a recognition on Corso's part of a philosophy that he already embraced but that he had not yet formulated or articulated. I believe, with John Fuller, that Corso is "a natural idealist."[13] More to the point is that with its imaginative action, its alchemical, transmutative character, Corso's poetry also represents an expression of metaphysical-social-political prophecy.

Although Corso has never written out his credo or produced a manifesto of his beliefs as such, he has come closest to doing so in his article "Variations on a Generation" in which he expresses his own hopes for a revolution of the spirit. Corso prophesies "a delicate shift of total consciousness" in which process art is central to human enlightenment and evolution. Ultimately, there will occur a "total alteration, personal work social political poetic emotive—demanded by alteration of consciousness," and there will be an end to "nationalistic madness . . . and to blindness and suicide, maniacal universal selfish competition."[14] Certainly, this is a utopian vision, no less sweeping nor less compelling than that of Shelley, to be embodied in poetic prophecy.

These two aspects, then, the imaginative and the prophetic, are the twin impulses of Corso's poetry, at once the poles and counterparts of his vision. The former aspect manifests itself as pure poetry, the poem as "Zeusian toy," while the latter aspect is expressed in Corso's polemical, discursive, introspective poems, the poem as Hermean message. In certain poems, of course, both qualities are present, diametrically and complementarily. Together they represent the record of a poetic exploration of the world, of the microcosm and the macrocosm, the ideal and the real, the inner and the outer.

An important feature of Corso's writing is its innocent impudence, its ingenuous whimsy, its sly, surreal humor. This element of comedy is central to his poetic vision as it serves to discredit and subvert the real, to point up the ludicrousness and absurdity of our vanities and obsessions, and to affirm our essential innocence. Corso's humor is never malicious and is often self-mocking, self-deflating. For Corso, the poet and the clown are one, engaged in the ultimate struggle of desire against death, vision against objective, external reality: "Their happy light is forged phalanx, charge!" ("Clown," *Birthday*, 55).

Corso's poetry constitutes an "Arcadian map" in that it insists upon our original and our final innocence. It informs us of where we have been, it acquaints us with where we are now, and it can serve to guide us to where we would wish to be. Like any reliable map, it represents all the features of the terrain, both the wonders and the dangers, both Arcadia and Hades. For, as Fredric Jameson suggests, if the real is by definition "that which resists desire," then "it also follows that this Real . . . can be disclosed only by Desire itself, whose wish-fulfilling mechanisms are the instruments through which this resistant surface must be scanned."[15]

Corso's central concerns may be discerned already in his earliest work, in the poems of his first collection, *The Vestal Lady on Brattle* (1955). The title poem announces the dominant theme of the volume: the destruction of beauty and innocence by the world. The aging, barren "vestal lady" of the poem inhabits a "grey ruin," where she pursues her "despaired" and "sunless" life of custom.[16] Daily, she drowns and consumes a child, nourishing, intoxicating herself on this cannibal fare. The poem suggests our daily murder of the child within us in order to maintain the habits of our ruined and sunless lives and it also represents the general hostility and inhospitability of the world to innocence and beauty with their inevitable annihilation by the real.

This theme is further explored and developed in other poems in the collection, such as "Greenwich Village Suicide," where a sensitive lover of "Bartok, Van Gogh / And New Yorker cartoons" destroys herself (or more properly is "suicided by society" as Artaud phrases it), and whose death is met with a complacent callousness by the world: "They take her away with a Daily News on her face / And a shopkeeper throws hot water on the sidewalk" (5).

Another variation on the theme occurs in "A Pastoral Fetish" where the deliberate destruction of beauty is perpetrated by a perverse, storm trooper person, who revels in crunching lilacs and dandelions beneath his boots and exults in the sticky smell of the "green blood" of the "murdered" flowers (31). Similarly, the poem "In the Early Morning" depicts a predatory "drooling Desirer" in his "long greasy coat" and with his "bloodstained nails" who waits in hiding to assault "the runaway hand-in-pocket / whistling youth" (13). The poems "Requiem for 'Bird' Parker, Musician" and "St. Lukes, Service for Thomas" both mourn the untimely destruction of two creative artists by those forces that Corso ultimately names as "uncreation."

Despite their nursery rhyme, fairy-tale quality and their disarming childlike tone, these early poems present a terrifying vision of a perverse and vicious world wherein the destructive, negative forces are predominant, devouring and preying upon the forms of beauty and innocence. Their flaws and stylistic uncertainty notwithstanding, these early poems make a forceful and affecting statement about the nature of life and the world.

Corso's next collection *Gasoline* (1958) exhibits a clearer thematic focus, greater stylistic assurance, and more developed technical skill.

Each poem in the volume seems to complement and clarify the other poems by reflecting on them and resonating with them. The collection thus forms a coherent whole composed of luminous, autonomous parts.

The first poem in the collection, "Ode to Coit Tower," employs two central images, the tower and the prison (Coit Tower and Alcatraz), to symbolize the two diameteric tendencies of human consciousness: the aspiration for ascent and liberation, the striving for vision, versus the urge toward confinement, constraint, and restriction. The tower represents the creative drive in the human spirit expressive of the urge for love and beauty, for transcendence; the prison embodies all that is cruel, blind, limited, and retrograde—a heavy, dreamless, "petrific bondage." Corso prays for "humanity's vast door to open that all men be free that both hinge and lock die" (12).

In the second part of the poem, the poet-speaker grieves for his own personal loss of vision. (There are direct parallels here to Wordworth's "Ode: Intimations of Immortality" and Coleridge's "Dejection: An Ode.") He mourns for "that which was no longer sovereign in me" and for the loss of "dreams that once jumped joyous bright from my heart like sparks." In contrast to the young children he watches who still possess the "eucharistic" "treasures" of imagination and vision, Corso longs to repossess "that madness again that infinitive solitude where illusion spoke Truth's divine dialect" (11–13). The poem concludes with a desperate sense of irredeemable loss, a despair at the poet's inability to sustain vision in the face of the vicissitudes of adult life. And yet the poem is itself testimony that vision and the imaginative faculty do not disappear altogether, although they may be markedly diminished in power and intensity. Some ember of this divine fire remains latent in the spirit and must be nourished and cultivated. For though there are prisons in the world and in the mind, there are also towers.

There are echoes of Corso's "Ode" in other poems in the volume. In "Puma in Chapultapec Zoo" the poet again depicts the unnatural confinement of that which is by nature free and self-sovereign. The caged puma emblematizes the general condition of sentient consciousness in the material world, as does the poet's friend in a faraway city "locked in some small furnished room." In "Sun" Corso views the universe itself as a confining prison into which the sun shines as through a hole in the enclosing wall of darkness. He celebrates the presence of light as the divine element that inspires humankind to reverence (as Helios, Apollo,

Rha, Sol, etc.) and to transcendental aspiration. Like the prisoners chained in Plato's cave, we must liberate ourselves from the world of darkness and follow the sun's "beckoning finger" to that realm of being "where all beyond is true Byzantium" (26).

Other poems in *Gasoline* are more qualifiedly affirmative than "Sun" or are characterized by a more pessimistic vision. Images of violence, destruction, and death, of isolation and alienation are prevalent: a battlefield, gangsters, a dead Italian baby, the aerial bombardment of Rotterdam, the murder of kindness, the cannibal devouring of beauty, the downfallen rose, the miserable fate of the hapless yak, the rejection and death of the sensitive Arnold, the doomed Mexican child, the windmill "alone, alien, helpless" in a windless, cactus landscape ("Mexican Impressions," 23), the tortures of Christ, wounded deer stalked by wolves. As in *The Vestal Lady on Brattle*, the dominant motif of these poems is the destruction, the devouring of all that is beautiful, innocent, kind, or sensitive by a cruel, benighted world that resists and rejects these qualities.

The disparity between the ideal world of the imagination, the realm of pure spirit, and the fallen, material world of physical existence is treated in the poem "In the Fleeting Hand of Time."[17] Corso employs images of light, radiance, illumination, warmth, and color, and of classical and medieval grandeur to suggest the ineffable splendors of the world of the spirit, while a grim landscape of "icy asphalt doomed horses / weak dreams Dark corridors" and "giant gray skyscrapers" expresses the graceless, hopeless, merciless character of the physical world. In such a world the poet (and the spirit) is a prisoner, an exile, and a victim (*Gasoline*, 15–16).

But just as the poet held by "the fleeting hand of time" eventually finds "conditional life," so these poems in *Gasoline* seem to offer at least tentative hope (16). In such poems as "Ecce Homo" and "Ucello," Corso affirms the transfiguring power of art that can be nourished by the sufferings and horrors of the world and that can transform them into beauty and truth. This is an important counterpart to the process that Corso depicts in so many of his other poems, where the opposite obtains.

Further evidence of such hope is provided by the language of the poems themselves with their zany humor, their vitality, and their immense energy—their enthusiasm, exuberance, and excitement. Characterized by unexpected usages and turns of phrase ("windless monkage," "visionic eyehand," "dome heirloomed," "ventrilóquial telegram"), wild juxtapositions and coinages ("seaharp," "wheatweather," "joyprints," "hungersulk," "deathical"), and an intoxication with words and a love of myth, Corso's poetic vision is itself a revivifying force, restoring language to innocence, celebrating wonder and mystery, remaking the world.

In *The Happy Birthday of Death* (1960) Corso presents the poet and the poetic imagination in a more vigorous, assertive role in the world. No longer simply a victim, the poet here assumes the authority of the power he or she serves, and the poet exerts force in opposition to the forces of "uncreation." In common with Shelley's view of poets as "trumpets which sing to battle" and as "the unacknowledged legislators of the world," Corso affirms and exercises the power of poetry to censure and to incite against, to resist, and to sabotage the real.[18]

Corso's assaults on "uncreation" take the form of a series of long poems, which, by alternating rhetoric and wild bursts of imagery, are meditations on and explorations of aspects of human life. The subjects of these longer poems in *The Happy Birthday of Death* range from the seemingly trivial, such as "Hair" (about vanity), to the most solemn, such as "Death," and include "Marriage," "Bomb," "Food," "Clown," "Power," "Army," and "Police." By means of humor and an ability to present common topics in new and startling perspectives, Corso deflates our pretentions and exposes our fears; he mocks them and makes them ridiculous. He forces us to consider things we would prefer to ignore, and he compels us to look closer and more carefully at things with which we think we are familiar. His goal is to debewitch the reader and the world, to exorcise from the spirit the demons of the real, so that we can again perceive the essential magic and mystery of existence.

Together with the justifiably famous "Marriage," the most successful (and for a time the most controversial) of the poems in the series is "Power."[19] This poem is central to Corso's vision. The poem turns upon Corso's special sense of the meaning of the word *power,* the definition (or redefinition) of which emerges in the course of the poem's development. Corso's understanding of the contradictory duality inherent in the word *power* is nearly exactly parallel to that proposed by Eric Fromm:

> The word "power" has a twofold meaning. One is the possession of
> power over somebody, the ability to dominate him; the other mean-

ing is the possession of power to do something, to be able, to be
potent. The latter meaning has nothing to do with domination; it
expresses mastery in a sense of ability. . . . Thus power can mean
one of two things, domination or potency. Far from being identical,
these two qualities are mutually exclusive. . . . Power in the sense
of domination is the perversion of potency. . . .[20]

The very purpose and declared intention of Corso's poetic exploration
of power is "wanting to change the old meaning of Power / Wanting to
give it new meaning my meaning." Corso celebrates creative power, the
power of the spirit, the power of the imagination (Coleridge's "esemplas-
tic power"); and he repudiates destructive power, refutes power as
coercion, as oppression (cf. Mao's dictum that "power comes out of the
barrel of a gun"). "Life is the supreme Power," Corso asserts, and "in
Power there is no destruction." The ultimate human powers are vision
and laughter. The first can make the "awful blank acreage" of the physical
world "pastoral" with myth; it can restore us to Arcadia. The second
power permits us to triumph over the anguish and suffering of life: "a
laugh / That drops my woe and all woe to the floor / Like a shot spy"
("Power," 80).

Those who seek or who wield despotic, destructive power (as in
"Army" and "Police") are self-defeating and self-destroying in their
ignorance of the real nature of power: "A thirst for Power is drinking
sand" ("Power," 78). Power in the physical world is not only mortally
injurious to those who attempt to possess it, but it is finally completely
illusory. The only true and ultimate power, the ground and source of all
identity and existence, is the redemptive, transcendent power of love.

Of the shorter lyrics in *The Happy Birthday of Death* collection, there
are celebrations, observations, poems of pure imagination, and cries of
despair. In "Notes after Blacking Out," the first poem in the volume,
Corso proposes a form of Keatsian "negative capability": "All is answer-
able I need not know the answer" (11); but in "1959," the last poem in the
collection, the poet expresses profound disillusionment with life, a sense
of utter hopelessness and frustration: "There is no mystery" but only
"cold history" (90). A similar vacillation of mood is evident between
"How Happy I Used to Be," which, like "Ode to Coit Tower" in *Gasoline*,
mourns the loss of the childhood faculty for vision and imagination, and
"Seaspin" or "Poets Hitch-Hiking on the Highway," which are seemingly effortless exercises in pure imaginative creation and joyous invention.

The poems "Giant Turtle" and "A Dreamed Realization" honor the irrepressibility, adaptability, and persistency of the Life Force as it is expressed in the survival of particular animal species (and, by extension, in all life). There is a similar optimism in "1953," which depicts a prison escape accomplished through a return to innocence and a cultivation and exercise of magic. There is a faith implicit in these poems, as well as in others in the volume, that the forces of life, the powers of laughter and imagination, are stronger than the forces of repression, destruction, and negativity and that they will ultimately triumph over them.

But a more sober, solemn note is struck in "Bomb," which envisions the total destruction of the earth through nuclear warfare, the final victory of the agents of "uncreation." And in other poems Corso expresses his dismay and despair at "this sad inharmonious weird predicament" of existence ("All Life Is a Rotary Club," 72), where each man conceals a monster within and where "horned Reality its snout ringed with tokens of fear" reigns enthroned in human minds and hearts, "pummeling child's jubilee, man's desire" ("Police," 86).

In sum, the vision of *The Happy Birthday of Death* is predominantly affirmative and optimistic. The poems strive to restore wholeness and vitality to human life, to promote and effect a victory of desire over external reality, but it is evident that Corso's resolve, his urgency, and his dynamism are not achieved without considerable inner struggle, profound doubts, nor without occasional lapses into despondency. His innocence is not naïveté or ignorance but an achieved state of spirit that must be cultivated, nourished, and maintained.

Corso's vision reaches its fullest expansion and achieves its clearest expression in *Long Live Man* (1962). The poems in this collection represent a culmination of his art and of his apprehension of the cosmic process and of humankind's place in the universal order. An important clue to Corso's poetic perspective in the volume is provided by his personal creation of the photographic illustration that appears on the front cover of the volume. While seeming to depict a nebula or galaxy, this is, in fact, a magnification of the poet's own semen.[21] This literal representation of the relationship between the microcosm and the macrocosm, and their mutual identification, is fundamental to the poet's view of the mysterious but harmonious and coherent design of the universe.

The first poem of the volume, "Man," provides a context for the poems that follow and presents a concise statement of the central themes of the collection. "Man" celebrates humankind evolving as a species, mastering the physical world, and evolving spiritually. To the poet language is of paramount importance in the evolutionary progress of the human mind and spirit. Chaos is primal and persistent, always destructively "groping behind" the scenes, manifesting itself in war and oppression, murder and madness. The evolutionary spirit expresses itself in creative genius, such as that of Beethoven, and in spiritual wisdom as embodied in Christ, "the victory of man." The created world and the phenomenological universe are themselves stages in a cosmic spiritual evolution in which humankind plays a central role as the highest evolved consciousness, "the victory of life."[22] The world is "the factory of the soul / The soul putting on a body like a workman's coveralls" (9). (There is a parallel here to John Keats' conception of the world as "a vale of soul-making.") Humankind is the agent and instrument of the Life Force, the evolutionary principle, but as such we are also the butt, the victim, the dupe, and the most effective implement of resurgent chaos.

Corso develops these themes in other poems in *Long Live Man.* In "Greece" he again defines the two opposing tendencies of human consciousness: the adventuring, explorative, questing spirit, as exemplified by the space program, and the destructive, annihilative impulses, as manifested by the "New York children . . . murdering each other" (20). The poet's journey to Greece is a pilgrimage in homage to, and in quest of, the original motive power of civilization—the mythic consciousness of the ancient Greeks. Amid the artifacts and landscapes of the now outmoded vision of the classical world, he senses the imminence of a new emergent vision. He hails a forthcoming "great event," a new age, and exhorts us to heed the new divine message ("Hear! Hermes is at the door / —who will take the message?") and to strive to realize it (22).

This new vision or cosmic myth (representing a rebirth of the most ancient myths) is articulated in this collection in "Reflection in a Green Arena," "Sura," "Gone the Last Danger on Earth," "Eden Were Elysium," "God? She's Black," "Seed Journey," and "Masterpiece." In these poems Corso affirms his belief in the creative energy of life, which is transformed, multiplied, but never lost. All of creation, history, and each individual life is a "masterpiece," an indispensable element in the greater "masterpiece," the unfolding of the cosmic plan ("Masterpiece," 60). Even death is a part of the life process, merely "a hygiene," an occasion for regeneration and rebirth ("Man," 9). Corso prophecies a joyful apocalypse, an end of all suffering and evil, "the clear distillation of night into dawn" ("Gone the Last Danger on Earth," 45). In this ultimate victory of light and life, "light must return / And reprieve the earth with its merciful stain" ("Sura," 42).

Doubt, however, is remorseless, and there are poems in the collection, such as "Writ in Horace Greeley Square" and "For —," in which Corso confesses his own bewilderment, ambivalence, doubt, even disgust, and despair at the evil, the sorrow, and the horror inherent in life. Overwhelmingly, though, the tone of *Long Live Man* is ebullient and affirmative. Corso's earlier recurrent image of the persecuted child or the wantonly destroyed ideal may be found still in such poems as "Suburbia Mad Song" and "Death of the American Indian's God," but a measure of Corso's more optimistic view of humankind and life is the series of five poems eulogizing the life and works of Saint Francis. He is celebrated as a true hero of the spirit, an ideal person who embodies the victory of compassion and love over selfishness and demonic destruction, the triumph of truth over chaos, of the Arcadian over the infernal.

"The agency of my sight darkens," declares a mythological persona in "The Geometric Poem," one of the central poems of *Elegiac Feelings American* (1970).[23] The phrase might well serve to characterize the dark vision of the entire collection. Published eight years after *Long Live Man,* the two volumes could scarcely be more dissimilar. As the title of the collection indicates, the tone here is serious, sorrowful, even grave. There is none of the humor that characterized the poet's previous work to be found here, but rather there is fear, sadness, anger, and profound pessimism.

The title poem is an elegy for Jack Kerouac, who is seen by Corso to exemplify the poet-prophet, the innocent idealist, rejected, scorned, and destroyed by a crass, materialistic culture. Corso here reverts to the imagery of his earliest poems where children are abused and devoured by monstrously unfeeling figures. Kerouac, the "Beat Christ-boy," is another child-victim. He is likened also to a tree that is first truncated, then starved in cold and foreign ground. The larger implications of the elegy extend to the fateful significance of this continuing rejection of beauty, truth, and vision by America and by the world. The poem has the solemn, ominous tone of a jeremiad (12).

In "Spontaneous Requiem for the American Indian," Corso considers the historical roots of this hostility to idealism by the pragmatic, utilitarian elements of American culture. This poem mourns the child-like, nobly primitive, indigenous peoples of North America, who had achieved harmony with the natural environment but who were vanquished and decimated by a blind, rapacious, mechanistic-rationalistic culture. The consequences for American civilization of this and similarly destructive acts are enumerated in the poems "Lines Written Nov. 22, 23 — 1963 — In Discord," "The American Way," and "America Politica Historia, in Spontaneity." America, for Corso, was to have been the new Arcadia, but it has instead become merely another empire, mad with material greed, obsessed with military power, denying its own vision and ideals.

Extending the theme further still in "Mutation of the Spirit," Corso explores the atrocities of human history from ancient Rome to the present "God-closed Age" (20), in which we witness "this piteous surrender of the spirit" (22). Again and again, throughout history the innocent and the joyful are destroyed; the "little white gowned rose girl" is "broken on the spoor" (19). The pastoral satyr with his syrinx is eradicated; "the Arcadian shepherd is famished thin" (24).

In "Immutable Moods" the poet reaches a nadir of despair and hopelessness, invoking the "old dead gods" to undo their creation, to "black out / blot out complete" the ruined, bloodstained world (116). Nor does "The Geometric Poem" offer any hope or consolation. The poem's central theme of a quest for a redemptive, transcendent knowledge, a "trismegistusian light" (43), a perfecting geometry, a "Sonic Eye" of vision (63), remains unresolved. The poem itself fails to cohere or to quicken to life; it forms only a jumble of mythological, historical fragments.

Appearing in 1981, eleven years after *Elegiac Feelings American,* Corso's most recent collection of poems is titled *Herald of the Autochthonic Spirit.* The poems in the volume bear the very distinct impress of the poet's experiences during the intervening decade, most particularly those of his addiction to heroin and his subsequent self-induced detoxification and rehabilitation. Though in comparison to Corso's early work, the mood of this volume seems subdued and regretful, there is also a new resolution apparent here, a renewed sense of purpose that informs his poetic vision and pronouncements with force and authority.

As the title of the volume suggests, the poet here reassumes and reaffirms his role as "ambassador of Power," as Hermean messenger, as herald of the creative spirit of the universe that is immanent in every human, indigenous to every land. But Corso begins by confessing his remissness in the performance of his sacred office of poet. In "Columbia U Poesy Reading — 1975," the first poem in the volume, Corso records in allegorical form the story of his near capitulation to the forces of "uncreation" within himself, and to the struggle waged in his mind and his spirit between his urge for oblivion (heroin) and his urge to create. Summoned by the Muse, Corso is accused by her and her companions (Ganesha, Thoth, and Hermes) of dereliction of duty, of forsaking poetic creation for the anodynic languors of opium. Denying the charge, excusing and justifying himself at first, he finally succumbs under their combined indictment: "'You have butchered your spirit!' roared Ganesha / 'Your pen is bloodied!' cawed the scribe Toth / 'You have failed to deliver the Message!' admonished Hermes." Realizing and admitting his fault, Corso vows to "expiate / all that's been sadly done . . . sadly neglected . . . ." He renews his commitment to poetry, his allegiance to beauty and truth. The implications of this victory go beyond the poet himself, representing a victory of the human spirit over the insidious, poisonous forces that would overwhelm and annihilate it from within.[24]

Corso celebrates his victory over these forces and the repossession of his vocation in the poems "Sunrise" and "Ancestry." He approaches his poet's task with a new humility, describing himself as "an olding messenger boy in "Sunrise" (6), but he proudly traces the distinguished pedigree of his profession from earliest myth and history down to his own appointment in "Ancestry" (20). By a fortuitous correspondence, Corso's middle name, Nunzio, means "messenger," so that his occupation seems foreordained and a fulfillment of his destiny and of his deepest self.

In "Return" from *Herald of the Autochthonic Spirit,* Corso delineates the stages of his growth as a poet. This entails a cyclic development from his earliest efforts through his eclipse to his reemergence. At the outset, imaginative creation for him is natural, effortless, and innocent:

> The days of my poems
> were unlimited joys
> of blue Phoenician sails
> and Zeusian toys.

Then the fall occurs and the middle period is "poemless," dreamless, a descent into a silent netherworld of opiates. This phase culminates in a long winter of struggle to rein in the runaway "wild horses" of the drug and to redeem his spirit from bondage. Through a sustained effort Corso recovers his powers and regains the "blue Phoenician sails / and Zeusian toys" of the poetic imagination. Thus, he completes his circular journey of self-discovery, returns to his original motive energy, and unites his past and his future (8–10).

The idea of a return to the origins and roots of one's being, to the true self, occurs again in "Poem Jottings in the Early Morn," where Corso exhorts his children (and by extension, all of us) "to return to primal sources / and there reclaim / all our natural losses—" (55). A related theme is developed in "What the Child Sees," "Eyes," and "Proximity." These poems argue for a return to original, pristine vision, the perception of children and mystics whereby the inner eye emanates and superimposes "truth upon all the lies" of the external world, the world of appearances ("Eyes," 37). (There is a parallel here to William Blake's distinction between "Spiritual perception" and ordinary sight by means of the "Corporeal or Vegetative Eye" as expressed in his "A Vision of the Last Judgment": "I look thro it and not with it.") Corso has again resumed his tactic of contradicting the real with the unreal, of repugning the material world with the imagination.

Corso's poems continue to be informed by his acute awareness of the violence, destruction, and suffering of the world and by his sense of a malevolent force active in the human heart. In "Many Have Fallen" and "Bombed Train Station, 80 Killed," he again probes the sources of human destructiveness, asking "Who knows what masks / bombers wear beneath their faces?" ("Bombed Train Station," 27). But in contrast to the pessimism and disillusion that characterizes so many of the poems in *Elegiac Feelings American,* Corso is again able to express faith in an ultimate redemption of the world and in the inevitable and final victory of the spirit. This faith is reflected in "Inter & Outer Rhyme," "Spirit," "Destiny," and "When We All . . . ." Though the tone of these last poems may seem somewhat chastened in comparison to the ardor of the poet's youthful idealism, it has gained the solidity and vigor of mature conviction.

Concerning his conception of the role of the poet in the world, Corso has written: "Someone must 'Christopher-Columbus' the mind, the great expanse of consciousness, and this the poet does. But unlike Columbus who discovered a new world a world that was there, the poet must make a new world — it is not there until he himself puts it there and discovers it for all peoples and time."[25]

Corso's six volumes of poetry represent the log of his long voyage of interior discovery: the map of new continents of vision and desire, including the dangerous whirlpools and doldrums, the horse latitudes and sargasso seas that must be navigated in order to reach these new worlds and make landfall.

His poems not only inform us of the universal struggle of light and darkness, creation and destruction, but also embody and enact that struggle manifesting the ultimate victory he prophecies.

Out of the stricken landscape of our age, Corso has brought us a vision of Arcadia. Out of the Plutonian underworlds of prison and heroin addiction, he has delivered his Hermean message of hope and liberation.

6

Homeward from Nowhere:

Notes on the Novels of

John Clellon Holmes

The body is hip. It is only the mind that knows Nowhere.
John Clellon Holmes
Nothing More To Declare

Night and homelessness are central motifs in the fiction of John Clellon Holmes, metaphors for the state of the human psyche in our century. The convulsive violence and vicious destructiveness of our age are seen by him as expressions of a spiritual void, a vacuum at the heart of humanity. For Holmes, the psychic climate of the postwar world is one approaching an absolute zero of the spirit; we are at Nowhere: benighted, dispossessed, in exile, and overcome by darkness. The motive of his work is to discover an end to the night, to find a way home.

Go, the author's first novel, opens with an image of spiritual nostalgia, as Paul Hobbes, the central figure of the story, yearns for a return to innocence, longing for humankind to live "naked on a plain" (3). In stark contrast, though, to this Edenic ideal, Holmes portrays a world where (in Matthew Arnold's phrase in "The Buried Life") men and women "live and move trick'd in disguises," sharing only mutual fear and shame, a desperate ennui, and the secret craving for love. Such is the state of the soul not only of the mass of men but also of the group of alienated young writers and bohemians on which the novel is centered. They are significant, however, for their attempt to transcend their condition, for their having undertaken a quest for a more authentic life, and for their search for some measure of meaning and peace.

The poles of *Go* are nihilism and vision, embodied respectively by the characters Bill Agatson and David Stofsky. The other characters of the novel, including the protagonist, occupy points along a continuum between these two extremities—between denial and affirmation, between fear and love, between zero and infinity. And the poles themselves sometimes meet, coexisting in the same person and ultimately in all humankind.

Agatson, the negative pole, the "black prophet" of the novel, is a demonic, destructive, drunken monster of a man (195). His outrageous and often cruel antics derive from "a fatal vision of the world" and from his "inability to really believe in anything" (19). His death, near the end of the novel, is as absurd and meaningless, as squalid and wasteful, as was his life. Shortly before Agatson's death, Hobbes observes an unguarded expression on his face that seems to epitomize his dark, anarchic life: "He looked like a man who is witnessing the vision of his whole unredeemable existence, seeing it as a savage mockery; but more, perceiving that *all* of life is a blasphemous, mortal joke at everyone's expense, a monstrous joke in which everything is ignoble, ludicrous and without value or meaning" (273).

And yet, Agatson, the monster, the nihilist, is ultimately seen to be an inverted idealist, a sort of saint turned inside out, an unconscious martyr to an unbelieving age. Precisely because he cares so deeply, he wills not to care at all. His essential sensitivity and vulnerability are glimpsed only when he involuntarily relaxes his will, as when he falls asleep once after a marathon binge revealing in sleep "a curious private softness" (74), a "boyishness," and an "innocence" (75). Only one other time does he let his mask slip for an instant in public, when he realizes that he has gone too far in baiting and mocking Verger, and he becomes suddenly contrite and gentle. Otherwise Agatson is determined to play the monster. But as Stofsky perceives, the monster in each of us is in reality no more than "a runny-nosed little boy"—pitiful, miserable, and strangely vulnerable (109).

Stofsky is the counterpart to Agatson. If Agatson may be seen to embody the psychic malady of our age, then Stofsky embodies the cure. Poet and mystic, Stofsky is an earnest quester who experiences a visionary breakthrough, a revelation of the essential duality of being: the material and the spiritual. He sees that the level of ordinary consciousness is characterized by "a chemical piercing fright," but at a deeper level, beneath the dread, there is "an impersonal, yet somehow natural love, cementing the very atoms" (83). This love is the Divine Presence, the Holy Spirit. As a result of this vision, Stofsky embarks on a life of charity and humility, extending compassion and consideration to all. He sees that the only proper and practical response to the "secret lovelessness" of the world and to the helpless, frightened "creatureliness" of man is love, sympathy, and service to others (179).

A measure of the spiritual strength of Stofsky is the noteable lack of success of other characters in the book who strive for vision or enlightenment. They achieve only a partial and, therefore, dangerous degree of success in their spiritual endeavors. Bill Waters, for example, though he attains a vision of eternity, succumbs to madness. Daniel Verger, despite his advanced theological studies, remains spiritually immature, and when he is unable to requite his amorous yearnings for May, becomes self-pitying and self-destructive. Finally, Ancke, who through his sufferings achieves a form of egoless resignation, a degree of detachment that could be turned to good advantage in a spiritual context, cannot summon the necessary discipline nor capacity for exertion and so remains passive, unable to raise himself from a life of criminality and addiction to opiates.

Nor do the paths to meaning and enlightenment followed by other more central figures in *Go* seem to lead them beyond their restlessness and confusion. The vitalism of Gene Pasternak, who champions the simple and natural life of the body over what he perceives as the sophistries of abstract thought and intellectualism, provides him with no enduring contentment or fulfillment. His love affair with Christine begins in "innocence" but ends in bitterness and pain (59), while his cross-country journeys only bring him back to where he started. He finds no livable truth. In a similar manner, Hart Kennedy's transcendental hedonism generates ecstasies and insights, but ultimately his Dionysian energies show themselves to be equally capable of veering off into nastiness and violence. Both Pasternak and Kennedy seem to be on the right track in their rejection of the rational mind and in their cultivation of the instincts, but their attempts to live fuller, truer lives are imperfectly realized and must be accounted as failures.

Other than Stofsky, the only character to grow and change in a positive manner in the course of the novel is Paul Hobbes. In the beginning, Hobbes feels "brittle and will-less," aimless, and frustrated (3). His marriage to Kathryn is troubled and precarious, and his relations to others are often uneasy, as his motives and reactions are frequently misunderstood. Reticent and unassertive, he is more of an outsider, an observer, than a participant in "the beat generation" (211). Earnestly searching for a direction, a position, a perspective on life, Hobbes is hindered by his emotionally reserved nature. "In the face of an avid passion, Hobbes snapped shut like an oyster on a grain of sand; but like the oyster, the passion festered inside him" (69). Similarly, he feels a simultaneous attraction to and an alienation from both the "hip" world of mystery and kicks and the "square" world of reasonableness and responsibility.

A series of shocks jolt Hobbes into self-examination and greater awareness. Confrontations with Stofsky and Pasternak and Kathryn, the rejection of his novel on which he had staked so much, and the death of Agatson are catalysts in Hobbes' psyche. He begins to perceive the falseness, the shallowness, and the essential selfishness of his relationships to others.

> How insufferable everyone was. . . . They came to fear emotions, to think of human needs as a sign of weakness, and to view isolation, not as a curse and a blight, but as a protection. For the first time, he saw these attitudes in himself. . . . And suddenly his part in all relationships seemed made up of actions blind and cowardly and base, even though they were unconscious. (292)

Humbled with this new awareness of himself, Hobbes undertakes a further journey into the dark labyrinth of the self, and there in the maze of motives and emotions, he confronts his personal monster. Hobbes' monster manifests itself in the form of a sudden, sickening realization of the "reality of horror, without meaning, with no certain end" (309). Hobbes' monster is the void itself. In the dim, foul men's room of a waterfront saloon, he regards himself in a shattered mirror, a metaphor for his fragmented self. Reading the obscene inscriptions on the walls, Hobbes is overpowered with a knowledge of "the barrenness of the heart" (310). He understands how tenderness and the longing for love become perverted into cruelty and lewdness. With awful clarity he sees the cause of Agatson's wild despair.

> Certainly, somewhere, some time this fatal perception must have entered him like a germ and corrupted his heart and mind. And

> Hobbes suddenly knew that someone who believes this vision is
> outraged, violated, raped in his soul, and suffers the most unbear-
> able of all losses: the death of hope. And when hope dies there is only
> irony, a vicious senseless irony that turns to the consuming desire to
> jeer, spit, curse, smash, destroy. (310)

Terrified and appalled by this infernal epiphany, Hobbes exclaims, "I
must get out of here!" (310). He wishes to escape not merely the rank
latrine and its scrawled obscenities but metaphorically, the state of his
mind and spirit. His exclamation is more than a cry of fear and revulsion;
it is a vow to amend his life. He must work to extricate himself from the
dark hell of lovelessness and selfishness. The novel concludes with
Hobbes' tentative reconciliation with Kathryn and with an image of his
continuing search for a spiritual home, recalling his longing at the outset
of the story for an Edenic home: "'Where is our home?' he said to himself
gravely, for he could not see it yet" (311). In the end, Hobbes, more than
any other character in the book, represents the burden of his generation—the terrible urgency of the spirit to "get out of here," to get out of
hell, to redeem itself (310); and Hobbes most fully embodies the
bewildered bereftness and lostness of the soul in an age of murder and
perdition.

Much of the meaning of *Go* derives from its nervous, ominous mood,
its atmosphere of decay and dissolution: the dreary, phony, sad bars of the
city; the hostile streets; the glimpsed vignettes of violence, indifference,
and affectation, of pretense and evasion; the endless, desperate, joyless
parties; the desolate, crumbling cityscapes; the squalor and the sordid-
ness—all seen in the infernal illumination of neon lights and streetlights
in a perpetual night. In this dark and this ruin Holmes' hipsters pursue
their spiritual quest: lurking, furtive; "connected by the invisible
threads of need, petty crimes of long ago, or a strange recognition of
affinity"; conspirators in a "revolution of the soul" (36). They are the
"children of the night: everywhere wild, everywhere lost, everywhere
loveless, faithless, homeless" (310); yet ever searching for a breakthrough, a vision, a center, an answer, ever seeking for some way
homeward from Nowhere.

Since mystical revelation, such as that experienced by Stofsky, is not
accessible to most people, other forms of communion and spiritual
enlightenment must be sought in the faithless wasteland of the postwar

world. For the Beat Generation in *Go,* the chief means of transcendence, truth, and grace is jazz. In the fluent, organic rhythms of bop they recognize the lost language of the loins and of the heart; they hear the cry of the human in a dehumanized age.

> In this modern jazz, they heard something rebel and nameless that spoke for them, and their lives knew a gospel for the first time. It was more than a music; it became an attitude toward life, a way of walking, a language and a costume; and these introverted kids (emotional outcasts of a war they had been too young to join, or in which they had lost their innocence), who had never belonged anywhere before, now felt somewhere at last. (161)

Through this music, at once erotic and ethereal, the music of the body and the spirit, the music of revolt and celebration, *Go* leads into and is linked with Holmes' next novel, *The Horn.*

The Horn is a bildungsroman told in reverse: the life history of jazz saxophonist Edgar Pool, known reverently to his fans and fellow musicians as "the Horn." (Pool is a fictional composite of Lester Young, Charlie Parker, and others but essentially a product of the author's imagination.) The central narrative of the novel moves forward in time from dawn to dark on Pool's final day of life, while a series of tributary narratives move backward in time tracing significant events in his life from the most recent to the earliest. Pool is a living legend in the jazz world, a seminal genius of bop, but he is dissipated, impoverished, broken in health and spirit. His object on his last day is to find a way home, to raise enough money to return to his hometown.

Pool is in many ways an extension of Agatson in *Go:* embittered, cynical, mocking, ironical, outrageous, and self-destructive. He is described as "the Black Angel," a man who has "fled from the light" and who has turned inward on himself in his fierce pride.[1] Like Agatson, there is a demonic quality to Pool, a desperate, driven quality. With his "cold eyes and destructive lips and closed heart" (38), he is likened to "a ruined prince intent upon doom" (107). Unlike Agatson, though, Pool is a musician, an artist, a creator who can turn even his rage and despair into art; and he is thus, in the end, able to redeem himself in despite of himself.

Redemption for Pool occurs only in the fleeting, final minutes of his life when he experiences a "falling away of all veils" enabling him to see himself and to see others clearly at last, to see the world not through the distortions of his fatal, satanic pride but lucidly with love (207). Only in the last minutes of his life does Pool extend kindness and compassion to others; only then does he regret his hauteur and pretense; and only then does he regain the full, true power of his art and understand it at last. In this sense, Edgar Pool does find his way home.

If Agatson in *Go* is seen as a sort of martyr, crippled by his lack of belief and acting out the destructive fantasies of a whole community of unbelievers, then Pool is a martyr of a similar sort but for opposite reasons. His is the martyrdom of a prophet unheeded for so long and forced to endure such neglect and humiliation that at last he loses his faith. Ironically and to his further embitterment, when he has lost his faith, others suddenly embrace his former prophecies and testimonies, leaving him "an atheist old man maddened by the certainties of youth" and feeling himself mocked by images of his earlier self (38).

Three interlocked clusters of images convey the thematic movement of *The Horn*: religious imagery, musical imagery, and the imagery of birds and of flight.

Religious similes and metaphors occur throughout the story, especially in connection with jazz, which is described in terms of a "testament" (10), a "sacrament" (202), and as "holy" (36) and further characterized as a "mystery" and a "prophecy" (154), and as a "ritual" enacted on an "altar" by ecstatic "suppliants" (155).

Music itself is, in turn, a metaphor for the spiritual search of humankind. It brings light to darkness and is the expression of truth. All music is a part of "the one song" (47), "the one continuing song" (243) that evolves in "apostolic succession, song to song, man to man" (76). The musician is "God's own fool" (25) (in both senses) and his music is ultimately "always deeply on God's side" (231), a celebration of the created world and of the spirit.

Imagery of flight and of birds is also central to *The Horn*. Allusions to types of birds (such as the goose, the hummingbird, the albatross, the eagle, etc.), to the anatomy of birds (wing, beak, plumage), and to their songs (their squawks and honks) are frequent in the text. The bird imagery is most often applied to jazz musicians, while imagery of flight is applied to the music itself. Pool's saxophone, for example, is compared to "some metallic albatross caught insecurely in his hands, struggling to resume flight" (8). The bird and flight motif suggests transcendence, the soaring of the spirit beyond the limits of the body and the material world, rising and gliding in perfect joy and freedom. In this way, the motif unites the religious and the musical imageries in mutual reinforcement.

The single image that most concisely encapsulates the theme of the novel is song as a defense against the cold, music as a defense against death by freezing. This image emerges from an early experience in the life of Edgar Pool, recalled many years afterward by his boyhood friend Metro. As boys on the bum, riding in an empty boxcar in the dead of winter, they were caught in an "arctic blizzard" (167). In order to generate heat and to stay alive, they sang—spontaneously and defiantly against the cold and the night and, by this means, surviving and triumphing.

The incident serves as a metaphor for the human situation: we are all alone and far from home, frightened and cold, traveling through a storm, heading, like Pool and Metro, through "the exact magnetic eye of that wild, uncaring night, into an absolute shrieking dark" (167). And, like Pool and Metro, we must also find the creative force, the source of song within ourselves, and we must learn to sing or we shall freeze in "the bitter dark and cold" of this godless age (167).

The knowledge that the state of ultimate human nakedness and vulnerability is coupled with an innate redeeming power informs Pool's art and is its secret motive power despite his attempts to deny it. He acknowledges this redeeming power again only as he is dying on stage, and he tries to communicate it to others with his dying words, his final message: celebrate. Pool's saxophone is the symbol of the continuity and the enduring presence of such power and its celebration. At the beginning of his career as a musician, he redeems his first horn from a pawnshop; and at the end of his career, he returns his last horn to a pawnshop. But his pawned horn will, we are told, be redeemed again by a new celebrant, "dreaming a new dream, hoping a new hope, loving a new love" (242); and this singer will "fashion on it a new song—a further chorus of the one continuing song" (243). In defiance of the inertia, the despair, and the surrender emblematized by the pawnshop, the instruments of renewal and hope, of celebration and truth, are passed from hand to hand, from human to human. Like the boys in the boxcar, we can only freeze if we give up, let go, if we allow ourselves to freeze.

Perhaps by way of emphasizing the essential continuity of *Go* and *The Horn,* Holmes develops points of intersection in the two novels. Both share, of course, certain locations and a similar milieu—the New York city night world of jazz and in particular the jazz club called the Go Hole. Gene Pasternak and Paul Hobbes from *Go* make two brief appearances in *The Horn*. They are first glimpsed listening to bop outside a record store (150) and later seen in the audience at the Go Hole on the night of Edgar Pool's final gig (232). In both instances they are appraised by the jazz musicians as true communicants, as exemplars of an understanding and appreciation of jazz that is inspiring to the musicians. Their enthusiasm is seen as a necessary nourishment to the artist who, in turn, gives sustenance to the audience. Thus is "the one continuing song" born out of the hearts of all humankind, not just the musician; it is given and received in equal amount, a mutual human endeavor.

Thematically, too, the two novels intersect, both representing aspects of the postwar search for belief, for a unifying vision. In *Go* Holmes describes the goal of the quest as being "some end of the night (the night that was a corridor in which they lurked and groped, believing in a door somewhere, beyond which time and the discord bred of time were barred)" (240). In *The Horn,* Walden Blue, the successor to Pool, is described as having "groped blindly" for some form of belief as he plays his horn and as feeling that "down in his heart waited a single note of music that he felt would shatter all discord into harmony" (16). The terms of description and the ends of both quests are significantly similar.

Both novels also affirm that the means to transcend discord and darkness lie not in the rational mind, not in the ego, but in the unconscious, the body. In *Go* Stofsky speaks of having rejected Aristotelian logic and of cultivating instead "a breakthrough into the world of feeling" (65). In *The Horn,* Metro, the "prophet of joy," achieves his ecstatic affirmations by moving beyond the mind, knowing that "only beyond such breaking loose would all things finally be reconciled" (154). His wild, joyful, celebratory music says "a clear and untranslatable 'Yes!' to everything that was not of the mind" (155). To resist alienation and dehumanization and to achieve a psychic reorientation that will restore integrity and coherence to human life, Holmes proposes the energies of the unconscious, the mysterious life of the body.

Holmes' third and last novel, *Get Home Free*, is a sequel to *Go*. The book follows the lives of certain characters from *Go* in the aftermath of the events of that novel. *Get Home Free* also shares motifs and themes with *The*

Horn and may be seen as extending and resolving the concerns of its two predecessors and thus completing a sequence of interrelated novels.

Get Home Free consists of two central, separate episodes divided by an interlude and framed by a prologue and an epilogue. The structure of the two episodes and of the novel as a whole is informed by the archetypal pattern of the night journey: the movement of the psyche through dissolution to a new wholeness, through darkness to light—a process objectified by the temporal movement from night to dawn and daylight. The novel is also unified by the motif of returning to one's geographical home and of finding a spiritual home.

The prologue, titled "New York: The End," is a sort of epilogue to the events of *Go*. The desperate energy of the immediate postwar era is now dissipating; there is an air of exhaustion, of "hopelessness and waste," as the forties end and the fifties begin.[2] And with the new decade there is a widespread feeling of apathy, a sense that the moral and metaphysical issues have somehow been obviated. Correspondingly, there is a reassertion of self-interest, self-gratification, a reentrenchment of convention. Personifying the new zeitgeist, the spirit of the fifties, is the character Tertius Streik: brash, insensitive, venal, hedonistic, cynical, and utterly, ruthlessly, unashamedly materialistic. (His name suggests an allusion to baseball: the third strike, the batter's failure to hit the ball, the end of hope for a home run.) Streik's self-satisfaction and his preoccupation with pleasure, career, position, and money is the antithesis of Agatson's despair and Stofsky's mysticism in *Go*.

The prologue also serves to define the specific problems of the main characters Verger and May. Having come together after Agatson's death, Verger and May are now nearing the end of their love affair. There has been "a failure of intimacy between them," a failure that encompasses both sexuality and true heart-to-heart communication through tenderness and openness (16). They are mutually alienated—alienated from their country (Verger rails and raves against America) and, of course, ultimately alienated from themselves. Their failure to love is linked with the horrors of the recent war and with the tensions of the cold war, with the universal human failure to love. "What's *wrong* with us?" May asks, "What happened to everyone?" (27). Verger replies, "Good Lord, what can I say. It sounds so pompous. . . . But Hiroshima, Belsen, the foolishness at Torgau, all that—it reached here somehow, right here . . ."

(27–28). The note of disintegration and disjunction introduced and sustained in the prologue reaches its culmination at the end of the section when Verger and May separate.

In the first of the two episodes that form the core of *Get Home Free,* Verger, having left May, leaves New York City too and returns to his hometown in rural New England "to come to terms with a stalled life" (55). There he encounters and becomes acquainted with Old Man Molineaux, a local eccentric and reprobate, the town drunk, and the object of much scandalized gossip. A curious affinity develops between the old man and the younger man, and through his association with Molineaux, Verger gains self-awareness and maturity; he discovers or recovers his own identity.

Old Man Molineaux is the heir to an American tradition that goes back to Washington Irving's Rip Van Winkle and comes down through Henry David Thoreau. Molineaux is a free spirit, fiercely independent, stubborn, defiant, a ne'er-do-well and a social outcast, undomesticated, at home in the forests and the fields, a friend of dogs, and an enemy of the authorities (the constables and the politicians), of propriety (the prim, church-going ladies and the respectable productive citizens), and of all convention and orthodoxy. Molineaux is the embodiment of the wild-outlaw-anarchic spirit that has always been the true informing energy of the American republic.

Significantly, Molineaux is in imminent danger of being involuntarily institutionalized, committed to the state hospital upon the recommendation of the town physician and with the consent of his family. The decision to confine this proud, wild, solitary man is entirely appropriate to an age of conformity and complacency and secret anxiety, an age dazzled by affluence and hypnotized by "the Great Gray Eye" of television (90). With the collusion of Verger, Molineaux evades the forces of normality for a time, and when at last he is cornered and forced to capitulate, he does so on his own terms. Molineaux manages to turn his defeat into a sort of victory, transforming his retreat into a tactical withdrawal. By feigning or, at least, by playing up his physical infirmities, he succeeds in preserving his self-esteem and in gaining the opportunity to spend the winter in the comfort of the hospital rather than in his primitive shack. The Old Man may be caught for the time-being, but he remains unreconstructed, unregenerate, unrepentant, and ultimately irrepressible. With the cunning and craft of an old campaigner he continues "the unequal struggle" against society (134), keenly, intuitively aware that, as Emerson states, "society everywhere is in conspiracy against the manhood of every one of its members" and that "whoso would be man must be a nonconformist."

Molineaux has also gained a disciple and an heir in Verger, who, during the course of their adventures, assumes "a filial protectiveness" for the Old Man, and for whom Molineaux becomes a sort of spiritual father (98). In protecting and defending Old Man Molineaux, Verger learns to accept and to affirm the same wild, anarchic, rebellious spirit in himself. He thus becomes the successor to Molineaux, just as the Old Man is himself successor to "the Old Leather Man" of his youth. After passing through a long, drunken night of wandering and misadventures with Old Man Molineaux, Verger manages in the end to bring him safely home. Through this act, he comes safely home himself, finding his true home and his true family by embracing the tradition of "*wild* America . . . Indians, sailors, bums, crazy damn fools with funny notions in their heads" (101). His night journey over, Verger has succeeded in getting home free.

May, too, makes a night journey, undergoing a process of self-refinement and regeneration. Like Verger, May has reached the dead end of herself in New York City and, in an "exhaustion of spirit," returns to her hometown in rural Louisiana (146). But, as did Verger in New England, May feels herself an outsider, a stranger in her community, stifled by the polite inanity and dismal conventionality of her family and her friends. And finally, like Verger, May, too, discovers "*wild* America" and reaffirms her own sense of individuality and of identity.

Abandoning her stuffy, unadventurous, hometown companions of the evening, May spends a night in the fertile chaos of a dilapidated country house inhabited by a collection of nonconforming, blithe, and unrestrained hipsters and free spirits. The house is a sort of oasis of untamed energy, sensuality, and individuality, a sanctuary of "careless anarchy and underground freedom of whim" (187). In the course of a long night of alcohol, marijuana, music, conversation, dance, arguments, and strange encounters (including three sexual propositions), May reaches "a bottomless weariness, beyond despair" (230). She passes then, at dawn, into an almost transcendent state of heightened receptivity to, awareness and acceptance of the ongoing and ever renewed and renewing miracle and mystery of existence:

> I was translucently open to it—the gnats, like a fine cloud of golden specks, swarming in a ray of early sunshine; the wild asters meek and fragile in the glistening grasses; the cock that crew with lazy conceit over near the bayou; all the verdure, and the growth, and the awakening—tiny hidden worlds from which we are mostly excluded by our formulating intelligence—all there in the dewy sanity of the morning. (234)

There is in this passage a sense of having at last reached the end of the night, the dark night of the soul, and of having moved out of Nowhere to here, to being on the earth, in the world, to a feeling of community of life, communion with creation. There is a sense of deliverance and repristination, of refreshment and restoration, a quality of having been returned to the senses, to the body. May has come through and has found a fulcrum, a meridian, a beginning.

Another character from *Go,* Paul Hobbes, also reappears in *Get Home Free*. Hobbes, too, has left New York, and, like Verger and May, he is embarked upon a night journey through his psyche. Hobbes is one of the racially-mixed company staying at the old Louisiana farm house. He is divorced, drifting, having forsaken words and writing for music and abandoned intellectuality for an exploration of the dark mysteries of the body. "We've lost touch with something—," Hobbes tells May, "something wild and natural, call it bliss or reality, a capacity for spontaneous love, whatever—but it's the only thing that can renew the consciousness when it's exhausted by anxiety" (198). Learning music under the tutelage of Little Orkie, sexuality under the tutelage of Orkie's sister Billie, submerging himself in the unconscious and the instincts by means of drugs and alcohol, and trying to learn to read the map of his own nervous system, Hobbes is still in midvoyage, at midpassage. His night journey has not yet been completed.

Music is, once again, an important motif in *Get Home Free,* a metaphor again for the spiritual search and aspiration of man and a vehicle of expression for certain elusive truths and for a knowledge beyond language. Embodying the wisdom of music is the blind, black singer, Little Orkie, with his message of joyous affirmation: "It's all all right." Orkie possesses an unfallen, Adamic innocence (appropriately, he works as a gardener), and his music reflects a prelapsarian "nakedness" of spirit and a strange, orphic reconciling power (162):

> The voice itself seeming to make its own peace with life's betrayals, the voice speaking for the body out of which it came, and for its humors and agitations and bafflements, a little mournful with the subsiding sob that lingers for a while in a cheered child's first hesitant laugh; somehow suggestive, too, of the grief that purges as usually only art can purge; a voice without an emotional flaw, with no failure of feeling, and, as a result, almost unearthly to hear, because we are so unused to hearing anything so utterly earthly exposed to the disbelief of strangers. (163–64)

Though blind, Orkie is intensely aware of, involved in, and responsive to the world around him. He retains, as May observes, a childlike sense of wonder at the world and a relatedness to it: "He's still part of it" (234). Orkie serves as a sort of spiritual teacher or guide for both Hobbes and May, an exemplar of simple, sincere, and unself-conscious faith and grace. He may be seen as the musician that Edgar Pool might have been without his fatal pride: an enraptured celebrant of life.

The last section of the novel, "New York: The Beginning," brings May and Verger back to the city again (Verger by way of Europe) and, as the title indicates, brings them to a new beginning of their lives. Both have achieved maturity and a new self-reliance and composure, a sense of identity. They recommence their affair but on the basis of immediate desires and spontaneous passion without reference to received patterns or abstractions of love or commitment or a long-term relationship. Free of such formal and impersonal conventions with their often distorting and inhibiting pressures and preconceptions, Verger and May discover a new sexual compatibility and a new intensity of erotic desire, one that flourishes "without a word, without a thought" (246). The sheer heightened physicality of their lovemaking serves to bring them closer together at a psychic level than ever before and constitutes a form of transcendence. "Their two desires fused into that single cleaving need in which the mind is extinguished at last . . . and the astounded moan of pleasure comes abruptly of itself, abolishing something—some illusion of the isolated self" (249). In their new union May and Verger have rediscovered an elemental, sacramental, regenerative energy; they have found a way leading homeward from Nowhere.

The title of the novel, *Get Home Free,* suggests the successful resolution of the quests that were begun in *Go* and were pursued in *The Horn.* Verger and May come home in at least three ways: they come home to themselves, attaining their identity, their individuality, and discovering a tradition, a community in which to participate; they come home to their homeland, reconciling themselves to the "creative turmoil" of America, its violence and anger, its joy and aspiration, its continuing potential for evolution (248); and, finally, they come home to that wholeness, that mysterious unity of being which exists beyond the exile of the isolate ego.

John Clellon Holmes' three novels propose three different but complementary ways of countering human destructiveness and of finding a solution to our common crisis of spirit. These ways or paths out of Nowhere are mysticism, art, and sexuality. Although these may, at first sight, seem to be irreconcilable and incompatible, ultimately they may be seen to share some essential qualities and characteristics. Each involves a surrender of the ego to a greater entity or energy; each in its way represents a form of communion with the numinous; each is rooted in the unconscious; and each draws upon the deepest creative energies of our being. Like Blake and Lawrence, Holmes perceives the subversive, liberating nature of sexuality and art—both expressions of Eros, both reflections and revelations of eternal beauty and bliss—and discerns the deep congruence and affinity of sexuality and spirituality—both expressions of the same urge to transcend the subjective self.

Holmes' novels record and interpret the inner conflicts and problems of the immediate postwar period, a crucial juncture of contemporary history. He focuses upon representative members of the generation that came of age during the Second World War and during the cold war that followed, the Beat Generation, which was the first to register the effects of the collective trauma of the war and to react to it, seeking the cause and the cure of their condition. In the acute response of his fiction to the social, moral, and metaphysical issues of postwar America and in his resolute quest for remedial means and measures, strategies for renewal, for the realization of a new consciousness and for a new human wholeness, Holmes' work is prophetic and possesses an enduring pertinence to our time. A bold explorer of the antipodes and terrae incognitae of the psyche, Holmes has shown us that the night and the void can be traversed and that a homeward passage can be effected.

7

From the Substrate:

Notes on the Work of

Michael McClure

Let that which stood in front go behind!
and let that which was behind advance to the front and speak.
                              Walt Whitman
                              "Respondez!"

*E*xtravagant, extreme, even excessive: the writings of Michael McClure aim at nothing less than a rediscovery and a redefinition of humankind. McClure's work is essentially alchemical: a process of reconciliation and transmutation. Beginning with the apparent contradictions of mind and body — mysticism and materialism, spirituality and sensuality, atavism and transcendence, human and nonhuman, energy and structure — the poet forges a new harmony and wholeness, a new coherence. McClure's poems, plays, and prose are the record of his struggle for personal liberation and of his evolving bio-alchemical vision. The following notes represent an attempt to trace the main direction and the major developments of his work over the last thirty years.

The most convenient and appropriate point at which to begin a consideration of Michael McClure's oeuvre is his autobiographical novel, *The Mad Cub*. The book presents an account of the poet's adolescence and young manhood and of his crucial passage through a prolonged and acute mental-physical and metaphysical crisis to a state of self-renewal and the affirmation of a secular faith, a faith in life. McClure's bildungsroman, his portrait of the artist, is in many respects a key to his work, providing an introduction to his concerns, his imagery, and his vision.

As the title implies, the central imagery of *The Mad Cub* is drawn from the animal world. Throughout the book, the narrator, Pete, likens himself and the other characters to various beasts, including pigs, goats, horses, bulls, wolves, calves, and rats. The numerous animal similes serve to convey the essential theme of the novel: human beings are mammals. This assertion is by no means as simple as it may at first seem. It serves as the foundation of McClure's vision. For the narrator it provides a release from his physical afflictions, from his neurasthenia, his alienation, his despair, and his madness, and it represents the principal datum for a new orientation to his own life and the life of the world.

Predominant among the animal images in the text is that of the lion, which is employed as a metaphor both for superconsciousness/divinity and for authentic identity, full physio-psychic being: "God is a vast robed figure of beauty who moves in space and simultaneously *is* space. He has a gentle maniacal face like a lion's. . . ."[1] "I'm sick of all the things that have held me down and dragged me and disgusted me with life. . . . I want to grow and become the lion I truly am" (79). With its heraldic, mythological, and astrological associations, the image of the lion serves to unite the individual and the universal, the microcosm and the macrocosm.

The development of the narrator from "mad cub" to "lion consciousness" (123) is finally achieved by a summoning forth of beast consciousness by means of "growling and imitating an animal and roaring" (156). Following this cathartic experience, the narrator is at last capable of self-understanding and self-acceptance and of the untrammeled expression of love for others, especially for his wife and daughter whose affections he has abused and alienated in the rage and pain of his sickness. His final vision of, and joyous identification with, the physical-metaphysical processes of the cosmos is expressed as a poem. The narrator rhapsodizes and celebrates a sense of sacramental unity with stars and nebulae, with mountains and trees, and (as in Joyce's *Ulysses*) he concludes his paean with a grand, universal affirmation: "YES".

The situation of Pete in *The Mad Cub*—"suspicious of everyone" (5), false, competitive, self-destructive, obsessed with sex, unable to express or to accept love, frustrated and blocked with unrealized potential—may be seen as emblematic of the human condition in general, perhaps more especially in Western culture. Pete's salvation through mammal consciousness is more, then, than a personal solution, it is a proposal for a transformation of human consciousness. To resist and arrest the psychic disintegration of man and to redeem and realize true human nature involves, for McClure, reclaiming our animal identity, coming to terms with the prelogical, primitive spirit of the senses, the unconscious, the body.

The Mad Cub provides a précis of McClure's themes, as well as a compendium of motifs and images which are further developed in his other works. The image of the self-divided man as embodied in Pete's physical appearance ("I look thin and romantic because of my skinny face. Secretly I'm fat. There's flab around my belly and my chest sags a little" [54].) is important in this regard. So, too, are the characters of Billy the Kid and Jean Harlow who are figures in the narrator's private mythology. Also significant here is the growling and roaring, the expression of the preverbal intelligence. Finally, the three-part movement of the book (the presentation of the problem, the achievement of a resolution, and the portrayal of liberated, visionary consciousness) corresponds to what may be seen as the three main phrases of the author's entire literary production.

The first phase of McClure's work is characterized by a sense of disequilibrium, of confusion, of torment, of alienation, of diminishment, of constraint, and of restriction, while at the same time, he exhibits a bold determination to resist all such limitation and negativity and to strive toward liberation, toward wholeness and health. In this regard, I recall reading that the first step in the alchemist's enterprise is the discovery of "a great crack in the heart of things." From this point the process of transmuting the corrupt to the incorruptible may begin.

McClure's first published poems are two villanelles titled "2 for Theodore Roethke," printed in the January 1956 issue of *Poetry.*[2] It is noteworthy that a poet later remarkable for radical poetic experimentation should display such technical mastery in this intricate, elaborate form. McClure's villanelles are polished, deft, and elegant; he exhibits faultless control of the rhymes and repetitions and achieves richness, complexity, and resonance of imagery. The two villanelles are probably so titled and dedicated because of the common concerns and sympathies of the two poets. Roethke was at that period also writing poems of personal suffering and transformation, and he, too, distrusted intellection and celebrated nature and the unity of all things.

The first of the villanelles, titled "Premonition," contrasts the "I" speaker's present psychic state, one of darkness, noise, fear, discomfort, and confusion with his aspirations to ascent, flight, song, sight, and light. Two opposing clusters of images are the vehicles of the conflict. Physical imagery, that of the body (bones, heart, toes, eyes, feet, ears, blood, skin, and skull) contends with imagery of flight and ascent (sky, clouds, height, birds, and the verbs "spiralled up," "ascend," and "climb"). The state of the body is "wingless" and "tight," burning and aching with the intensity of its desire to ascend, to fly.

Although perplexity and distress are established by the condition of noise and the statement that "the echoes from the sky are never clear," more hopeful indications are given in the affirmation that "what sings inside me climbs above my fear" and by the repeated lines declaring, "I work toward light." The "arsenics of sight" by which ascent is accomplished in the poem would seem to suggest a process of death and rebirth, while the "Great Bird" suggests a mythic force or spiritual energy, the very embodiment of transcendent freedom (the Holy Ghost) whose bite is blessing. The arsenic and the bite unite as images of an ordeal or death of self that must precede enlightenment or liberation. Significantly, it is in the heart and the body, not the intellect, that the longing for light and for flight is felt.

The second, untitled villanelle is much darker in mood. The body and the senses are again prominent but in a distinctly negative respect. The images of the body are here set in opposition to those of the natural world (copse, earth, mole, rock, plant, ouzel) and also to a mythic, mysterious level of existence encompassing the secrets of nature (Elysium, song and romance, and the undine [an alchemical allusion: a water nymph, from the writings of Paracelsus]). The body is imaged as "corpse," very strongly suggesting its lack of vitality and energy. McClure reinforces this image by words and phrases applied to the senses, such as "defeat," "in the way," "dumb," and "numb." There is a strong sense of awkwardness, clumsiness, bluntness, insufficiency of the senses as tools. The phrase "these stocks of body" may refer to the body as being lifeless, dull, and stupid or may constitute a metaphor of the body as pillory or stocks—confining, imprisoning.

McClure establishes a further conflict in the poem between the wayward and the straight or between elemental mystery and logical positivism, between nature and civilization, between the unconscious and the rational, analytical faculties. The image of the mole seems to suggest a regenerative force within the psyche, perhaps the deepest self, associated with the deep "poundings of the earth" or the impulses and truths of the unconscious mind. The present state of the self in the poem is as yet one of "weighted trance," of loss and of death-in-life, of alienation from nature and from the powers of the unconscious, of separation from mystery and mythic consciousness. The mole has not yet succeeded in rescuing, redeeming the "I" speaker, and the strict order of the rational mind still prevails over nature and the life of the imagination.

Aside from their beauty of expression, these early poems of McClure are significant for their delineation of the poet's physio-psychic crisis in terms of patterns of images. The formal restraint and the poetic artifice of the villanelle form seem an attempt to contain and control the intensity of the conflicts. The two poems serve not only to describe the problem but also to prefigure its eventual solution: the Great Bird and the mole represent mythic, elemental forces — redemptive energies capable of transforming the self.

The issues of these early poems are more closely examined and more fully developed in the collection *Hymns to St. Geryon and Other Poems.* What is immediately striking about the poems in this volume is their metrical structure and the visual impact of their typography. Rather than beginning at the left margin, the lines are centered on the page, creating a vertical axis. The arrangement of lines along this axis creates an effect of both equilibrium and dynamism, both a centripetal and a centrifugal poetic action. The lines are without regular meter and of unequal length, measured by their meaning and music, and more nearly approaching natural speech rhythms than the poet's earlier verse. Dramatic emphasis of particular words and phrases is achieved by the use of capitalization. Pauses are indicated by spacing. The total effect of McClure's prosodic adaptations and innovations in these poems is a heightened sense of experience, an intensified discharge and transfer of energy, a greater urgency, vitality, immediacy, and force of expression.

Geryon is the monster of Fraud in Dante's *Inferno,* Canto 17. He is "the beast that makes the whole world stink," the embodiment of duplicity and corruption: "His face was innocent of every guile, benign and just in feature and expression; and under it his body was half reptile."[3] Geryon is sainted by McClure because we have sanctified and canonized Fraud in our lives, in our civilization. Geryon represents the fraudulent lives we lead, our poisoned bodies and senses, the patterns and preconceptions that obscure the world from us, the monstrous denial of our energy and true nature, the monster of measurement, habit, and custom that constricts and dams our vitality. But Geryon is also for McClure a very personal demon: "He seemed to be my patron. I had a luminous handsome face and a rather gross and flabby body. I felt that I was a kind of living hypocrisy or fraud."[4]

A motif common to a number of poems in this collection is that of enclosure or confinement by walls or barriers and the necessity of effecting a breach, breaking through, breaking out. The first poem of the volume, "The Breach," describes the urgent, desperate assault (hurling, crushing, knocking) against the barricade of custom, the stronghold of habit, and a fleeting, timeless moment of penetration into clarity, into visionary consciousness. Other such ecstatic occasions are recorded in "The Mystery of the Hunt" and in "Poem" — moments when we perceive in common things with "the secret behind them," moments when "the mystery is unveiled,"[5] when we can see all living matter from algae to mammals as "creatures of grace — Rishi / Of their own right" ("Poem," 3). (A rishi is an illuminated sage.) It is noteworthy that, far from rejecting the phenomenal world (as do certain mystical traditions), McClure embraces it with rapturous attention, finding that the path to the noumenal is through the phenomenal and that ultimately the two are identical.

McClure is very much aware of the inadequacy of language, even the heightened, imagistic language of poetry, to communicate the absolute otherness and intense suchness of self-transcendent perception, of visionary experience. "THIS IS NOT IT," and "this is failure . . . ," he protests in disappointment and discouragement ("The Rug," 12), concluding that at best "the image is only a fiery shadow ("The," 13). But, though "the poem / is confusion," the poem for McClure is a necessary gesture, a mode of self-discovery, self-creation ("And there is no end to it / to the covering," [32]). Writing poetry is an act of being, an act of love; and as such, it is an assault on apathy and inertia, an indictment against mediocrity, compromise, complacency, sham, and inauthentic life.

As in his early villanelles, McClure continues in *Hymns to St. Geryon* to sense the presence of a liberating energy within—a spirit or motive power, an instigator. "THE SELFS FREE HERO," he names this spirit ("The Gesture," 17), and "THE HERO INSIDE" ("Canticle," 24), and in another poem's title declares, "HE MOVES US THO WE DO NOT KNOW HIS NAME" (27). This hero, this power, survives and resists all our evasions and denials of life, all the tricks of limitation and abstraction that we marshal against direct experience and perception. This motive power is wiser, deeper than the intellect and expresses itself through the body, the senses, and the emotions, through gesture and act, especially the act of physical love: "my body moves to you yearning. / Tho my head is full of images" ("Moving to cover the other proportion falls away," 31). It may occasionally manifest itself in dream or vision or in one of its guises:

> I am visited by a man
> who is the god of foxes
> there is dirt under the nails of his paw
> fresh from his den.
> We smile at one another in recognition.
>
> ("Peyote Poem," 36)

Thus the metaphor of confinement has a double meaning: we seek to liberate ourselves from the prison of restricted being, and there is that within us that we keep in close confinement and that seeks liberation. The key that may open both prisons is the knowledge that "we are stars with our five / appendages" ("OR HE WHO MOVES US THO WE DO NOT KNOW HIS NAME," 28). That is, we must learn that there should be no hierarchy among our consciousnesses, that the organs, the limbs, the senses, the glands, and the brain form an equilibratory composite of awareness, a union of autonomous entities, and that by elevating one and denying another, we imperil the life of the whole.

But this concept of aggregate being is still tentative at this point of McClure's writing; it is neither fully defined nor realized. And so the poet's personal torment continues; he cannot discover a passage. He can but break out momentarily, only to find himself immured again: "Walls do not change to pearls" ("Walls do not change to pearls. There's no speed," 30). The concluding poem of the volume is titled "The Chamber," again suggesting enclosure, and its imagery is infernal. The poet feels himself confined in "DARK HELL," in "Hell without radiance," where "nothing is changed," where there is no transfiguring vision, no "Vita Nuova," but only "the dead, dead world" (46–47).

The motifs of hell and of enclosure and constraint are also prominent in *The New Book / A Book of Torture*. The first poem in the collection depicts a psychic state of "HELL PAIN BEWILDERED EMPTINESS," a sense of being fallen and fragmented, capable only of "half-desires . . . half-loves."[6] Darkness, sorrow, anguish, lostness, lovelessness, sickness, deadness, confusion, misery, fear, vacancy, pain, and stupor are the terms in which McClure describes his dark night of the soul. These poems are desperate cries, agonized probings of the spirit, alternating between expletives and prayers, between despair and determination. The struggle between the forces of pain and of vision, of sickness and of health, has intensified, and McClure images it here as "a war" ("Rant Block," 33) in which we "are battlegrounds / of what is petty and heroic" ("For Artaud," 23), a grim but "noble combat" waged in the body, mind, and spirit. In this collection some engagements are won, others lost; the outcome of the conflict is as yet uncertain, but it is fought right down to the last poem in the volume in which McClure still cries his resolution and defiance: "I DO / NOT SURRENDER" ("Mad Sonnet," 64).

Walls and barriers continue to be central images in *The New Book*, metaphors for the patterns and systems that enclose us, that separate us from true being, from beauty and freedom. Kicking in, smashing through, breaking down walls, is a refrain common to several poems here, together with the recognition that "there are no walls but ones we make" ("Ode for Soft Voice," 17). A group of images complementary to the above are those of constraint and obfuscation. Locks, seals, nets, webs, smoke, and vapor represent in these poems the complex of socially conditioned responses that repress our essential human identity, check our spontaneity, sensuality, spirituality, our latent energies and potentialities.

In "End-Fragment of a Hymn," McClure images the inner messiah as the Fenris Wolf and as Prometheus. Both these figures, it will be remembered, were bound by the gods (the Aesir and the Olympians, respectively). Together they represent the Beast-Redeemer, the forces of the instincts which have been suppressed and constrained by the high gods of the intellect, but which will one day free themselves from their bonds and destroy the rule of the gods who have restrained them. Prophecies of the liberation and the victory of these elemental, redemptive powers occur repeatedly in these poems. "I am the animal seraph" ("Rant Block," 32); "I AM BEAST" ("The Column," 34); and "I am black beast and clear man," the poet proclaims ("The Flowers of Politics, II," 39). But the apocalypse of the body is not enacted here; the "raised force" is only momentarily raised, then banished again, returned to its dark exile ("The Column," 36). The struggle for deliverance continues.

A decisive change in the conflict occurs in *Dark Brown* with an eruption from the substrate, a bursting forth of chthonic energy that shatters the walls and scatters the nets and webs. This is the beginning of the second phase of McClure's writing: the achievement of a resolution. In this vigorous, vivid book-length poem, McClure celebrates the resurrection of the "INTER-RED BULK SPIRIT," the awakening of the "sleeping Lion," the rising of "the deep and / singing beast."[7] McClure names this entity the *Odem* or undersoul. The word is German and may be translated as body-spirit, as distinct from *Geist,* which is the more ethereal soul. The coming of the Odem was prefigured in "Lines from a Peyote Depression" in *The New Book / A Book of Torture,* where the poet quoted a passage from Ecclesiastes 3:21 in German that was used as a text by Brahms in *Four Serious Songs.*[8] McClure also refers to the Odem in a journal entry for September 1959, which is used as a statement of poetics and as a preface to the combined edition of *Hymns to St. Geryon & Dark Brown.*[9]

The coming forth of the Odem may be likened to a rebirth for the poet. He feels cleansed, freed, ennobled, returned to pleasure and joy, to desire and love and hunger. He is "undamned"—released from envy, falsehood, deceit, and vanity; unburdened of customs, patterns, forms, and habits; free to be and to act and to grow in new clarity and truth. The Odem brings wholeness ("THE BODY THE SPIRIT ARE ONE") and renewing vision ("NEW EYES TO SEE I AM A SERAPH") (*Dark*).

The two erotic poems that complete the volume, "Fuck Ode" and "A Garland," extol "love INVENTED," "love made anew," and declare the truth of the body, the mystery of physical actuality, the poetry of the skin and the senses. The act of love is celebrated as sacramental, conferring grace on the communicants; it is shown as a sacred act partaking of the infinite: "Freed / of all lies the face is pure. The gestures are immortal" (*Dark*). The sexual act is represented both as the negation of constraint and enclosure and as the affirmation of expansion, extension, and union. McClure has written in his essay "Revolt" "the basis of all revolt in one phase or another is sexuality. The Erotic impulse is the impulse to destroy walls and join units together in larger and larger structures."[10]

The emergence of the Odem in *Dark Brown* is followed by its ascendance in *Ghost Tantras,* a sequence of ninety-nine stanzas composed partly (some stanzas entirely) in beast language. Beast language consists of pure emotive sounds phonetically transcribed on the page. There are growls of aggression, passion, and anguish, roars of joy and delight, grunts of pleasure and attraction, purrs of tenderness and affection, howls of sorrow, fear, and loneliness — all interspersed with lines of verse. Beast language is most commonly characterized by plosives (*g* and *k*), liquids (*r* and *l*), by the aspirate *h,* and by prominent and prolonged vowel sounds: *aaaa, eeee, oooo.* These sounds are distinguished by unconstricted breath and they vary in quality from deep and gruff to sonorous and melodious.

Ghost Tantras represents a magical, mantric use of sound and vibration, a linguosomatic tool. The poems must be read aloud in order to exert their peculiar power. They are physical-metaphysical exercises that release physiological and psychological tensions and that exhort the reader to rapture and vision. *Ghost Tantras* is a return to the earliest poetry, to primitive song that summons healing or helping powers and induces states of trance or vision. The poems are shamanistic invocations, incantations, evocations of the beast spirit, of mammal consciousness.

In terms of imagery, the dominant motif in these poems is sensory, supporting the central theme that "physicality is posesy."[11] Color imagery is most prominent, with bright, intense colors and an extreme sensitivity to subtleties of tone and hue. Qualities of light also figure very largely: flaring, shimmering, flashing, beaming, shining, gleaming, glimmering, glowing, radiance, brilliance, translucence, lamplight, candlelight, sunlight. Sound imagery includes the breeze through leaves, rainfall, rustlings, creakings, thumps, boomings and silence, the cascade of water, references to music and musical instruments. ("All sounds," McClure proclaims, "are unjudgemented love" [No. 56, 63].) Tactile images are also frequent: textures, temperatures, surfaces, erotic fondlings and caresses, and the response of the skin to stimuli such as "the motion of cool air" (No. 54, 61). Tastes and odors are also represented: nectar, honey, sugar; the fragrance of hemlock, musk, and copal; the scents of flesh, perfume, and smoke.

Significant to the theme of visionary perception, of seeing anew, discovering new correspondences, is the occurrence of synaesthesia in

Ghost Tantras. McClure writes of a "radiant chorus" (No. 42, 49) and of "satins of sounds," of "the ear's vista" (No. 51, 58) and "eyed feet" (No. 68, 75), of drinking stillness and hearing the feel of music, of "space sounds" (No. 31, 38) and "strawberry-peach darkness" (No. 3, 9), of "touch-scent" (No. 93, 100) and of "an ultimate chord. It started bright ivory yellow and swiftly turned to black" (No. 78, 85). These sense transferences are suggestive of a larger, fuller awareness and a higher degree of response, of an integrated, direct experience of physical sensation. The scales (in both the sense of measurement and encrustation) have fallen from the senses and we regain "what we once knew and have forgotten" (No. 72, 79).

Appropriately, where in earlier poems there were walls and barriers, there are now doorways, entrances, hallways, vistas, vastness, hugeness, infinity; and where there was infernal torment and torture, there is now the pleasure and grace of "multitudinous heavens" (No. 68, 75). "The heavy curtains are raised / by roaring," writes McClure (No. 82, 89), and on the other side of the curtains there is an Eden of sensory delight, where "we are incarnate joys," (No. 67, 74), attaining "total acceptance and god-belief" (No. 71, 78), and are blessed with liberty and tranquility in "A UNIVERSE OF ENERGETIC STILLNESS" (No. 18, 25).

McClure's plays from this period treat the same issues and themes as his poetry, and the two modes are mutually illuminating. *The Blossom, or Billy the Kid* is McClure's first drama, written in 1959 "between the finish of *The New Book / A Book of Torture* and my sexual poem *Dark Brown*" and first performed in 1963.[12] The play is more in the manner of an enquiry into the causes and nature of McClure's psychic conflicts than a resolution of them. That is, *The Blossom* is essentially diagnostic, a dramatic exposition of self-dividedness as a personal and general human condition.

The characters in the play are based on actual historical figures, participants in the Lincoln County War of New Mexico. The drama is set in eternity, though, and the characters do not remember either their deaths or their former relationships. As entities within the play, they embody various attitudes and perspectives, different aspects of the psyche.

Tunstall espouses boldness, courage, the nobility of action. Alexander McSween represents a more passive, fearful, restrained type of person, taking refuge in the forms of orthodoxy, such as the Bible and romantic ideals, denying his senses when they contradict his mental images and his conceptions. Mrs. McSween is sensuous, erotic, nurturing. The Mother, bound in bandages and rags and living in the darkness of her narrow chamber, seems to personify all the forces that limit and arrest growth and hamper freedom and action. In a sense, these characters may be seen as emanations or extentions of the Kid, the central figure of the play, who is caught between and torn by violence and love, pain and desire, horror and beauty, the coldness of space and the heat of action.

Flowers provide the unifying image of the play, symbolizing the growth and unfolding of the deep, true self, the spirit: "THE FLOWER RISES UP OUT OF THE EARTH BRINGING FIRE FROM COLD BLACKNESS."[13] Light and heat are important supporting images, significant of love, courage, the realization of freedom and authentic being. The Kid's growth of spirit during the course of the play may be measured by his pronouncements: "There is no warmth but the warmth I make" (*Mammals,* 25), and "I do not reflect light but cast light" (*Mammals,* 31).

The Blossom offers no final solution to the conflicts that it presents. Even after his second death at the end of the play, the Kid discovers that "there is no end. There is no end." The unfolding, blossoming of the spirit continues, "swelling at once to one eternal / last final act swelling" (*Mammals,* 39). The process of transmutation is one of successive stages of transition, a cyclic distillation of the spirit.

A more conclusive working out of the theme of self-dividedness takes place in *!The Feast!* (written and first performed in 1960). This play presents thirteen characters who may be seen as embodiments of forces in the psyche or components of the self: some are light, others dark; some are male, others female. With their robes of shining cloth, their long hair and pharaonic beards, and their strange names, they have the aspect of noumenal entities. There is a solemn, ritual quality to the play, a sacred and ceremonial ambience.

McClure alludes to the Last Supper in the thirteen figures seated together at a long table, set with black wine and loaves of bread and red plums. The central figure (at the table and within the play) is Yeorg, lion-pawed, the Beast Messiah. He delivers the main speeches of the play and his presence and his words serve as a catalyst for the dialogue and the action of the drama. His utterances are oracular; he declares that "the fur and blood / of living are denied by (the) closed vision" and that "the

Dumb rises to full voice and song." He prophesies that "the right hand shall bless the left."[14]

Yeorg's prophecy is fulfilled when, at the end of the play, the six figures seated to his left and the six figures seated to his right rise and exchange places and assume the names of their counterparts. The dialogue of the play is partially in beast language (preceding its use in *Ghost Tantras*) thereby raising what has heretofore been dumb "to full voice and song." At a symbolic level what has taken place in the course of the drama is a readjustment of forces in the psyche: the life of the body and the senses has asserted itself against denial and repression by the "closed vision" of the intellect; the Beast Messiah has risen to effect reconciliation and to establish a new balanced interrelationship among the constituents of consciousness.

The Beard (written and first performed in 1965), probably McClure's best-known play, provides a further treatment of the theme of psychic division, the conflict of spirit and body. Again, although thoroughly modern on the surface, the play possesses strong ritual, ceremonial elements and a mythic, magical quality that harks back to the sacred origins of drama. With its use of obscenity and explicit sexuality, its oneiric setting, primal situation, and incantatory dialogue, *The Beard* is at once contemporary and archaic, a work of poetry, potency, and mystery.

In common with *The Blossom* and *!The Feast!*, *The Beard* is set in eternity and the characters are ritually bearded with white tissue paper beards to indicate their status as spirits. Billy the Kid appears again as a central figure, in this instance, together with Jean Harlow. In contrast to the longer, lyrical speeches of the earlier plays, the dialogue here consists of short sentences delivered in a succession of quick exchanges. *The Beard* is altogether a more concentrated and austere work than its predecessors.

The terms of the conflict in *The Beard* are inherent in the two characters: the outlaw and the sex goddess. For the Kid, humans exist as "bags of meat," whereas for Harlow the flesh is "an illusion."[15] In the course of the play each character moves closer to the other's point of view, modifying his or her own, until at the end they arrive at a higher truth, finding accord and unity.

The dramatic action of *The Beard* proceeds from the opposition and affinities that obtain between man and woman—attraction and repulsion, aggression and tenderness, dominance and submission, truthfulness and dissimulation, and most importantly, between meat and spirit. The reconciliation of contrarieties, the resolution of tensions, in the play is achieved at two levels: as concept and as act. Both characters discover that meat and spirit are concurrent, not exclusive, categories of being, that they (we) are "sheer spirit taking the guise of meat" (16). They agree at last that they (we) are divine incarnations—beautiful, mysterious, and at perfect liberty, absolutely free. Desire is the key to the realization of our divinity and our freedom: it must be enacted. This enactment of desire is literally accomplished and symbolically imaged in the erotic tableau that concludes the play. Harlow's final, ecstatic cry of "STAR! STAR! STAR! STAR!" confirms the state of transcendence, of divinity attained through the union of head and genitals, spirit and meat (82).

At this stage of McClure's personal and artistic evolution, when he has definitely overthrown the forces of denial, negation, and restriction within himself and has achieved a psychosomatic equilibrium, his writing begins to undergo a shift of focus and emphasis, moving from the inner to the outer, from the personal to the universal. This change manifests itself in his work in an increasing concern with social and environmental-ecological issues (well in advance of the vogue of the latter) and in repeated strivings to articulate a vision of the process of life in the universe and of humankind's position in that process. This is the third phase of McClure's work: the attainment of freedom and visionary consciousness.

Poisoned Wheat is the earliest of McClure's revolutionary pronouncements: a manifesto in verse form but an antipolitical manifesto in which the poet assails the prevalent political doctrines and dogmas, denouncing capitalism, communism, and fascism for their essential insanity and their manifest cruelties and failures. McClure calls instead for a revolt against the repressive codes and "structural mechanisms of Society" that impede individual and collective human evolution.[16] He advocates "no single answer" but "a multitude of solutions" and declares that "POLITICS IS DEAD AND BIOLOGY IS HERE!" (24).

Poisoned Wheat is an impassioned, indignant denunciation (in the Blakean, Shelleyan tradition) of the organized barbarism of the state and of society. War, overpopulation, mass starvation, mindless consumerism, and the rapacious exploitation of natural resources are seen as the inevitable consequences of abstract political and economic theories that have been and continue to be imposed upon actual human, planetary realities. A direct correspondence lies here between the intellect's domination of individual human beings to the neglect and detriment of the unconscious, the emotions, and the consciousness of the body and the domination of the nations and peoples of the world by abstract theories and doctrines. Both are mutually reflexive aspects of a single tyranny that suppresses "the freedom creature" (2) and denies "mammal, sensory pleasure" (3).

Thus, appropriately, *Poisoned Wheat* is framed by Odemic *Grahhrs* as invocation and coda. In order to resist the guilt, fear, aggression, cynicism, and hysterical millennialism that are inflicted upon individuals or called forth by the crimes and failures of their social structures, McClure proposes the assertion of primal being, of mammal consciousness. This biological revolt consists of disavowing the patterns, projections, and preconceptions of the head (the state, social, political, and economic theories) and affirming, exerting the wisdom of the body: clearing the senses to see the world as it is, awakening the corporeal-spiritual energies of desire and love and tenderness and compassion. Biological revolt arises out of the need of the animal body to adjust to the influences and conditions of its environment, to survive, and to achieve a state of active equilibrium. This process is as natural and as necessary as the body's efforts to reject infection or poison.

The other dominant theme of McClure's middle and later work is cosmology. His writings persistently explore the processes of life, energy, and matter in order to discover and delineate essential patterns and configurations of the universe. McClure unites perspectives from biology, physics, myth, and metaphysics in his cosmological poems and plays, recognizing the insufficiency of any one viewpoint and the interfertility of more comprehensive, eclectic approaches. In a sense, this bio-alchemical vision of McClure, together with his use of concepts, images, and vocabulary drawn from natural science, may be seen as a contemporary renewal of a poetic tradition that stems from Lucretius, Erasmus Darwin, and Walt Whitman but which since the nineteenth century has fallen into disfavor and neglect. McClure infuses scientific themes with new energy and beauty and in so doing reclaims for poetry a large and fruitful territory.

"The Surge" from the collection *Star* is perhaps the earliest of McClure's enquiries into the nature of the cosmos (the theme has always been implicit in his work), and the poet himself in a prefatory note accounts the work a "failure," describing it as "not fully achieved" though he allows it represents a "step."[17] McClure's remarks notwithstanding, "The Surge" is an effective and compelling poem whose four parts form a coherent whole and convey a complete statement or meditation. "The Surge" is an effort to gain "a more total view" of the "Surge of Life," to achieve a mode of seeing or conceiving that exceeds those of philosophy and science, especially insofar as these disciplines reflect what are essentially male points of view and are thus inherently limited and partial (23).

The poet proposes love as a mode of understanding and declares that "the female / who is unprincipaled, sees further and into more." In evidence of this last assertion he describes a valentine "made by a woman as gift of love in a casual moment," a drawing which for McClure constitutes "a picture of the living Universe," an intuitive, artistic representation of the "Surge of Life" that "calls all previous images to abeyance" (23). In the poet's apprehension of it, the valentine depicts a dynamic, metamorphic, mysterious, equivocal universe, a cosmos of sensuality, love, joy, ascent, and progression. Nearly every creature or object in the drawing may be seen to be something else, expressing the interplay and interrelatedness among all things.

Inspired by this perception, the poet feels himself momentarily immersed in the Surge, experiencing it in a vision of the "roaring meat mountain" of mammals, men, and birds (25), and in the smallest particles of life and knowing it also as a "rosy, / full, flowing, and everspreading and con- / tracting, spilling flash" in infinite space (26). He sees too that "the cold seas beasts / and mindless creatures are the holders of vastest / philosophy," for they are fully engaged in the Surge while we humans are too often merely self-conscious observers of it. He recognizes that the universe is in need of neither explanation nor justification; it simply exists in, of, and for itself: "There is no answer / —and no question!" As human-mammals we should learn to accept and celebrate our part in the Surge: "We are bulks of revolt and systems of love-structuring / in a greater whole" (27).

References to Dante and Beatrice and to *Paradiso* serve both to unite the poem and to extend its meaning. "The Surge" makes clear that "in our male insistency on meaning we miss the truth" and that woman's view of the universe is at once more gentle and more bold than man's (25). As Beatrice guided Dante in *Purgatorio* and *Paradiso,* so may our male cosmology be enlarged and enhanced by the insights of woman. In the alchemical union of male and female mind, a new awareness, harmonious, and whole, will be created. The poem concludes with a prophetic declaration that humankind will undergo a transformation, attaining visionary consciouness: "Beatrice! Beatrice! *Paradiso is opening!* / WE ARE AT THE GATES OF THE CHERUBIC!" (27).

The informing concepts, energies, and emotions of "The Surge" are more fully developed and more completely expressed in McClure's book-length poem *Rare Angel.* The work originates, as the poet informs us in a foreword, "from the substrate" of muscle and nerve, from the cells and selves of the body, and it concerns "the interwoven topologies of reality" in which we exist and of which we are comprised.[18] *Rare Angel* gives form and shape to "the alchemy of being," to the intricately intertwining, rising and falling, expanding and contracting, constantly changing, cyclically recurrent, heterogenous agglomeration and inseparable wholeness of the phenomenal universe (31).

The poem consists essentially of catalogs of images—real and surreal, juxtaposed and linked—which are interspersed with poetic commentary and pronouncements. The verse lines are generally quite short—many are made up of only a single word—so that the poem is read more vertically than horizontally, creating (as McClure intends) an Oriental scroll effect and suggesting also the action of frames of film passing the eye in rapid succession.

Rare Angel proceeds by accretion, repetition, and sudden sweeping waves of words to represent the force of cosmic energy that incessantly forms and transforms all life and matter. The poem depicts a universe of which love is the motive power and luck the catalyst and agent of change; a universe of inconceivably myriad forms and of essential unity and indivisible identity; a universe composed simultaneously of spirit and matter, inseparably interwoven and interdependent; a universe that is an organism, self-creating and evolving; a universe that the poet proclaims as "the messiah" (20).

The concept of the universe as messiah is further treated in several poems collected in *September Blackberries,* including "The Basic Particle," "A Thought," "The Skull," "99 Theses," and "Xes." McClure has always scrupulously avoided the vague and indefinite vocabulary of religion and mysticism, preferring the more precise terminology of natural science, but as a poet using language as a tool to express the inexpressible, he occasionally avails himself of metaphors drawn from spiritual traditions. Concerning his special understanding of the term *messiah,* McClure explains in an essay: "For the artist or animal there is but one religion. . . . The religion is *being* itself. . . . In the religion of *being* the universe is the Messiah. . . . The universe is the Messiah because it is the possibility of our being. . . . Each life is a tentacle or finger of the Messiah or Tathagata experiencing itself and the universe through entrances of perception, movement and contact. But to assign the Messiah human nature any more than the nature of a sea cucumber is beyond reason."[19] In this sense, then, McClure declares in these poems that "MATTER IS SPIRIT!,"[20] that the universe "IS DIVINE" ("Springs," 66), and that we are all "Pseudopods of Messiah" ("The Basic Particle," 12). Microstructure recapitulates macrostructure, and each being and the totality of all being is "all one starry thing of selves and selves / of selves of selves of selves of selves of selves" ("Xes," 90), in which "we are ONE and ALL" ("Gathering Driftwood on Christmas Morning," 109).

September Blackberries is a rich and varied collection which contains a number of shorter poems of diverse moods and forms. McClure employs an aphoristic style (somewhat in the manner of the "Proverbs of Hell" section of Blake's *The Marriage of Heaven and Hell*) in poems such as "99 Theses," "Moiré," and "Springs"; he adopts an angry, rhetorical, polemic tone at times, as in the extended poem "We"; and he demonstrates considerable skill with short lyrics that are most often built around observations of natural phenomena: animals, flowers, birds, terrains, and landscapes. These latter poems are little gems of visionary attention, changing our perception of familiar things and providing glimpses, flashes of unknown beauty, elusive truths. An unobtrusive use of internal rhyme and end rhyme frequently distinguishes these lyrics, which in their stillness and luminousness contribute a sense of a deepening of the poet's vision.

Quietly, clearly, surely, McClure unites and strengthens the inter-weaving themes of his art in the pared-down poems of *Jaguar Skies.* The personal, the social, the environmental, and the cosmological themes are joined here as aspects of a universal unfolding and growth, a process of

progression, an ascent. The photograph on the cover of the volume is
worth remarking upon in this regard: it depicts a long flight of steps—
hewn in rock, weathered and worn—ascending to the dark, open door of
a temple-like building; behind and above the temple there are wind-
blown white and dark clouds and patches of clear sky. The photographic
image seems a visual counterpart of the poem "A Stepping Stone," which
states:

> We
> take
> the steps
> of alchemy
> from scale
> to scale;
> we cannot fail
> to burst
> to new plateaus
> of musky seeing
> as we stretch
> among the breezes.[21]

"New plateaus of seeing" and "acts of seeing" are very much what the
poems in this collection are about. Seeing, for McClure, is a mode of
action and not simply the passive reception of visual stimuli. True sight
involves a creative extension of the self, a level of will and attention that
must be attained and sustained. The "EYES ARE WIDE EXPLOSIONS"
("Ode," 50) that can be instruments of liberation: "THE WALLS OF
THE FRONTIER ARE DOWN FOR THOSE / WHO CAN SEE IT"
("The Bow," 15). In acts of seeing we can become "radiant momentary
gods" ("Hwa Yen Totalism," 37) when the world is transfigured to a
"living gold" of aura, haloes, and glows of energy ("Movies," 18).
McClure summarizes his counsel in "Mad Song": "Away with the frown /
and up with the eyelids!" (41).

The poems in *Jaguar Skies* explore the connections between the denial
and violation of the substrate of our individual psyches and our collective
destruction and exploitation of the substrate of the planet. McClure
writes of endangered primate species and of ravaged landscapes where

> everything is nine-tenths
> DEAD

> where
> once
> there was
> complex beauty
> of meat and plant
> that jeweled the plain.
>
> ("From a Pocket Notebook," 22)

The poet's own planetary consciousness is developed by his travels across the United States and to Africa, Europe, and South America that serve both to reinforce his sense of a global ecosystem and to increase his knowledge of the insult and misuse to which the planet and its inhabitants (nonhuman and human alike) are subjected. "We are here! / We are here!" in these bodies, on the planet, McClure urges us to realize ("Up Beat," 80), and we must accept and honor, nurture and care, for ourselves and our world and cease our grasping, ruinous abuse of the biosphere. "Save the substrate," he exhorts us,

> Let
> us
> prepare
> to love this place
> before we leave it.
>
> ("At Night on the River," 74)

There is a growing consciousness in these poems of shape and design as the expression of energy. McClure focuses on the multitude of forms and patterns assumed by life and matter, the architectures and structures of petal, bark, shell, fur, and flesh as they relate to the whirling, flowing, billowing, waving, spinning, rippling, and swirling of cells and molecules and atomic particles—the dance of energy. "THE DIVINE IS PRACTICAL" he notes ("Claremont Suite," 47), and "the physique / of our gestures / is truth" ("The Glow," 12). This concern with the reciprocity and complementarity of shape and energy is also evident in the metrical and visual designs of the poems themselves, which include intricate forms such as the sestina and the villanelle—poems whose lines mirror themselves in such a way that they may be read both backwards and forwards—and an increasing use of internal and end rhyme.

McClure's play *Gorf* is a vigorous, energetic, and original treatment of the cosmological theme in drama form, combining elements of Aristophanic and Elizabethan comedy with echoes of Shelley's *Prometheus*

Unbound and embellishments from vaudeville and modern musical comedy. To even begin to comprehend the cosmos, the play suggests, we must possess a sense of humor as well as a sense of wonder. *Gorf* exemplifies McClure's cartoon style of theatre as developed in his *Gargoyle Cartoons,* written in the late sixties and early seventies.[22] The play is looser in structure than McClure's earlier dramas and employs farcical and exaggerated characters, animal figures, and supernatural entities and embraces song, dance, parody, and pastiche, violence and terror, strange, dreamlike beauty, and wild and bawdy humor.

Gorf is a comic retelling of the cosmogonic cycle and of the myth of the Fall. The original unity of the universe, of all life, matter, energy, of time and space, is shown in the play to have been scattered into division. The multiple particles of the universe are attracted to each other though, and in the end, reintegration takes place and unity is restored. Humankind too, in the characters of Gert and Mert (parodic parallels to Adam and Eve) has fallen into a state of death-in-life. Gorf, a winged phallus, has been unjustly blamed for the Fall, when in fact, he is a regenerative principle. (Sexuality is often considered to be the original sin that caused the Fall of Man.) Gorf overcomes persecution, impediments, and trials, slays a monster octopus, and fulfills his vital, heroic role in redeeming humankind and rejoining the separate fragments of the universe into one body united in "ecstasy and transfiguration."[23]

The silly names of the characters, such as the Shitfer, Gorf, and the Blind Dyke, disarm our normal abstract, logical, limited modes of regarding the cosmos, sterility, and the life principle and in this way alter our perceptions and concepts. The playfulness of the play emphasizes the essential playfulness of the universe and its processes. (A concept intrinsic to Hinduism and Buddhism is the phenomenal universe known as *lila* or *leela,* the divine play or sport of God.) The comic-cosmic vision of *Gorf* succeeds in restoring a sense of proportion, optimism, and dignity to our consciousness of the role of human beings in the universe: we should feel at home in the universe; we belong, we are a part, but the universe is not to be measured or comprehended in human terms; and insofar as we (individually, collectively) further the Life Principle do we in the same degree contribute to the universal regeneration and joyous unfolding of the cosmos.

"The Rains of February," the opening poem of *Antechamber and Other Poems,* clearly establishes McClure's central concern of liberation. Not liberation as understood or as propounded by the political activist or the religious ascetic but an ontogenetic, ontological liberation, the freedom of really, fully being what one truly is—a sensory, visionary liberation:

> a liberation
> filled with buttercups
> and blue-eyed grass
> and golden tracks of spring
> upon the hill
> and air that's filled
> with the scent of rose
> and dill.[24]

In the poems of this collection (mostly short lyrics with the exception of the title poem) McClure continues to refine his poetic line, achieving ever greater simplicity and directness of expression and an almost haikulike concision and clarity. Thematically, a similar distillation is taking place, as the poet ever deepens and extends the issues of his art— defining, describing, delimiting, developing, and interrelating his information and insights.

The poems of *Antechamber* record and perform a sense of the unique- ness, rightness, suchness of things, and the mystery and the wonder of being. Each event, each perception, is a "new birth," a showing forth of innate beauty and significance, a revelation of noumenal essence, of

> Glittering
> gold
> trembling
> on darkness.

("The List," 6)

Vultures, raccoons, crocuses, sea lions, hummingbirds, gnats, roses, mountain peaks, and trees are all glorious "sculptures of molecules" ("Watching the Vulture," 2); each equally extraordinary, ineffable, divine. But, among people, "THERE ARE VERY FEW IN SEARCH / OF THE DIVINE!" ("Despair in the Morning," 11). The mass of humankind remains (and is content to remain) arrested, stunted, domes- ticated, caged, and estranged. Too many become "robots" or "ogres" who project their inner emptiness and sterility outward onto the world, reforming it in their own image: burning, grazing, fencing the forests and the chaparral, shattering the substrate.

In response to this "madness" and these "endless murders" of species and spirits ("Wildness," 7), McClure proposes a Mammal Patriotism, whose premise is the recognition that "BIOLOGY / IS / POLITICS". As Mammal Patriots, we must "build love / in creation of / what is organic" ("Poetics," 17), while accepting our place in the whole "flow / of the biomass" ("Watching the Vulture," 2). We must recognize our own aggregate being, of which our conscious life is only a small part, and realize our relatedness to, and identity with, all other life: "We are waves / and forces intertwined / in invisible totality" ("Antechamber," 68). Such a fundamental change in our perception of ourselves and the world would represent a revolution in the truest sense of the word and an evolutionary advance of major proportion. And despite all impediments, such a change is inevitable; for, as McClure affirms:

> spirit cannot
> be broken
> but ever grows
> toward flight.
>
> ("Freewheelin's Tattoo," 9)

In the title poem of the collection *Fragments of Perseus,* McClure speaks through the persona of the mythic hero Perseus, slayer of the Gorgon and of the sea monster and the rescuer of Andromeda. The work may be read both as a social-cultural statement and as a personal allegory. At one level, "Fragments of Perseus" represents the perennial and universal struggle for liberation in the person of the archetypal hero who slays the terrible monsters that threaten the natural order of the world and who rescues the life-principle from captivity and death. Perseus may thus be seen as the personification of biological revolt. Construed in this way, McClure's retelling of the myth is pertinent to the present environmental crisis and to all the life-destroying technological barbarisms of our era. In order to arrest the monstrous process of despoilment and the waste of planetary resources and the cycle of violence against and oppression of human and other living beings of the world, we must arouse and incite the heroic qualities within ourselves and our society. Like Perseus, we must secure the appropriate weapons and battle the ogres of havoc and blight and thereby redeem our age.

The poem also expresses a symbolic self-assessment, a retrospective inquiry by the poet into the life of his psyche. Considered in this manner,

Perseus represents the self; Medusa and the sea-monster—the crisis and trials of his earlier life; and Andromeda—his anima, his love, and his poetry. Such an interpretation is supported by Perseus' description of the Gorgon as

> the horror
> of
> my
> mind
>
> BLOWN
> UP
>
> with-
>
> in
>
> my body and MADE
> INTO FLESH![25]

If we read the poem in this fashion, we see that the poet's quest for psychic integration and for liberation of the self is still unfinished and incomplete despite the degree of individuation achieved, as represented by Perseus' heroic deeds. At the end of the poem, Perseus, addressing the sleeping Andromeda, declares:

> TO SLAY DRAGONS
> to free you is
>
> not
> enough
>
> when
> I
>
> am still chained
>
> to my rock of self
>
> above a howling sea. (17)

The process of attaining full selfhood and true liberation continues. As McClure has stated elsewhere: "REVOLT is a constant reformation of the body image until it is exactly Spirit (*Meat,* 89), and the ultimate aim of revolt is the creation, or rediscovery, of "a whole state of mind, beauty and being—the awakened creature!" (*Meat,* 107).

In such poems as "Listen Lawrence" (written in reply to Lawrence Ferlinghetti's *Populist Manifestoes*), "Action Philosophy," and "Stanzas Composed in Turmoil," McClure again addresses the themes of revolt and cosmology, specifying the dangers not only of ignorance of, or indifference to, ecological issues but also those of applying political solutions to biological problems. Political thinking remains for McClure inherently, inevitably ruinous and entirely counterproductive in its limited scope—an imposition of static and obtuse habits and patterns onto complex and protean states and situations. In "Listen Lawrence" he therefore urges people to leave the "CLOSET OF POLITICS" and emerge into "the light of their flesh and bodies!" A knowledge of the indivisibility of our bodies and spirits and of our essential unity with "our brother and sister beings" is the basis for the only real revolt we can undertake:

> A REVOLT
> that we only begin to
> conceptualize as we
> achieve it!
>
> (*Fragments,* 39–42)

A sense of the process of the cosmos and of the deepest core of our individual existence will lead us to realize that

> LOVE is the only answer
> that
>
> we've
> got.
> ("Stanzas Composed in Turmoil," *Fragments,* 82)

The publication in 1986 of McClure's *Selected Poems* represents a concise retrospective of his work over thirty years. Chosen by the poet himself, the selection gives a sense of the shape of his art, its coherence and its integrity, its variety and its quality, its originality. The volume also suggests a promise of the work that is to come, for McClure will not accept stasis; he will not cease to change, to grow, to progress, to refine and renew his vision even as he extends it.

McClure contributes a courage of enquiry and expression to contemporary poetry. His writing returns us to our senses, literally and figuratively. His vision is heuristic, holistic, and healing; it reestablishes broken links, clears channels and passages of energy, and promotes wholeness. His work continues a vital tradition that includes William Blake and D. H. Lawrence, and yet it is unique in our time.

Aniela Jaffé, a contemporary psychologist, describes the continuing crisis of human evolution in these terms: "Suppressed and wounded instincts are the dangers threatening civilized man; uninhibited drives are the dangers threatening primitive man. In both cases the 'animal' is alienated from its true nature; and for both, the acceptance of the animal soul is the condition for wholeness and a fully lived life. Primitive man must tame the animal in himself and make it his helpful companion; civilized man must heal the animal in himself and make it his friend."[26] The work of Michael McClure represents a very significant contribution to the furthering of such healing and wholeness.

Nearly two hundred years ago in his Preface to *Lyrical Ballads,* William Wordsworth predicted that at some future date the poet

> will be ready to follow the steps of the man of science . . . he will be at his side, carrying sensation into the midst of the objects of science itself. The remotest discoveries of the chemist, the botanist, or mineralologist will be as proper objects of the poet's art as any upon which it can be employed. . . . If the time should ever come when what is now called science . . . shall be ready to put on, as it were, a form of flesh and blood, the poet will lend his divine spirit to aid the transfiguration.[27]

He might have been describing the work of Michael McClure.

The alchemists of the Middle Ages, seeking the *aurum philosophicum* (philosophical gold) that would transform both matter and the psyche, called their enterprise the Great Work. The bio-alchemical vision of Michael McClure seeks to expel from the living body and the spirit of the world all that impedes natural growth and freedom, and to reconcile, unite, and exalt all life. "Beginning in the heart I work towards light," wrote McClure in his first published poem, "Premonition," and thirty years later, that Great Work proceeds.

8

Toward Organized Innocence:

Richard Fariña's Been Down So Long

It Looks Like Up to Me

Imagine a state of perfect immunity, a charmed existence, a life of absolute security in the midst of poison bacilli. Nothing touches me, neither earthquakes nor riots nor famine nor collisions nor wars nor revolutions. I am innoculated against every disease, every calamity, every sorrow and misery.

Henry Miller
Tropic of Cancer

*O*ne of the most central and persistent myths of American culture is that of the American hero as innocent and as unfallen. The celebration of this heroic innocence and the lamentation of its anomalousness, its precariousness, and its vulnerability are recurrent themes in our national literature.[1] Innocence as a strategy of resistance and a mode of affirmation has been cultivated with particular urgency in the postwar American novel. Richard Fariña's *Been Down So Long It Looks Like Up to Me* presents a variant expression of the myth of innocence, proposing the hipster as a new American Adam and projecting a vision of contemporary America as a blighted, despoiled Eden.

Set in the late 1950s, Fariña's novel traces the decline and fall of Gnossos Pappadopoulis, a hipster picaro. Gnossos is the son of Greek immigrant parents, raised in Brooklyn, streetwise but innocent. His innocence is of an uncommon variety, predicated not upon an ignorance of evil, but residing instead in his conscious refusal to internalize the knowledge of evil, to become tainted by or infected with evil. He insists upon maintaining a state of what he calls "immunity" or "exemption," a precarious and besieged innocence.[2]

Gnossos' immunity permits him to resist the consequences of the fall (complacency, resignation, corruption, depravity), and it enables him to view the world with an innocent eye, to discern the superficial, the pretentious, the meretricious, the vicious, the hypocritical, and the perverse. But there are negative aspects to his immunity as well. His refusal to relinquish his exemption necessarily precludes any true commitment, responsibility, or engagement. Gnossos' immunity also represents a dead end of personal and spiritual development; for (in Blakean terms) without first surrendering innocence, he cannot hope to progress through experience to organized innocence, the state in which evil has been transcended and innocence regained, the ultimate aim of the life journey.

The antithesis of immunity is, of course, infection or disease, and these opposing states provide the metaphorical poles of the story. To have succumbed, either passively or actively, to the evil of the world is to have become infected, diseased. The land itself is wasted by disease as Gnossos clearly perceives: "I've seen fire and pestilence, symptoms of a great disease" (26). The ultimate manifestation of the great disease is the atomic blast which Gnossos witnesses in the Nevada desert, seeing it as "a festering core" (101). A lesser manifestation of the same malady is Oeuf's clap, which Gnossos ultimately contracts, symbolizing his loss of immunity, his fall from innocence.

As the story begins, Gnossos is returning from an unsuccessful vision-quest, a search for spiritual knowledge; "Looking for the Connection who might tie all the loose ends of various experiences into a woven sign or pattern, some familiar rebus. A triangle perhaps. A fish. The symbol for infinity" (59). Instead of finding visionary enlightenment, Gnossos has (as we learn through flashbacks) experienced a series of negative epiphanies, revelations of violence and horror: an encounter with Louie Mother-ball, the false and corrupted shaman; the pitiless vengeance of the pachucos, brutalized victims of a materialist-consumer society; the encroaching control of the nascent police state; a vision of apocalypse in the atomic weapon test; and a vision of evil and death in an encounter with a wolf.

In spite of such experiences, Gnossos preserves his innocence, the tokens and talismans of which he carries in his rucksack including "a Captain Midnight Code-O-Graph, . . . a boy scout shirt, . . . a bottlecap from Dr. Brown's Cel-Ray Tonic, . . . and a 1920's baseball cap" (18). Appropriately, he also considers himself to be a virgin, his numerous amorous adventures notwithstanding. According to Gnossos' view, "membranes are spiritual"; that is to say that sex without love, without emotional surrender, is merely a form of masturbation (160). Thus, he insists that he remains "a spiritual virgin" (59).

To indicate the larger context of Gnossos' experience and to provide a frame of reference for his exploits, Fariña suggests, by means of similes and allusions, a number of parallels to literature and popular culture. The first of these is to A. A. Milne's character Winnie the Pooh. The novel's table of contents together with repeated references in the text suggest Gnossos as a counterpart to Pooh. Obviously, this parallel associates Gnossos with the world of childhood and innocence. Those readers who are familiar with Milne's stories will recall Pooh's endearing simplicity, his affectionate nature, and his complete lack of pretension and of defensive-aggressive egotism (as opposed to other inhabitants of the Hundred Acre Wood such as Eeyore, Owl, and Rabbit). In this sense Pooh (and thus, at least potentially, Gnossos too) represents an ideal of human behavior — harmonious, intuitive, self-reliant, an embodiment of primary and final innocence.[3]

Another parallel is evoked between Gnossos and the Homeric hero Odysseus. Aside from their common nationality, Gnossos resembles Odysseus in several particulars. Like his forebearer, Gnossos returns from an extended voyage, on "the asphalt seas" of modern America, a voyage on which he has endured perils and undergone trials and adventures; and, like Odysseus, he is presumed to be dead (17). As did Odysseus in the course of his wanderings and upon his return to Ithaca, Gnossos assumes many disguises and gives false names (including Ian Evergood, King Montezuma, the Holy Ghost, and Ravi Shankar) as a protective device. Odysseus' protective moly has its analogue in Gnossos' immunity, though the latter ultimately proves ineffective against a modern Circe (Kristin, who lives in the "Circe III" dormitory). There may also be glancing allusions to the Lotus Eaters in the figures of the addicted Taos Indians and the zombies and to the Cyclops in the one-eyed Heap. Stretching the parallel somewhat, we may say that, figuratively speaking, Gnossos steers between the Scylla and the Charybdis in his course between the self-interest and materialism of Oeuf on one hand and the egoless, transcendental mysticism of Blacknesse on the other. Certainly the formulaic epithets associated with Odysseus (resourceful, wily, of many devices) are equally appropriate to Gnossos.

Gnossos may also be seen as a sort of Grail knight in quest of a vision that will redeem "the great wasted land" (17) and as a hipster Huck Finn with a quadroon Jim as his companion, evading "sivilization." The novel also alludes repeatedly to the characters and superheroes of American popular culture from the radio serials and the comics: the Shadow, Captain Midnight, Superman, Linus, Snoopy, Plasticman, the Lone Ranger, Tom Mix, the Hornet, Green Arrow, Jack Armstrong, Captain Marvel, Batman, Mark Trail, and others. Gnossos identifies himself and is identified, by simile, with these heroic figures who represent a contemporary mythology and who embody the modern heroic impulse. Gnossos alone retains a Captain Midnight Code-O-Graph, and it is he who exhibits the greatest familiarity with the superheroes in the nostalgic discussion that takes place in Guido's Grill.

Fariña's use of allusion and parallel, though never solemn, is serious in intent. The parallels are a central element of the mythopoeic vision of the story. The classical myths, literary myths, the myths of childhood, and the myths of popular culture (together with Fariña's personal mythology) are shown to be aspects of a single mythic sensibility, a primary mode of response to the world and to human nature which exists in every individual and in every culture. Gnossos is one more incarnation of what Joseph Campbell has called the hero with a thousand faces, who represents the noblest aspirations of the human spirit.

Gnossos embodies the primitive, the natural human being; he is a sort of noble savage among the sterile conformists and consumers, the impercipient materialists, those spiritually dead but "deaf to their doom" (27), "the resigned" (31). In contrast to their unquestioning acceptance of specious values, Gnossos, the uncircumsized (both physically and psychically), the bearer of real culture and tradition, affronts and reprimands what Emerson, in his essay "Self-Reliance," called "the smooth mediocrity and squalid contentment of the times." He is an iconoclast (both figuratively and literally, i.e., his destruction of the crèche figures) transgressing all laws, codes, and proprieties by which blandness and hypocrisy are sustained. Gnossos deals only in the genuine: true food, true music, true vision, true ecstasy, true love. In a vacuous and insipid culture, as the incident with the checkout lady and the silver dollars testifies, the authentic goes unrecognized and is rejected.

Gnossos' primitive sensibility manifests itself in his preoccupation with omens, portents, and apparitions, his cultivation of visions, and in his ritualistic behavior, such as crossing his fingers "to avoid hex" (61) and clutching his genitals "to hex away the dangers of the underworld" (115). Dreams, "his mind's additional eye," are an important mode of knowing for Gnossos (154). They are a way of understanding his experience in the world, such as his dream of the abandoned and neglected pachuco (66), and a source of warning and premonition, such as his dreams of Kristin's betrayal (154). ("Come and weep and take my blood from me and dye your hair with it" [195].) Gnossos inhabits a universe of mystery and magic, of menace and rescue, a universe in which instinct and intuition are primary. Accordingly, his allies in the world are children and those who live on the edge and in a state of siege, such as the Black Elks.

Gnossos' ultimate enemy, his antithesis, his antiself, his foil and nemesis, is G. Alonso Oeuf. With his pretentious name and his affected speech, his impeccable tastes, his jaded appetites and his casual diabolicalness, Oeuf represents at once an archetypal and a very contemporary villain. Like Gnossos, Oeuf too desires immunity but in concrete, material terms rather than psychical or metaphysical terms. (Oeuf dismisses Gnossos' immunity as existing "only in a subjective sense" [175].) Oeuf seeks personal power, position, status, control, security — all the pleasures and the privileges of material reality. Oeuf sees in the world the same corruption and inertia that Gnossos sees, but unlike Gnossos who wishes to resist or redeem the evil of the age, Oeuf wishes only to manipulate and exploit it to his fullest advantage. A self-serving cynic, Oeuf is absolutely ruthless in the pursuit of his ends. He incites and then exploits the student uprising, arranges for the murder of Dean Magnolia, and incidentally contrives to bring about Gnossos' fall from innocence. Appropriately, Oeuf is diseased; and it is infection with Oeuf's clap that signals Gnossos' loss of immunity.

Gnossos' much beset and assailed state of immunity is not overthrown in a single dramatic assault but abates by stages, succumbing ultimately to subversion from within and force from without. The first stage of

Gnossos' fall occurs when he learns from Pamela Watson-May of the suicide of Simon, her fiancé. Simon's death is a consequence of Gnossos' earlier seduction of Pamela and serves to indicate that, his convictions notwithstanding, Gnossos is neither "inert" nor without "valence." He learns that his actions do, in fact, produce effects, do have results and repercussions for which he must be held accountable. Gnossos feels "an oily guilt" about Simon's death by which he is haunted throughout the story (99). Emblematic of this partial fall from innocence is the self-destruction of the Captain Midnight Code-O-Graph, found mysteriously sprung in two in his rucksack. "While he was turning it over in his hands it discharged its secret little Captain Midnight spring with a sudden boing, shuddered, and lay lifeless forever" (99).

Eventually, Gnossos uses shellac "to seal the sprung Captain Midnight Code-O-Graph against the mortal insult of rust," and, in a similar manner, he shores up his crumbling innocence (157). But it is only a patch job. The decisive stage of his loss of immunity takes place when, beguiled by love for Kristin and "bowing to her coy insistence, the promise of lewd extraordinary pleasures," Gnossos agrees to lend his name to the campaign against the college administration (199). Previously he had resisted Oeuf's comprehensive temptations to do so, importunings couched in terms of ideological necessity, personal advantage, and philosophical justification. Oeuf, of course, is serpent to Kristin's Eve, using her to seduce Gnossos so that he may be exploited as a crucial link in Oeuf's master strategy. Thus, unwittingly, but not without foreboding and forewarning, Gnossos becomes an accomplice to Oeuf's nefarious plot. Although Gnossos is at this point as yet unaware of having done so, he has forfeited his immunity.

Heffalump warns Gnossos repeatedly that he will "get dosed" eventually, and that is precisely what occurs. Through Kristin Gnossos contracts Oeuf's clap, a particularly virulent strain which is resistant to antibiotics. Only when the symptoms manifest themselves does Gnossos realize that he has been exploited and betrayed, that he has lost his immunity, and that he has become, both literally and metaphorically, infected. His first reaction is to attempt suicide. Then, after withdrawal and reflection, he decides to avenge himself, to meet evil with evil. At this point Gnossos burns his baseball cap, proclaiming that "it is the end of an era" (244). He now recognizes the essential depravity of humankind, the corruption and doom marked on each forehead, which he had previously failed to perceive. With the death of Heffalump, Gnossos' fall is complete. Heffalump represented Gnossos' better self: sensitive, vulnerable, open, engaged in life and in love. Gnossos is at last forced to internalize the knowledge of evil and death, and he casts the remaining tokens of innocence from his rucksack into Heffalump's grave. The extent to which his immunity has been rescinded and his exemption revoked is made explicit when Gnossos is arrested and called to account for all his past transgressions. Significantly, his draft exemption has also been revoked.

Despite Gnossos' fall ("bump bump bump, down the funny stairs" [269]), there are indications that his descent may be seen as a *felix culpa* or fortunate fall, the necessary precondition for attaining a higher state of innocence. In reality, Gnossos' immunity represented a state of arrested development, a desperately prolonged and protracted innocence which had become static and stagnant. This aspect of his immunity is suggested by Gnossos' constipation, which, although it is attributable to his repeated ingestion of opiates, also possesses a metaphorical level of meaning. Appropriately, his constipation ceases with "the cathartic announcement" of his love for Kristin (147). He also relinquishes his emotional virginity to Kristin in an "Epiphanal Defloration" of the heart (182). In spite of the fact that this results in "a dosing," Gnossos' gains are potentially greater than his losses, for he has learned to extend, to surrender, to make love in the literal sense upon which he has always insisted. That he does not altogether repudiate and renounce innocence after his fall is indicated both by his epitaph for Heffalump and later by his acquisition of "a freshly starched Cuban boy scout shirt" (257). Even after his arrest and induction, there is evidence for believing that Gnossos, like Huck Finn, will escape, will flee and evade his oppressors as he hears the call of "the asphalt seas" (269).

True immunity can only be achieved through innoculation, by being actually infected with the disease and developing the antibodies that ensure future resistance. Gnossos has been "dosed," but we may hope that his experience represents an innoculation. By his fall Gnossos has been returned to the place that W. B. Yeats, in "The Circus Animal's Desertion," named "the foul rag and bone shop of the heart," which is where "all ladders start." In his defeat and his possible future status as a fugitive, Gnossos is yet in a more favorable state of soul to receive the unitive vision he has been seeking (but to which his immunity was an impediment), to experience authentic human love (previously precluded by his "virginity"), and thus to strive toward organized innocence.

Innocence, in the universe of Richard Fariña's novel, is engaged in an unremitting struggle with the demonic, with the primal forces of evil, symbolized ultimately by the monkey demon.[4] The struggle manifests itself in the microcosm and in the macrocosm: within individuals, in communities such as Athené, in the nation, in the world, in the cosmos. Fariña depicts a dualistic universe, divided between innocence and evil, immunity and disease, allies and enemies. The various plots and conspiracies of the novel are, in fact, ultimately aspects of a single grand strategy: "Somebody has a plan. . . . I see the signs" (254).

The portentously named protagonist (gnosis: liberating, transcendent knowledge; spiritual enlightenment) and his allies (Heff, Blacknesse, Grün, the Black Elks) represent a regenerative force, opposing the agents and the incursions of the demonic. They challenge and partly check the advance of the interlinking conspiracies of the demonic and its manifestations in the defilement and pollution of the landscape, the spiritual moribundity of its inhabitants, the sterile architecture, synthetic food, and ersatz plants—all of the phenomena that Gnossos characterizes collectively as "the worm in the image" (60).

Gnossos, teller of tales, characterizes his practice as a "subversive art form" (37). Apart from his more direct acts of outrage, disruption, and retaliation, telling tales is his central means of sabotaging the grand plan of the monkey demon and his minions. Accordingly, the book itself represents such a subversive tale, enacting the message of resistance that it affirms and urges.

The novel proposes humor against horror, mythic sensibility against reductive rationality, love against power, energy against inertia, subversion against subservience, Eros against Thanatos, individual resistance against collective complacency, and spontaneous and natural affections against nervous conformity and joyless depravity. Fariña's seriocomic fable is cautionary and hortatory. We have, the author warns us, become accustomed, oblivious, or resigned to our fallen state. We have been down so long it looks like up to us.

9

The "Spiritual Optics" of

Lawrence Ferlinghetti

The Sun's Light when he unfolds it
Depends on the Organ that beholds it.
"What is Man?"
William Blake

The Eye of man a little narrow orb,
clos'd up & dark,
scarcely beholding the great light,
conversing with the Void.
Milton
William Blake

I remember clearly that what impressed me and attracted me in the poetry of Lawrence Ferlinghetti, when I first read it as an adolescent twenty-five years ago, was its quality of mystery. By mystery I do not mean obscurity or hermeticism nor do I mean mystification, but rather, that magical, mythic, secret, and visionary power at the heart of the work of certain poets, that property that causes a poem to resonate so deeply in the mind of the reader. I continue to respond to that mystery in Ferlinghetti's work whenever I read or reread it, and for that reason I want to consider his writing with close attention, not to explain the mystery but to approach it, to honor it.

My procedure is simply to follow what I see as the inner continuity of concerns in Ferlinghetti's writing, the correlations of thought and of emotion and of image within and among the works and to trace elements of the whole design as I perceive them.

As I read it, the work of Lawrence Ferlinghetti proposes what I call (borrowing the phrase from the title of an essay by Thomas Carlyle) a "Spiritual Optics," that is, a way of being and seeing, a mode of identity and vision. Ferlinghetti's writing embodies a myth or metaphysic which conceives an original unity of being from which human consciousness, individual and generic, has fallen. The fallen state is one of division and conflict where the mind struggles toward reconciliation and reunification with original being. The impulse toward reunification involves a twofold, interrelated process in each human psyche: the integration of the fragmented, fallen consciousness into a unity; and the reconciliation of subject and object, of ego and nonego, in the communion of creative perception.

The development and definition of this "spiritual optics" is the central problem of Ferlinghetti's poetry, prose, and dramatic work. In the following I want to examine this double theme and to consider its evolution in his writing, with particular attention to his prose narrative *Her,* which represents a grammar of the premises and concerns of his work.

Her is an interior monologue narrated by Andy Raffine, an American painter living in Paris. In the opening paragraphs of the story, Raffine characterizes his psychic situation in terms of "a transaction with myself" and "a battle with the image."[1] These two elements of his problem are mutually reflexive. The first, the "transaction," is a quest for identity, a search for the whole or completed self, which he images as a sexual union. And the second element, the "battle," is a quest for vision, for a true perception of existence, a perception beyond habit and preconception, beyond subjectivity and objectivity. The state of being and seeing in which he hopes to unite the masculine and feminine aspects of the self, unite subject and object in vision, he calls "the fourth person singular" (90).

Raffine has a sense of an original, true, whole identity experienced in childhood and shattered when he was orphaned at an early age. He views himself as fallen and fragmented, continually seeking to refine and refind himself. He also sees his situation as a microcosm of the human condition, that we are "all of us, all splintered parts of the same whole" (40). In Raffine's view everyone, whether consciously or unconsciously, is engaged in a quest "searching for something all had lost," a condition of original human unity that is now "a lost community . . . a far country" from which we are exiled (76).

Accordingly, the world in which we live, the fallen world, is divided into the forces of redemption and liberation that would restore humankind to unity and the forces of repression and oppression that, perhaps unknowingly, enforce alienation and divisiveness. Poetry, music, visual art, eroticism, affection, ecstasy, compassion, beauty, communication, and love represent the reintegrative principles. Egotism, power, authority, dogma—as embodied by the military, the police, the clergy, the customs authorities, and others and as reflected in "regulations and protocols and codes and restrictions and taboos and constitutions and traffic regulations and accepted maxims and venerated proverbs"—represent the principles of conflict, impediment, and disunity (58).

Raffine is, potentially, a redemptive, regenerative figure who could, through his life and art, help to bring about "the true Liberation" ending "the prolonged Occupation of the world" (46). He could articulate the "final, irreducible secret" in paint, catalyze "the long overdue millenium of art and life" (88). Raffine is represented as a sort of Fisher King figure and is associated with fish imagery throughout the text ("the fishy king none other than myself, my name a brand of canned salt fish" [27]). He is sexually wounded, pursuing a female Grail in the figure of "Her."

Raffine's sexual wound is not physical but mental. It consists of his view of women as either virginal-maternal or as insatiable devourers. This fixation prevents him from consumating a sexual union. Repeatedly, at crucial moments of erotic encounter he fails, held back in fear by his illusions, abstractions, preconceptions, never learning to use "the one true key of love that could unlock all the doors" (104).

Similarly, Raffine fails continually in his art; his "orgasm" in paint is checked by an inevitable return to habit and cliché. He is unable to "break away into the free air of underivative creation" (111) and is frustrated in his attempts to "enact the new" (112).

Both Raffine's sexual and artistic failures are extentions of his essential failure to achieve identity and vision, a failure which ultimately results in his death.

Raffine's quest for identity and vision closely parallels the process of individuation as described by Carl Jung involving encounters with shadow and anima.

According to Jungian psychology, the shadow is a projection or personification of "the hidden, repressed and unfavorable (or nefarious) aspects of the personality."[2] The shadow is not altogether negative though; it also possesses creative qualities and virtues, "values that are needed by consciousness,"[3] including "even the most valuable and highest forces."[4]

Raffine's shadow in *Her* is Lubin, waiter at the Café Mabillon. Lubin is an ambiguous figure, whose face is "two masks, a mask of comedy superimposed on one of tragedy" (16), whose jaw "was meant to cup a violin, or to clench a bone" (65). Ferlinghetti compares him both to "a great bird of prey" (18) and to "a great shy dog" (64). Lubin is at once vulgar and wise, ragged and elegant, blasphemous and reverent. (There is a close resemblance, deliberate on the part of the author, between Lubin and Dr. Matthew O'Connor of Djuna Barnes' novel *Nightwood*.)

A drunkard and a debauchee, Lubin serves as confessor and counselor to the naive and idealistic Raffine. The identification between the two figures exists in both a paternal relationship (Lubin describes himself to Raffine as "your wandered father"[66].) and a twin relationship (doppelgänger, alter egos, opposite and complementary). To Lubin, Raffine is "my own past" (66), while he sees himself as "the billous tag-end of your future" (67) and in memory as "an earlier Andy Raffine" (68). Lubin's most important function is to disabuse Raffine of his notions concerning the virginity of "Her" and to serve as a mediator between Raffine and "Her." Lubin foresees disaster for Raffine, but his counsels and warnings to him are unheeded.

The second stage of the individuation process, according to Jungian psychology, "is characterized by the encounter with the *soul image*, . . . the complementary contrasexual part of the psyche" — for the male, the anima. The anima may manifest itself in a variety of forms including "a sweet young maiden, a goddess, a witch, an angel, a demon, a beggar woman, a whore, a devoted companion, an Amazon, etc."[5] Andy Raffine's anima takes the form of most of the named figures above, constantly metamorphosing. Like the shadow, the anima has two aspects, benevolent and malefic. In its sublime aspect the anima is often "fused with the figure of the Virgin," while in its infernal aspect it often presents itself in the figure of the femme fatale or a witch.[6]

Raffine's search for his anima is rooted in his childhood experience of the death of his mother, thus his insistence on purity and virginity.

Another recurring virginal figure of Raffine's anima is "a little girl with a hoop in a dirdnl dress" (11), whose piece of white string that is "as purely white as innocence itself" becomes defiled by mud (17). These two images are inhibitory, obstructive, and finally destructive for him. During the most critical sexual encounter of the book, his failure is attributable to his fixation with such virginal purity, for he involuntarily recalls "that first face" and notices a soiled piece of white string on the floor beside the bed (118). The ultimate symbol of the manifestation of the maternal-virginal aspect of Raffine's anima is the statue of the Virgin on the cathedral Notre Dame, between whose breasts he climbs before falling, figuratively "tangled up and trussed" in string, to his death (156).

The baleful aspect of Raffine's anima is the concept of woman as the emasculator, the insatiable whore, the devourer. Raffine views women in terms of female archetypes such as the Sirens, exhausting helpless men "in perpetual orgasm" (55); the Mona Lisa, "that eternal dame having just eaten her husband, note the famous enigmatic smile of containment if not contentment" (88); Salome, "she wants more than my head she wants my body on a spit" (102); the Queen Bee, "no sooner is the union completed than my abdomen opens and my organ detaches itself" (109); and the ominous old crone flowerseller who reappears throughout the book, with her mad, raucous laugh, reminiscent of the "layer-out" figure of Robert Graves' Triple Goddess.

Raffine fails to integrate and reconcile the positive and negative qualities of his anima, fails to balance or direct the energy. In consequence, both aspects are destructive to him and result ultimately in his death. His failure is most apparent during the central romantic-erotic encounter of the story which takes place in Rome.

Raffine travels to Rome in a desperate endeavor to flee his "half-life" and to seek to achieve genuine identity and perception (84). He attempts to "see without the old associational turning eye that turns all it sees into its own" (93). Two brief unconsumated erotic encounters (one with a prostitute, the other with an Italian peasant girl) convince him of the necessity of liberating his psyche from his abstractions and preconceptions concerning women. He characterizes the restrictive grip of these habits of mind as a bird perched inside his head: "the crazy sad bird I carried in my head as the idea of woman . . . the parrot of love who kept repeating all the phrases and phases of it" (107). His quest culminates in an involvement with an American girl in a hotel in Rome. Raffine vows to himself that he will avoid all the old patterns and associations and "this time begin with the real and stick to it" (113). And, for a time, he succeeds: "Instead of a hazy image out of somebody else's painting or out of my own, I saw the girl in sharp outline, a clear incisive line . . ." (113–14). But as they are about to make love, Raffine realizes that they remain "anomymous bodies" to each other, each imposing a pattern upon or evoking an image from the other (118). Raffine cannot escape the imprint of his early experiences, the memory of his mother, his fixation with purity. They do not make love, do not comfort, warm, or awaken each other, do not save each other. Raffine recognizes that he remains on the "carrousel" of inauthentic identity and perception, revolving continually through the same experiences, never able to grab the brass ring of true selfhood and vision (119).

Still blindly and desperately seeking a union with the feminine to complete his "transaction" with himself, Raffine returns to Paris. There he ascends the cathedral Notre Dame by means of a scaffolding, embraces the statue of the Virgin, and falls to his death. Raffine's final, fatal fall is, like Finnegan's, a reenactment of the Fall of Man—"a falling away through a failure of contact through a failure of life" (147). The events of the story have taken place during the Lenten season, during Passion Week, and Raffine dies on Good Friday, a parody Christ, "a friday fish to hang upon the old hook" (149), an unhealed, unredeeming Fisher King who has lost his "battle with the image" (7).

The final images of the narrative may, however, indicate a *felix culpa,* or fortunate fall, a redemption in death for Andy Raffine: "God grips the genitals to catch illusionary me . . . he plays the deepsea catch he reels me in O god" (157). There is an echo here of a phrase of Lubin's: "The hand that grips the genitals, love plays the deepsea catch . . ." (68), which is later recalled and expanded by Raffine, "Love plays the deepsea catch, it's love will reel it in . . ." (139). Raffine is identified with fish both by means of his name, "a brand of canned salt fish," and by means of recurring fish imagery: "fished up . . . Fishface . . . swimming . . . fisheyed" (66–69) and again, "my sardine can alack . . . a fart of a fish . . . my sardine boat . . . your fishy fellow" (86). Thus, Raffine becomes "the deepsea catch" that is "played" throughout the book to be reeled in by God or by love in the end. Ferlinghetti employes a pun (a frequent device in *Her*), perhaps a double pun, involving the use of the word *reel.* Aside from its surface contextual meaning of being drawn in as a fish on a line, it may also refer to the image of "the unwinding reel" of cinematic film that Raffine uses as a metaphor for his life and his identity, a film projected frame by frame and then recoiled (10). In the meeting of the two metaphors, fish and film, there may be another meaning created, a sound pun, a homophone. Raffine is not only reeled in (like a fish or a film) but, perhaps also, *realed* in as well; that is to say, reeled into the real. In this case, Raffine's final exclamation, "O god," may be understood not as a cry of despair but as an affirmation. He may, in death, have achieved the fourth person singular.

Her is a complex, resonant work whose themes are developed through recurring images and associations. There are paired opposites such as blindness/sight, key/lock, obesity/Lent, climbing/falling, virginity/licentiousness, sleeping/waking; and there are associative pairs or clusters such as shadow/haze/dusk/fog (suggestive of ordinary perception, that is, cliché, habit) and gramophone/film reel/carrousel (suggestive of the endlessly repetitive nature of ordinary perception and experience). In addition there are multivalent images such as string, fish, bird, film reel, door, statue, flowers, mirror, window, flushing toilets. Puns and literary allusions are frequent in the text.

Her represents the myth or metaphysic of Ferlinghetti's writing, the cosmography of his poetic imagination. His view of existence has much in common with that of the English romantic poets, particularly William Blake, but it is nonetheless distinctively and uniquely that of the author himself. According to Ferlinghetti's myth, human beings are fallen (from unity to disunity, from true perception to false and limited perception) and are, as a consequence of their fall, self-divided. Their inner divisions are reflected in the world they create that is divided between power and love. Authentic (or visionary) perception and authentic being (which in combination, constitute what I have named a "spiritual optics") are the means by which unified human identity may be regained and a return to the prelapsarian world accomplished. Ferlinghetti's art evolves out of his desire to communicate this vision and to uphold and advocate the cause of unity against disunity, love against power. Thus, the theme of vision and the absence of vision is, in its various aspects and applications, central to virtually all of Ferlinghetti's writing.

Lawrence Ferlinghetti's dramatic pieces, collected in *Unfair Arguments with Existence* and *Routines,* are extentions and expansions of the central myth articulated in *Her.* There is a particularly close relationship between *Her* and the play *The Soldiers of No Country* where the characters of Denny, Toledano, and Erma parallel those of Andy Raffine, Lubin, and "Her." The situation of the characters in a cave recalls certain of the images of *Her* and may ultimately derive from Plato's allegory in which the cave represents limited perception, the world of reflected reality, shadows. The cave is described in the stage directions as "womb-like," that is, a cave out of which we must be born.[7] Denny's complaint is similar to that of Andy Raffine: "Nobody's listening, we're just talking to ourselves. . . . They don't even see you . . . seeing only themselves or someone else, not you but another . . ." (*Unfair,* 9–10). Images of mirror, bird, white string, virginity, the Virgin, darkness and light, loss, a lost country without "evil or hate . . . only a blind urge to love". (*Unfair,* 19) also unite the play with *Her. The Soldiers of No Country* seems more optimistic than *Her,* however, ending with Erma emerging from the darkness of the cave into the light and with a powerful image of birth.

The images of cracked binoculars, blindness, and the unwillingness to see in the plays *3,000 Red Ants* and *Alligation* evoke the eye and sight motifs of *Her.* In *The Victims of Amnesia* the conflict occurs between a Night Clerk, a benighted authoritarian who likes to play at being a conductor or a soldier, and Marie Mazda, associated with miracle, mystery, and light. *Motherlode* portrays another "sounding of the same eternal situation" wherein "prospecting for love, we dig flesh . . ." (*Unfair,* vii–ix). The piece represents again the human quest for the lost and mythic "mainland" or "the land of lovers" (*Unfair,* 91), the prelapsarian world from which we are exiled. The quest motif occurs again in *The Customs Collector in Baggy Pants* in which the object of the search is the lost "diamond of hope," associated also with erotic or generative powers, the power to love, "twin gems . . . King of Diamonds," which are also lost and must be recovered (*Unfair,* 109). The figure of the customs collector and the flushing toilets of this piece recall identical images in *Her.* (There is, of course, a pun involved in the word *customs* in this context. The Custom's Agents represent the inner forces of custom and habituation that allow no contraband impressions or perceptions to pass.) Further images from *Her,* climbing and falling, are central to the final play of the volume, *The Nose of Sisyphus.* The opposition between vision and blindness, freedom and repression, spirit and animality, is configured in this instance as the conflict between Sisyphus, a heroic, redemptive figure, and Big Baboon, a menacing embodiment of all that is base and retrograde in humankind.

The shorter dramatic pieces of *Routines* reflect and explore particular aspects of existence as repetition, as habit, and as pattern. In his preface to the plays, Ferlinghetti declares that "life itself . . . [is] a blackout routine . . . [we are] lost in the vibration of a wreckage (of some other cosmos we fell out of)."[8] This metaphysical premise, already established in *Her* and developed in *Unfair Arguments with Existence,* provides a sense of the unity and continuity of the various "routines" as attempts to locate and describe the ground of our experience, with the ultimate intention of aiding us in transcending our condition.

The "question of identity" is the problem treated in *Our Little Trip (Routines,* 9). Whether identity may be said to exist at all, whether it is attainable, and whether it is important are the issues raised by the Question Man, a dispassionate, reductive, intellectual relative of Big Baboon. The Question Man views human existence in terms of mechanics, physical properties, mental capacities, and operations, without metaphysics, without mystery, without meaning. The male-female relationship is again presented as being intimately involved with the process of identity. The central image of the piece is that of a man and a woman whose faces are wrapped in a single long bandage which attaches them to each other. We first see them "dressed conventionally," straining away from each other (*Routines,* 6). Later, after an interval, they return to the stage naked except for the bandage around their faces and "now strain toward each other," finally rewinding themselves completely, pressing against each other and caressing (*Routines,* 9). Their actions suggest a resolution to the question of identity, a casting aside of conventions, of defenses, a return to the true and original state of the soul, an integration of the masculine and feminine principles.

Male and female relationships are also the subject of *His Head* and *Swinger,* but these pieces seem only to describe conflicts without suggesting resolutions. They are, together with the other philosophical and political routines of the collection, provocations to the reader or to the audience, problems, questions to make us "think of life" and to precipitate "revolutionary solutions or evolutionary solutions" (*Routines,* 23). As Ferlinghetti reminds us, "Routines never end; they have to be broken" (*Routines,* 50).

Ferlinghetti's first volume of poems, *Pictures of the Gone World,* records epiphanies and vignettes of vision and satirizes and exposes elements of the conspiracy against joy and vision. In these poems, lovers, children, artists, and poets oppose librarians, cultural ambassadors, museum directors, priests, patrolmen—those who can neither love nor see because they have "been running / on the same old rails too long";[9] those who have "no eyes to see" the beauty of the world because they are preoccupied with trivialities and superficialities (No. 20); the predatory and acquisitive; those who have no identity outside of "their hats and their jobs" (No. 26); those who have

> fatally assumed
>
> that some direct connection
>
> does exist between
>
> language and reality
>
> word and world.
>
> (No. 27)

The poems are also united with *Her* and to the plays by common imagery, including statues, mirrors, doors, virgin, and string.

A Coney Island of the Mind continues and expands the theme of vision with a unifying image of the eye. "The poet's eye obscenely seeing" discerns reality from illusion, the mysterious from the meretricious, the eternal from the temporal.[10] "The poet's eye" may be developed through response to literature or to visual art (Goya, Bosch, Chagall, Kafka help us to see) or may be retained from childhood "when every living thing / cast its shadow in eternity" (No. 19, 34). As in *Her,* humankind is engaged, consciously or unconsciously, in regaining "the lost shores" where there are "green birds singing / from the other side of silence" (No. 21, 36). Human beings are "all hunting love and half the hungry time not even knowing just what is really eating them"; they are "always on their hungry travels after the same hot grail" (No. 29, 44–45). In the paradise we seek there will be no clothes, no altars, no hierarchy or authority, but only "fountains of imagination" (No. 13, 28). And though we are confounded as to how to gain admittance to the castle of the "Mystery of Existence" where "it is heavenly weather" and "souls dance undressed / together," the poet assures us that "on the far side" there is "a wide wide vent . . . where even elephants / waltz thru" (No. 16, 31). We continually overlook the epiphanous possibilities of the obvious, the miraculous qualities of the commonplace.

In his "Oral Messages" section of *A Coney Island of the Mind* Ferlinghetti declares again and clarifies his opposition to tyranny, boredom, exploitation, nationalism, and war and reaffirms his faith in "a rebirth of wonder" and a "total dream of Innocence" ("I Am Waiting," 49–52). If we would return to "the true blue simple life / of wisdom and wonderment," we would reach the "Isle of Manisfree," the just and joyous society ("Junkman's Obbligato," 54–59). In "Autobiography" and "Dog" Ferlinghetti urges us to attention and observation of the world, to see what is around us with the innocent eye of the dog, to see directly, unintimidated, without abstractions or preconceptions, but instead "touching and tasting and testing everything" ("Dog," 68). And in "Christ Climbed Down," Christ is associated with "the poet's eye," potential in every human being, the ability to reject the superficial, to discern the essential. In a commercial, consumer society, artificial and hypocritical with a vacuum of values, Christ must seek rebirth, a Second Coming in the soul of every human: "In the darkest night / of everybody's anonymous soul / He awaits . . ." (70).

The image of a dormant, potential, redemptive force waiting in the world, waiting to be awakened in each separate psyche and in the collective human psyche, becomes the central motif of "The Great Chinese Dragon," which is one of the key poems of *Starting from San Francisco.* The dragon of the poem represents to the poet "the force and mystery of life," the true sight that "sees the spiritual everywhere translucent in the material world."[11] The dragon is guarded and restrained by the police, the agents of the conspiracy against joy and vision, who recognize and fear its apocalyptic power. The poem concludes with the image of the dragon buried in a cellar, awaiting "the final coming and the final sowing of his oats and teeth" (64). The dragon may be seen as the visionary imaginative potential within each human mind, restrained by the rational faculties and the collective regenerative qualities of humanity, repressed by the forces of authority, egotism, and materialism. (Appropriately, the ultimate etymological root of the word *dragon* is the Greek verb *derkesthai,* which means "to see.") Also closely related to the premises of *Her* are the concepts of the poem "Hidden Door" which rejects the "pathetic fallacy / of the evidence of the senses / as to the nature of reality" and explores the mystery of "our buried life," the attempt to rediscover the "lost shore of light," to find again the "mislaid visionary self" (31–35). A number of images from *Her* and from the plays recur in the poem, including the blind man with tin cup, key, door, climbing and falling, palimpsest, vulva, and mirror. The poem "He" describes a poet-prophet who is "the mad eye of the fourth person singular," who has achieved "unbuttoned vision" (36–41).

The Secret Meaning of Things is, as the title indicates, a further enquiry into visionary consciousness, an attempt to achieve and to convey a mode of observation that "leaves behind all phenomenal distinction," enabling the eye to perceive essences, inscapes, the mystery and the eternalness of temporal phenomena.[12] The volume is notable for two poems in particular, "After the Cries of Birds" and "Moscow in the Wilderness, Segovia in the Snow," which can be seen as companion pieces. In the first of the two poems, Ferlinghetti prophesies "a new visionary society . . . a new pastoral era" in America, the reconciliation of occidental and Oriental culture and thought, the American frontier translated into a metaphysical frontier, the new manifest destiny in "the wish to pursue what lies beyond the mind / . . . to move beyond the senses" (32–39). In the second of the poems, another prophecy, the Russian spirit, in the image of an ancient armadillo "asleep for centuries / in the cellar of the Kremlin," at last awakens to music, to ecstasy, and to vision (47–48). Considered together the two poems represent a prophecy, as described in Revelation, of "a new heaven and a new earth" achieved through the medium of the awakened eye.

The title to the volume *Open Eye, Open Heart* is again significant to the pervasive theme of vision. The phrase is taken from the poem "True Confessional" in which it refers to a way of seeing with the eye of "the inside self."[13] Images of light, "shining . . . bright . . . skeins of light . . . luminous," oppose those of darkness, "cobwebs of Night . . . shadow"; the "inside self" is contrasted to the "outside with its bag of skin" (4–5). In such poems as "Sueño Real," "The Real Magic Opera Begins," and "Stone Reality Meditation" the nature of reality is the central issue. These poems reflect an increased awareness of the ephemerality, the transitory nature, of material form with its "fugitive configurations" (21) that occur in "the eternal dream-time" (16).

The artist or poet, as in "An Elegy on the Death of Kenneth Patchen," is still seen as a redemptive figure who struggles against "the agents of

Death" (38) and who opposes the "various villainies of church and state" (45). Ferlinghetti again depicts art as the medium of awareness and of visionary consciousness. He mentions, in this connection, references to music by Telemann, sculpture by Giacometti, paintings by Ben Shahn, and the writings of Lorca, Whitman, Blake, and Lawrence. The absence of vision is recorded in the poem "London, Rainy Day" where "life's eternal situations / stutter on . . . Nothing moves in the leaded air," and the transcending, transforming power of the inner eye is inactive: "The blue rider does not appear" (46).

The "Her" figure, anima, muse of vision, psychic complement, appears again in *Open Eye, Open Heart,* glimpsed, lovely and elegant, in a restaurant or encountered in a Ramada Inn in Kansas, with her "far-eyed look" (13). The "Eternal Woman" remains a disturbing presence for Ferlinghetti, at once magnetically attractive and yet dreadful in her demand for absolute abnegation (29). "Tantric Ballad" treats the theme of man and woman as "counterparts," who in sexual union form a lotus flower, a perfected form (125).

The external and internal relationship between the masculine and the feminine and its relation to identity and vision is again a dominant theme in the poems of *Who Are We Now?* Man and woman relationships are the subject of several poems in the volume, including "People Getting Divorced," "Short Story on a Painting of Gustav Klimt," "At the Bodega," and "The Heavy." In "The Jack of Hearts," Ferlinghetti's paean to the prophet-visionary who can redeem "the time of the ostrich," who can awaken and enliven "the silent ones with frozen faces," the hero with open eye and open heart has found

> the sun-stone
> of himself
> the woman-man
> the whole man.[14]

And in "I Am You," the poet praises and prophesies what Plato called the Spherical Man, the original and final human:

> Man half woman

> Woman half man

> And the two intertwined

> in each of us androgynous
> . . . .
>
> in the end as in beginning.

(19–20)

Further prophecies of ultimate harmony, ultimate unity, ultimate victory, occur in the poems "A Vast Confusion" and "Olbers' Paradox." In the first of these Ferlinghetti describes "a vast confusion in the universe" in which "all life's voices lost in night" and then envisions

> Chaos unscrambled
> back to the first
> harmonies
>
> And the first light.

(44)

"Olbers' Paradox" is a metaphoric appropriation of the theory of an early astronomer Heinrich Olbers that "there *must* be a place / where all is light" and that the light from that place will one day reach the Earth (45). For Ferlinghetti the theory represents the final victory of light over darkness, the Great Awakening, the apocalypse of the fourth person singular:

> And then in that symbolic
> so poetic place
> which will be ours
> we'll be our own true shadows
> and our own illumination.

(45)

In this manner the problems of identity and vision which were posited in *Her* are resolved in prophecy.

And in the concluding poems of the volume, "Eight People on a Golf Course and One Bird of Freedom Flying Over" and "Populist Manifesto," Ferlinghetti reaffirms his belief in the inevitable and final triumph of the indestructible, resurrective phoenix of life, truth, and vision over the conspiracy of politics, industry, religion, the military, the media, bankers, and the police and reiterates his faith in poetry as a primary instrument of enlightenment: "Poetry the common carrier / for the transportation of the public / to higher places" ("Populist Manifesto," 64).

The theme of "spiritual optics" that is articulated in the work of Lawrence Ferlinghetti is coherent and consistent but not static. Rather, it lends dynamism and invention to his writing, varying focus, tone, and response, permitting dramatic expansions and reductions of experience, fitting the poems to each other and to the plays and to *Her* in such a manner that they reinforce one another's meanings. The theme develops in the course of the work—from the diagnostic, essentially pessimistic *Her,* with its abortive poetry revolution and failed quester-hero, through the cautious hope in the plays and the early poems, with their continuing struggle from blindness to vision, from darkness to light, from power to love, from quotidian life toward "a renaissance of wonder" (I Am Waiting," *Coney,* 53), to the prophecies of the later poems which foresee a Great Awakening, the union of the masculine and the feminine principles, the reconciliation of Occident and Orient and of opposing ideologies, and which herald the emergence of a visionary society, "a new pastoral era," and the final victory of light over darkness.

10

Friendly and Flowing Savage: The Literary Legend of Neal Cassady

The friendly and flowing savage, who is he?
Is he waiting for civilization, or past it and mastering it?
. . . .
Wherever he goes men and women accept and desire him,
They desire he should like them, touch them, speak to them, stay with
them.

Behavior lawless as snow-flakes, words simple as grass, uncom'd head,
laughter and naiveté.

Walt Whitman
"Song of Myself"

Neal Cassady (1926–1968) achieved within his lifetime the status of a modern folk hero, a contemporary legend. Both during and after his life, that legend has found expression in a number of written works, on film, and in popular song. In the following I am concerned specifically with Neal Cassady's literary legend; that is, with the manner in which he is depicted as a character in literary works. Cassady's own autobiographical writing, his published correspondence, the recordings and transcriptions of his monologues, and the works of memoir and biography that treat his life are inapposite to my purpose, which is to assess the particular values, the myth, and the mystery which he represented for the various authors who were inspired to write about him.

The earliest work in which a character based on Neal Cassady appears is John Clellon Holmes' novel *Go,* first published in 1952. The character, called Hart Kennedy, is a secondary figure in the book. He enters the story suddenly about a third of the way through the novel, appears intermittently for about a hundred pages, and then hastens away again. As in many of the subsequent works in which he appears, the Cassady figure is profoundly ambiguous, manifesting both positive and negative aspects, inspiring admiration and disapproval on the part of the other characters in the works, on the part of the author, and on the part of the reader.

The physical description of Hart Kennedy emphasizes the negative, manipulative-opportunistic aspects of his character: "small, wiry Hart, who moved with itchy calculation and whose reddish hair and broken nose gave him an expression of shrewd, masculine ugliness" (114). He is further described as having eyes that are "continually sizing everything up" (117). And Hart's actions in the story bear out the suggestions of his physiognomy. He exploits every situation, every friend, and every acquaintance in the service of his amoral hedonism. He is dishonest, irresponsible, inconstant, callous and on one occasion, shows himself capable of violence. Such is the confusion and destructiveness of his life that his wife, Dinah, remarks that "you can't stick close to him if anything matters to you" (149).

And yet, together with his negative and destructive qualities, Hart represents an intensity and an excitement, a responsiveness to life that provokes awe and imitation among many of the novel's characters. He is a catalyst—initiating, inciting action, urging others on to pleasure and abandon. His ebullience and exuberance are infectious. He communicates an awareness of existence as possibility, as promise, and as wonder that denies the self-limiting cautions and conventions by which most people live their lives.

In the context of the story Hart embodies a type of response to what Holmes sees as the spiritual predicament of postwar man. Hart's response is extreme, primitive, almost atavistic; indeed, he is likened to "an euphoric savage who erupts into a magic rite at the moment of his seizure" (139). He is a prophet of the libido, of the instincts and appetites. His desperate hedonism is not, however, an end in itself but rather the means to an end: the transcendence of personal consciousness and time. His message, incoherent and inarticulately expressed, is of the perfection and essential unity of all experience:

> Hell, you can't explain it; all this intellectual terminology drags me
> now. It isn't that really . . . it's nothing you can explain that way.
> It's just getting your kicks and digging *everything* that happens. Like
> everything was perfect. Because it really is, you know? . . . It's just
> that *everything's* really true, on its own level. See? . . . Everything's
> really true. I mean the same as everything else. (144–45)

Paul Hobbes, the main character of the novel, finds Hart's conduct to
be frequently dubious and blameworthy and his ideas specious. Hobbes is
capable at best of only a grudging acceptance of Hart and his wife, whom
he regards as "amoral, giggling nihilists" (166). The other two central
figures of *Go,* Gene Pasternak and David Stofsky, revere Hart, though
Stofsky finds cause to remonstrate with him for his callousness. Finally,
there is no attempt in the novel to reconcile or resolve the creative and
destructive aspects of Hart Kennedy, but by virtue of his duality and
ambiguity, he becomes something of a mythic figure in the story,
something elemental, a force more than a man—ultimately an enigma.

Probably the best-known and certainly the most extensive of the
portrayals of Neal Cassady in literature is his appearance as the character
Dean Moriarty in Jack Kerouac's novel *On the Road.* Moriarty is, aside
from the narrator, the central figure of the story. His character is fuller,
more nuanced, and significantly more sympathetic than that of Hart
Kennedy in *Go,* though the essential ambiguity of the character is at least
equally profound.

The relationship between the narrator of *On the Road,* Sal Paradise, and
Dean Moriarty is that of neophyte to adept. As the novel opens, Sal,
though still a young man, has reached the end of himself. He has ended
his marriage, suffered a serious illness, is weary and has the feeling that
everything is dead. At this critical point of his life he meets Dean
Moriarty and with that meeting his life begins to change direction. For
Sal, Dean represents a psychological and spiritual reorientation, a new
pattern of conduct, and a new system of values, including spontaneity,
sensuality, energy, intuition, and instinct. In contrast to Sal's eastern,
urban-intellectual friends who are "in the negative, nightmare position
of putting down society and giving their tired bookish or political or
psychoanalytical reasons" (11), Dean, "a sideburned hero of the snowy
West," affirms and celebrates life (6). Dean retains an eager receptivity to
experience that Sal associates with childhood innocence; and from the

beginning of their friendship, Sal believes of Dean what he later states in his defense: "He's got the secret that we're all busting to find" (161).

Dean brings Sal into contact with his own lost self, guides him in reestablishing the primacy of his instincts and intuition, instructs him in nonrational modes of knowing. He aids him in disencumbering himself of systems of thought in order to perceive and to experience directly and without preconceptions: "Everything since the Greeks has been predicated wrong. You can't make it with geometry and geometrical systems of thinking. It's all *this*!" (99). Dean initiates Sal into the religion of "IT," which is the transcendence of personal, rational consciousness and the attainment of a synchronization with the infinite.

Dean also attempts to instill in Sal his own sense of energetic receptivity to events, his joyous passivity to life. Dean advises a total acceptance of oneself and of the world without resistance or despair, an attention and a response to circumstances that amount to a cosmic optimism. Throughout the story Dean assures Sal of the inevitable rightness of things as they are and as they will be: "I am positive beyond doubt that everything will be taken care of for us" (100). "Everything takes care of itself. I could close my eyes and this old car would take care of itself" (132). And again later: "I *know* that everything will be all right" (153). "We know what IT is and we know TIME and we know that everything is really FINE" (172). The key concepts of his code are affirmation and ecstatic resignation, expressed in his refrain of "Yes!"

But together with his irresistible charm, his irrepressible energies, and his hip mysticism, there are other features of Dean's character that make him an ambiguous figure in the book. There is, from the beginning, an element of the con artist in him, as Sal recognizes, something of the self-seeking trickster, the amoral hipster looking for kicks, the young man on the make. His treatment of people often parallels his treatment of cars: using them, breaking them under the strains of his demands, and then abandoning them. Dean is alternately innocent and demonic, tender and destructive, and Sal responds to him with admiration and with fear. Sal identifies Dean both with his "long-lost brother" (10) and with the Shrouded Traveler of his recurrent nightmare. He sees him both as "a new kind of American saint" (34) and as "the Angel of Terror" (193). Sal's ambivalence is manifested most clearly during the climactic Mexican adventure when, while euphoric with marijuana, he sees Dean as God, and then later after his illness and his abandonment by Dean, he states: "I realized what a rat he was . . ." (249).

Dean is neither altogether angelic nor altogether demonic. He is energy, both positive and negative. He can be benevolent, libidinous, sage, or baleful. Always he operates beyond the boundaries of rational consciousness. In the manner of a mystic, he can communicate directly with such other surrational persons as the idiot girl with her visions, the ecstatic spastic in the Denver bar, the wild, sweating bop musicians, and the fellahin of Mexico whose spoken language he does not know. Dean is as protean, as powerful, and as unknowable as the human subconscious mind with which he may be identified — as a votary, a prophet, and as an embodiment of its energies and mysteries.

Dean may be seen as a parallel to the shadow figure of Jungian psychology. The shadow is the personification of the latent unconscious traits, the hidden and repressed aspects of the personality, both favorable and unfavorable, destructive and creative. "The shadow usually contains values that are needed by consciousness but that exist in a form that makes it difficult to integrate them into one's life . . . sometimes everything that is unknown to the ego is mixed up with the shadow, including even the most valuable and highest forces."[1] In the novel, Dean serves as Sal's shadow, and in a larger context, the Cassady figure may be seen to represent the shadow of postwar American society.

In addition, Dean represents an earlier American spirit (the American Adam, the American innocent) that has been stifled by what Huck Finn termed "sivilization," the insipid, insidious systematizing of life. Parallels between Huck Finn and Nigger Jim, and Sal Paradise and Dean Moriarty, between the river and the road, are numerous. The trailblazer, the pioneer, and the cowboy are also very much part of his makeup. Sal describes him as "a young Gene Autry — trim, thin-hipped, blue-eyed" (6) and as "a wild yea-saying overburst of American joy," "an ode from the Plains," "a western kinsman of the sun" (11). The irony and tragedy of his situation is that there are no geographical frontiers left for him in industrial, suburban America. The remarks of the poet Gary Snyder speaking about Neal Cassady are particularly relevant to this point.

> My vision of Cassady is of the 1890s cowboys, the type of person who works the high plains of the 1880s and 1890s . . . he is the Denver grandchild of the 1880s cowboys with no range left to work on.

Cassady's type is that frontier type, reduced to pool halls and driving
back and forth across the country. . . . Cassady was the energy of
the archetypal west, the energy of the frontier, still coming down.
Cassady is the cowboy crashing.[2]

Dean may also be considered in light of what W. H. Auden has termed
"the American child-hero" who is "a Noble Savage, an anarchist, and,
even when he reflects, predominantly concerned with movement and
action. He may do almost anything except sit still. His heroic virtue
. . . lies in his freedom from conventional ways of thinking and acting:
all social habits, from manners to creeds, are regarded as false and
hypocritical or both. All emperors are really naked."[3] This characterization is entirely applicable to Dean Moriarty; indeed, it would seem to be
a description specifically of him. In this manner, the Cassady figure
represents something archetypally American, something closely connected with American literature, American history, and with deep-
seated patterns of the American psyche.

More than being a resurgence of the American revolutionary and
frontier spirits, Moriarty also represents for Kerouac a fulfillment and a
culmination of American identity and an evolutionary step. He is
"something new, long prophesied, long a-coming" (34). Kerouac sees
him as a precursor, a potentially redemptive, visionary figure: "the
HOLY GOOF" (160) whose spiritual condition is "BEAT—the root, the
soul of Beatific" (161).

There are also significant affinities between the character of Dean
Moriarty and Norman Mailer's idea of the hipster expressed in his essay
The White Negro. Mailer characterizes the hipster as "a philosophical
psychopath" (Alan Harrington classified Neal Cassady as a psychopath in
his *Playboy* article "The Coming of the Psychopath.") for whom "movement is always to be preferred to inaction" and whose quest is for "the
apocalyptic orgasm." The fundamental decision of the hipster's nature,
according to Mailer, is to seek "to open the limits of the possible for
oneself." The metaphysic of the hipster is a belief in "God who is It, who
is energy, life, sex, force, . . . the paradise of limitless energy and
perception just beyond the next wave of the next orgasm." For Mailer, the
hipster represents "the first wave of a second revolution in this century,
moving . . . toward being and the secrets of human energy." Parallels
with the character, conduct, and ideas of Dean Moriarty are unmistak-

able. Indeed, so similar are Kerouac's Moriarty and Mailer's hipster that the essay makes (unintentionally) one of the most perceptive criticisms ever written of *On the Road.*[4]

Kerouac was, however, dissatisfied with his rendering of Neal Cassady as Dean Moriarty, and a year after writing *On the Road,* he began another book in an attempt to more closely and completely delineate the man in whom he saw such heroic qualities. *Visions of Cody* is an ambitious and original novel that essays a total portrait of a human mind and soul from within and without. The author approaches Cody Pomeray (the novel's pseudonym for Neal Cassady) through a careful depiction of the places and scenes of his life, through a detailed account of Cody's boyhood and young manhood, through transcriptions of recorded conversations between himself and Cassady, and through abstract language and stream-of-consciousness imagery that attempts to communicate the very rhythms and sounds of Cody's soul.

Despite its beauty of expression and truth of observation, *Visions of Cody* fails to contribute substantially to the characterization of Cassady already achieved in *On the Road.* The endeavor testifies though to the complexity and significance that Kerouac sensed in Cassady and the intensity of his desire to record an accurate and comprehensive image of him.

Neal Cassady also appears (usually under the pseudonym of Cody Pomeray) in a number of Kerouac's subsequent works, components of *The Duluoz Legend,* though never again as a main character. Throughout Kerouac's writing he remains a somewhat ambiguous figure. In *Book of Dreams* (1961) he is a fearful presence—sullen, silent, cold. In the screenplay and film *Pull My Daisy* (1961) he appears as Milo, an essentially anarchic-poetic spirit trying to fulfill the demands of a working, family man. Cody makes a brief, minor appearance in *The Dharma Bums* and a more substantial one in *Desolation Angels* where he is still revered by the narrator as "a *believing* man" (*Desolation,* 138). Only in *Big Sur* is he a real presence again, his energy and his optimism undiminished—"a grand and ideal man" (55). But he has become something of a tragic figure to Kerouac, "a martyr of the American night," an ex-convict, reduced to grueling physical labor and later jobless (57). The narrator recognizes that Cody has failed to fulfill his enormous promise as a man. Watching him chop wood furiously but ineffectively, the narrator views the activity metaphorically—"vast but senseless strength, a picture of poor Cody's life" (84). Ultimately though, whatever his ambivalence and reservations about his hero, Cody remains for Kerouac an angel, "so much like St. Michael" (100), still emitting an angelic, golden aura, "that strange apocalyptic burst of gold" that seems to derive from "the golden top of heaven" (101). The spiritual energy of Cody's psyche far exceeds his occasional and minor failings as a man.

For the poet Allen Ginsberg, Neal Cassady represented a man in whom spiritual and sexual energies were harmonious and complementary — "the ultimate psycho-spiritual sexo-cock jewel fulfillment."[5] As such Cassady was an ideal to be celebrated, and after his death, elegized.

An important early Ginsberg poem in which Neal Cassady appears, as "N.C." and "Neal," is "The Green Automobile" from the collection *Reality Sandwiches: 1953–60.* The green automobile of the poem is the vehicle of the imagination, of poetic vision. Ginsberg acknowledges Cassady as "the greater driver" of that vehicle. Together in the green automobile, the poem affirms, they will ascend "the highest mount," driving up "the cloudy highway," and will attain a state of vision, experiencing time-in-eternity, discerning the eternal in the temporal. Ginsberg sees "N.C." as a "sexual angel" and a "native saint." He declares, "Neal, we'll be real heroes now / in a war between our cocks and time."[6]

A close parallel exists between the sort of homoerotic comradeship and visionary partnership that Ginsberg eulogizes in "The Green Automobile" and that celebrated by Whitman in his *Calamus* poems (1860) and prophesied in *Democratic Vistas* (1871): a redemptive, adhesive, democratic brotherhood, a "virile fraternity" of "manly love."[7] For Whitman such relationships would in time manifest themselves in America, counterbalancing the nation's materialistic tendencies, and would be of a character "fond and loving, pure and sweet, strong and life-long, carried to degrees hitherto unknown — not only giving tone to individual character, and making it unprecedentedly emotional, muscular, heroic and refined, but having the deepest relations to general politics."[8] Ginsberg also sees his relation to "N.C." in such terms, heralding an era of "princely gentleness" and "supernatural illumination" ("Green Automobile," *Sandwiches,* 14).

Neal Cassady is one of the dedicatees of Ginsberg's volume *Howl and Other Poems* and in the title poem figures prominently in the catalog of outcast and persecuted spiritual questers. As "N.C." he is named "secret hero of these poems" and celebrated as "cocksman and Adonis of Denver," a sensualist whose ultimate purpose in "ecstatic and insatiate" copulation is to achieve spiritual enlightenment (12). The poem "Wild Orphan," in the same collection, would also seem to be drawn from the life of Neal Cassady. The poem depicts an orphaned boy, lonely, growing up among "dead souls", but who "imagines cars / and rides them in his dreams" (42). He is a boy of rare spiritual power which will eventually find expression in "a cock, a cross, / an excellence of love" (43). As in "The Green Automobile," both poems of the *Howl* volume emphasize Cassady's role as "sexual angel," an embodiment of great sexual and spiritual energy without tension, division, or contradiction.

A theme similar to that of "Howl" informs Ginsberg's poem "The Names," collected in *As Ever, The Collected Correspondence of Allen Ginsberg and Neal Cassady,* which laments the deaths of American "saints," martyred by a materialistic-militaristic-rationalistic society. Cassady is named as one such martyr, condemned to a living death in the frustration, suppression, and gradual dissipation of his natural energies and joy. Again, the heroic proportions of Cassady as the "Angel" of desire and of "cock kindnesses," the "Lamb" of suffering, "patience & pain," are celebrated and are contrasted to the repressive and insensitive nature of the society in which he is abused and persecuted (211–12).

Cassady is elegized in a group of poems in *The Fall of America* in which Ginsberg assesses the personal significance and defines the larger metaphysical and social contexts of Neal Cassady's life and death. Cassady is seen in these poems as a hero of human consciousness and spirit whose thoughts and acts opposed maya (illusion, ignorance) and its manifestations: "If anyone had strength to hear the invisible / and drive thru Maya Wall / you *had* it."[9] The poems contrast the ephemerality of the maya manifestations, such as tyranny, violence, fear, and acquisitiveness, to the eternality of acts of tenderness, of passion, and of compassion, such as were performed by Cassady. In this respect Cassady's life was that of a teacher, a liberator. Ginsberg consoles himself for his sense of grief and loss with the discovery of a new dimension of personal relationship to Cassady: after the sometimes confused affections of "flesh forms," there is the endless, pure, and direct discourse of "spirit to spirit" ("Elegy for Neal Cassady," 77).

Interestingly, the work in which Neal Cassady is most unequivocally depicted as a mythic figure, a living legend, is neither fiction nor poetry, but Tom Wolfe's nonfictional *The Electric Kool-Aid Acid Test.* Wolfe's book is an account of the adventures of Ken Kesey and the Merry Pranksters in which Cassady is a central figure. Wolfe emphasizes in the book the religious nature of the group's experience, the parallels that may be drawn to the historical process of the foundation of new religions around the *Kairos,* or supreme experience, and its prophet. In Wolfe's account Kesey is clearly the prophet, but Cassady is both his precursor and his closest disciple.

At the outset Cassady is valued by the group only as "the holy primitive . . . the *natural,"* admired for his *On the Road* reputation but not (except by Kesey) esteemed intellectually.[10] Later, however, all reservations concerning him are forgotten, when as the driver of the Prankster bus, he exhibits exemplary resourcefulness and dependability and manifests his intuitive astuteness and spiritual understanding. As Kesey explains to the others, "Cassady doesn't have to think anymore" (160).

As a member of the "mystical brotherhood" of the Merry Pranksters, Cassady continues and consummates his role as the "HOLY GOOF" in *On the Road.* He distinguishes himself as a spiritual clown, a mystical acrobat, "a monologuist . . . spinning off memories, metaphors, literary, Oriental, hip allusions" (16–17), a mystagogue, a living parable, and a man in continual and rapid pursuit of "the westernmost edge of experience" (362).

Cassady's name in the Prankster group is "Speed Limit," in recognition not only of his driving skills but of his ability to approach the infinite present, the eternal now. As Wolfe explains there is "a sensory lag" built-in to the human mind: "the lag between the time your senses receive something and you are able to react. One thirtieth of a second is the time it takes, if you are not the most alert person alive, and most people are a lot slower than that. Now Cassady is right up against the $\frac{1}{30}$th of a second barrier. He is going as fast as a human can go . . ." (145). The Pranksters equate the "sensory lag" with the concept of samsara or maya of Eastern religions and the "Now" with satori or enlightenment: "It was as if Cassady, at the wheel, was in a state of satori, as totally into this very moment, Now, as a being can get . . ." (102).

This conception of time and being (a recurrent topic of Dean Moriarty in *On the Road* in his pursuit of IT) corresponds in many respects with Bergson's idea of "pure duration."[11] The self, according to Bergson, could, by means of a union of intellect and intuition achieve a state of consciousness in which its own inner essence and its identity with the cosmos, become fused in a single experience of perpetual becoming. A more direct parallel exists between Cassady's endeavor and that myth that the critic Leslie Fiedler finds central to American culture: "the hope of breaking through all limits and restraints, of reaching a place of total freedom. . . ."[12] For Cassady such a place is not geographical but a state of being. The manifest on the Prankster's bus, of which Cassady is driver, reads: "Furthur" and that is Cassady's spiritual destination: beyond the limitations of the body, beyond the restraints of the mind, and into the total freedom of pure being (69).

Cassady's role as catalyst is now extended to that of a cultural catalyst, his energies inspiring and helping to define the shape and direction of postwar American culture: "Here was Cassady between . . . [Kerouac and Kesey] . . . once the mercury for Kerouac and the Beat Generation and now the mercury for Kesey and the whole—what?—something wilder and weirder out on the road" (103).

Present at all the epiphanous moments of the Prankster experience — the cross-country bus trip, the Acid tests, exile in Mexico—Cassady helps bring the adventure to its termination by officiating at the Acid Graduation Ceremony. His death, occurring soon thereafter, concludes Wolfe's account of the Pranksters and lends a note of finality, and perhaps also of futility, to their endeavor.

A character based on Neal Cassady but considerably fictionalized, not drawn from life as in the previous works considered here, appears in Robert Stone's story "Porque No Tiene, Porque Le Falta." The character, named Willie Wings, is identifiable as a Cassady figure by his prodigious amphetamine use, his being "a very good driver," his pet parrot, his inspired monologues, and a number of other personal characteristics and attitudes.[13] But he is also endowed with attributes and traits that are entirely fictional, such as his possession of a pistol and his occasional aggressiveness and hostility.

Willie Wings, a middle-aged speed freak and ex-dealer, is an ambiguous character, though ultimately he may be seen as the moral center of the story. His friend Fencer considers him "an avatar" (203), while the main character of the story, Fletch, neither likes nor respects him, believing that "his mind is running off its reel" (203). For his part, Willie Wings does not like or respect Fletch either; he is contemptuous of Fletch as a "literary" type and accuses him of living "unawares," not living "the conscious life" (206). Wings considers Fletch "dead" in perception, "like a dead nerve in a tooth" (207).

The issues of the story are courage and imagination, known here in combination as "corazon." In the beginning Fletch lacks "corazon" utterly. He is paranoid and a heavy drinker whose chief wish is for stasis, constancy, and safety. Like the cockroach in the song "La Cucaracha" to which the title of the story refers, Fletch "doesn't want to travel on," so to speak, because he lacks the metaphorical marijuana of the imagination; that is, creative courage. In contrast to Fletch, Fencer and Willie Wings approach life with daring and fantasy, experiencing the world as a mystery, events as symbols to be read. Their lives are correspondingly enriched with hazard and adventure, dangers faced, and perils overcome. In the course of the story Fletch learns (or regains) the sort of "corazon" necessary to endure and prevail in life and thereby wins the respect of Willie Wings who pronounces, "I had you wrong, brother. You really are a poet" (226).

Willie Wings, as his name implies, maintains such a degree of grace and fluidity of thought and action that it may be likened to a flight through life, almost a transcendence of the conditions of living. Imagination (true poetry for him, not "literary" poetry) is the key to both physical and psychic survival for Willie Wings. He expresses his code or philosophy through the parable-anecdote that he relates (for Fletch's edification) concerning the man alone in the hotel room whose masturbation becomes an act of imagination and spiritual affirmation, an act of poetry. For Willie Wings boredom and inertia are far more dangerous than uncertainty and insecurity and surviving intact (with joy, humor, fantasy, style) far more important than merely surviving.

Neal Cassady also serves as the basis for Ray Hicks, the hero of Robert Stone's novel *Dog Soldiers*. Hicks is an idealized Cassady figure, fictionalized to a much greater extent than any previous character based on Cassady—a Cassady as he might have been. Nevertheless, Ray Hicks is clearly recognizable (as the author intends) as having cardinal aspects of his character and personal history inspired by those of Neal Cassady. He is a quintessential Cassady figure—perhaps in some measure a truer, deeper portrait than those drawn from life.

Hicks, like Dean Moriarty, has significant affinities with Mailer's "philosophical psychopath." (He is introduced in the novel reading a volume of Nietzsche, and a few pages later we learn that his closest friend considers him a psychopath.) He is, at once, a man of strict physical and mental discipline and yet impulsive, erratic; a man of scrupulous personal honor and honesty involved in immoral and illegal activities. Hicks thinks of himself as "a kind of samurai," "a serious man" who has chosen out of all the numberless illusions of the world "the worthiest illusion."[14]

Obvious parallels exist between the relation of Hicks to his former Zen Master, Dieter Bechstein, and that of Neal Cassady to Ken Kesey, as described in *The Electric Kool-Aid Acid Test*. Kesey's place at La Honda with its painted trees, outdoor mobiles, speakers and lights, is the model for Dieter's similarly equipped mountaintop *rosha* at El Incarnacion del Verbo, "the last crumbling fortress of the spirit" (274). The Merry Pranksters are fictionalized as and elevated to the brotherhood of "Those Who Are" (212).

As in the case of previous Cassady figures, Hicks is possessed of both physical and spiritual energy. Dieter says admiringly of him, "He was your natural man of Zen. . . . He was incredible. He acted everything out. There was absolutely no difference between thought and action for him. . . . It was exactly the same. An enormous self-respect. Whatever he believed in he had to embody absolutely" (271). Ultimately, Hicks assumes the role of a sacrificial figure, becoming "the pain carrier," the bearer of the suffering of the world (330). His death alone, walking on a desert railroad track (as Neal Cassady died), bearing his "weight" or burden, is his final sacrificial act, a fusion of his physical and spiritual disciplines.

Using the same man as inspiration, Robert Stone creates two disparate characters: Willie Wings and Ray Hicks. At the deepest level, however, they have in common their personal integrity and their advanced but imperfect spiritual development. In their different ways both men embrace "the worthiest illusion" (poetry for Wings, human love for Hicks) and actively oppose the agencies of negativity (the Sinister Pancho Pillow and such devils as Antheil and Danskin). And both Wings and Hicks share a fluidity of psyche, a quality of attunement with and attention to the total environment, the inner and the outer, the visible and the invisible worlds. They manifest a singular ability to maneuver in the moment, to respond quickly and correctly to the flow of events, to flow with the events. They have recognized the unpredictability of life, its lack of constants and fixities, and they have mastered the flux, knowing, though, that their mastery is only temporary, knowing that it must end, that defeat is ultimate and inevitable. In this recognition and in their response to the terms of life, Wings and Hicks share a code, a style which is, again, very similar to that of "Hip" as defined by Mailer. Both men act out of "a dialectical . . . dynamic conception of existence" in which the alternatives are "to stay cool or to flip," to control or to be defeated. Finally, only the particular strategies of Wings and Hicks differ. Their views of existence and the essential nature of their response to it are the same.

Neal Cassady is incarnated as "Sir Speed" Houlihan in two works by Ken Kesey: the play *Over the Border* and the short story "The Day after Superman Died." In the former he is a central figure, and in the latter he is the subject and the pivot of action and meaning, although he is present only in the memories and the minds of the other characters.

Over the Border is Ken Kesey's poeticized version of the experiences of himself and the Merry Pranksters, here called Devlin Deboree and the Animal Friends. The essential situations, events, and characters are clearly recognizable from Tom Wolfe's account but are here altered, embroidered, recombined. The title refers to the group's flight to and exile in Mexico and also to their state of consciousness, over the border of rational, ego consciousness and in the terra incognita of the personal subconscious and the collective unconscious. The title also suggests the ultimate goal of the group, a sort of neo-Nietzschean transcendence of the human condition, and may also be read as suggesting the nature of their failure, crossing over the border of common sense and human mercy into megalomania.

Houlihan is a key figure among the Animal Friends. His relation to Devlin Deboree is very similar to that of Lear's Fool to Lear. His earthy, antic metaphysics are the ballast of the group. His humor and sensuality represent a sense of proportion that counterbalances Deboree's insidious messianism. Houlihan's personal characteristics are very much those of some earlier Cassady figures: catalytic, kinetic, irrepressible in his energy, eloquent and humorous in his endless free-association monologues, resourceful, imperturbable in the face of adversity. His presence dispels stasis and immobility and inspires humor and courage. As Dieter said of Hicks, Houlihan embodies implicitly what he believes to the extent that he is a living parable. And in the manner of many of his fictional predecessors, he flows with events, maintaining a Taoist balance, participating simultaneously at the physical and metaphysical levels of existence.

Flight is the central motif of the play, in both of the principal meanings of the word: as escape and as movement through the air. The Animal Friends escape from the forces of law and authority (restraint and limitation) in the United States and in Mexico, and they rescue their comrades from imprisonment in Mexico. Their aim of transcendence is both an escape from the confinement of rational, ego consciousness and a soaring flight in the limitlessness of the Infinite Mind. Houlihan personifies the group experience of flight in both of these senses. He is imprisoned in Mexico but escapes from the prison into the sky (by means of a helicopter). And the group's ultimate failure in their quest for transcendence, their "aerodynamic error," as the play's narrative voice characterizes it, is epitomized by Houlihan's kite, which soars for a time but then, through a miscalculation, an overextension, plummets into the sea.[15] "Houlihan forlornly reeling the drowned carcass of the kite up the cliff, calling over his shoulder through a hole in the electronic noise: 'The sharks got 'im mates.'—holding aloft the bedraggled skeleton: 'I went out too far . . .'" (*Garage,* 157).

The question of whether or to what extent the Cassady figure is psychopathic arises again in *Over the Boarder* with reference to Alan Harrington's article—"some *Playboy* hack calling your buddy a psychopath" (*Garage,* 65). Kesey addresses the issue by allowing the deceased spirit of Houlihan to speak in his own defense. "Joyce was blind in one eye. Would you let James Joyce go down for posterity with Here Lies a One-Eyed Man as his only epitaph? Nothing about his style, his genius, his innovative influence?" (*Garage,* 65). Obviously, Kesey views this as a trivial matter, a minor imperfection at worst, and utterly irrelevant to the real significance of Houlihan's life. Through his Devlin Deboree persona, the author promises to consider this larger issue, the meaning of Houlihan's life, at some future date.

Kesey fulfills his promise to treat the significance of Houlihan's life in his story "The Day after Superman Died." The title refers to the death of Houlihan, and the narrative focuses on the consequences of his death for Devlin Deboree and by extension, for the world at large. The movement of the story is from denial to affirmation, from despair to renewal of faith. The central motif is the eye, or sight—obscured vision versus clear vision.

The story opens with images of death, conflict, weariness, sorrow, tension. It is a "blighted afternoon" of harsh, raw light and "eye-smiting smoke."[16] A day on which there seem to be "no satisfactory answers" to questions, doubts, and accusations, both external and internal (150). The imagery and the mood culminate in the revelation of Houlihan's death. For Deboree this knowledge is the final, ominous sign that "the movement," or "the revolution" in which he believes, is losing.

Far worse for Deboree is the apparent nonsense of Houlihan's final words: "Sixty-four thousand nine hundred and twenty-eight." Deboree is, in his despair, "begging for some banner to carry on with, some comforter of last-minute truth quilted by Old Holy Goof Houlihan, a wrap against the chilly moss to come." But Houlihan, "the Fastestman-alive," has left only "a psycho's cipher" (168). Deboree cannot avert the conclusion that Houlihan's senseless death invalidates all that had gone before: "That it had *all* been a trick, that he had never known purpose" (189).

The turning point of the narrative occurs when Deboree learns the circumstances of Houlihan's death, the context in which his last words were spoken. Drunk and doped, Houlihan had accepted a challenge to count the railroad ties between two Mexican villages; he died in the attempt. His last words were a record of the extent of his endeavor. For Deboree this knowledge constitutes "the banner" for which he had hoped: "Houlihan wasn't merely making noise: he was *counting*. He didn't lose it. We didn't lose it. We were all counting" (192). Such sudden renewal of hope and purpose precipitates a sort of satori or illumination in the stricken psyche of Deboree. He experiences a profound sense of acceptance, the joyous passivity and receptivity, the cosmic optimism that was Houlihan's message in life and his legacy in death.

In the context of Kesey's story, Houlihan is identified with "the movement," "the revolution," relating more to the Taoist term of the Great Awakening of the consciousness or the spirit rather than to the political sense of the terms. In the movement Houlihan is "Hero, High Priest of the Highway, . . . Hoper Springing Eternally" (176). Despite his failures and shortcomings, his life is seen as an example for others pursuing similar spiritual goals: "that faith that saw him through his lapses had become a faith for everybody that knew him, a mighty bridge to see them across their own chasms" (189).

The larger implications of the story seem to be that Houlihan is a key figure in an American (and international) cultural-philosophical-spiritual movement, that the movement is an important step in human evolution, and that this step represents, in turn, an important phase in cosmic evolution. In this manner, Kerouac's prophecy of Cassady as "a new kind of American saint," possessor of "the secret that we're all busting to find," would seem to have been fulfilled, a quarter of a century later, in Kesey's canonization of Houlihan.

The Cassady figure, as represented in the works of fiction, the poems and plays in which he appears, is protean, disparate. A common denominator of his various incarnations, however, would seem to be his psychic (consciousness and spirit) energy, which is manifested in one or another of its aspects in every appearance.

There is a clear development of the figure in terms of this psychic energy in the course of the works in which he is depicted. His movement is, to borrow Kerouac's image, from Beat to beatific. Hart Kennedy is obviously primarily a hedonist, but he is struggling toward an essentially mystical insight concerning time, consciousness, and reality. Dean Moriarty, though no less of a sensualist, is more pronouncedly mystical in orientation. He is a young man beginning to form his experiences and his perceptions into a new coherence. Ginsberg's "N.C." is a man who has resolved his contradictions, who has attained a degree of mastery in directing the poetic imagination—unequivocally a spiritual hero. Robert Stone's figures have achieved personal discipline and formulated codes by which they live. They are able to direct their thoughts and actions in accordance with what they perceive as the flow of existence. Tom Wolfe's "Speed Limit" Cassady and Ken Kesey's Houlihan represent the final unfolding of the character: the Holy Fool, the cosmic jester, master of the flow within and without, teacher of courage and faith.

What the Cassady figure represents in American literature and culture is a populist mysticism: the reemergence of a heterodox, syncretic, religious impulse that has previously found expression in such figures as Whitman and Henry Miller. The Cassady figure is an embodiment of transcendental primitivism—the American response to the cultural-spiritual crisis of Western civilization to which such movements as dadaism, surrealism, and existentialism have been the European response. His alliance with the renewing forces of the unconscious, his cultivation of surrational intelligence, his leverage through passivity, and his ability to determine the flow of events and to move with it closely resemble elements of various oriental, spiritual disciplines. In this sense the Cassady figure represents a marriage of West and East, helping to accomplish the spiritual circumnavigation of the globe prophesied by Whitman in his "Passage to India," evolving toward a new synthesis, a new paradigm. Whitman's admonition of "O farther, farther, farther sail" has become the manifest on the magic bus driven by the Fastestman-alive: "Furthur." The modes of locomotion (physical and metaphysical) may have altered greatly in the century between Whitman and Cassady, but the destination remains the same.

11

Conclusion

Passage indeed O soul
to primal thought
Walt Whitman
"Passage to India"

*D*iverse and variegated as they are in so many respects, the writers of the Beat Generation nevertheless possess a shared spirit and governing purpose that confers upon them a distinctive group identity. Among the most characteristic qualities and the most significant aspects of Beat literature are the affinities it possesses with elements of primitive ritual and archaic thought and with archetypal patterns of consciousness. These affinities with the primordial and the mythic are central to the Beat enterprise and essential to a more complete understanding of the nature of Beat writing and of its pertinence to the life of our times.

Since the time of the emergence of their writings during the late 1950s, the Beats have been assailed by critics for their primitivism.[1] Although the term has been applied invidiously to their writing, it is not inaccurate when it is understood in the context of the tradition of romantic primitivism that begins with Jean-Jacques Rousseau and in the line of the primitivist tradition in the visual arts which includes artists such as Gauguin, Picasso, Brancusi, Klee, and Pollock.

The Beats manifest primitivist tendencies and sympathies in their writing by affirming instinct, feeling, energy, the unconscious, and nonrational modes of intelligence and perception. Their art, in common with that of primitive cultures, often centers on the spirit of myth and magic and engages primal forces both creative and demonic; it is, like the mythico-ritual art of the archaic world, shaped by inner necessity and directed toward the psychic needs of the community. Additional primitivist attributes of Beat writing include its spontaneous and improvisatory character, its incorporation of elements of folk and popular culture, and its revivifying of the oral/aural tradition in poetry. The ends as well as the means of Beat literature are essentially primitivist for its fundamental aim may be said to be the recovery of the mythopoetic sensibility and sacramental vision as modes of relating to the world and to the cosmos.

Unlike their earlier counterparts in the visual arts, the Beats did not seek to emulate primitive magico-religious models but endeavored rather to rediscover within their own minds and spirits the same source of motive power and creative energy that animated primal art. In so doing they inevitably kicked over the traces of established literary taste and decorum, challenging all the received values, the accepted forms and inherited conventions, all the neat boundaries of formal, official literature. The Beats sought not so much new modes of expression as ends in themselves as they did a new idiom of consciousness. Necessitously, of course, the latter made imperative and proceeded from the former, so that both in terms of technique and theme, the Beat movement served to expand the parameters of American literature.

Before proceeding to a consideration of certain more specific aspects of Beat primitivism, it would be well to focus upon the particular juncture of circumstances to which their art is a response, the social and psychic conditions against which they reacted and rebelled.

The twentieth century has been an age of constant crisis, a time of permanent emergency, but the post–World War II era has seemed to many to represent the culmination of all the negative forces of Western civilization in a final, desperate state of ultimate terror and destructiveness. This condition may be seen as being threefold in nature, an interrelated and mutually reflective complex affecting every level of life: physical, psychological, and spiritual.

The physical menace is obvious and absolute: the impending danger of thermonuclear annihilation. The advent of the bomb seemed to represent the ultimate expression of Thanatos, the ascendancy of humankind's collective death wish, and seemed also to herald imminent apocalypse. Beat writing was (aside from science fiction) the earliest literature to register the new postwar, atomic malaise. Already in Jack Kerouac's first novel, *The Town and the City* (1950), the author presents a nightmare vision of the end of the world precipitated by "the atomic disease," a newly mutated deadly virus of decay: "The molecule will suddenly collapse, leaving just atoms, smashed atoms of people, nothing at all . . ." (*Town,* 198). In a similar manner, William S. Burroughs in his first novel, *Junkie* (1953), records a horrific vision of a postapocalyptic America. "One afternoon I closed my eyes and saw New York in ruins. Huge centipedes and scorpions crawled in and out of empty bars and cafeterias and drugstores on Forty-second Street. Weeds were growing up through cracks and holes in the pavement. There was no one in sight."[2]

Indeed, the image of the bomb and of its aftermath is pervasive in the literature of the Beat Generation. In "Howl" Allen Ginsberg writes of "listening to the crack of doom on the hydrogen jukebox" (*Howl,* 10), while in "America" the poet irately enjoins the nation: "Go fuck yourself with your atom bomb" (*Howl,* 31). Imagery of nuclear peril is recurrent also in Ginsberg's subsequent work, including his recent "Plutonian Ode."[3] Gregory Corso explored the terrors of atomic apocalypse in his extended poem "Bomb" which was shaped typographically upon the page in the ominous form of a mushroom cloud (*Birthday,* foldout between 32–33). Lawrence Ferlinghetti, who witnessed the hideous and shocking aftermath of Nagasaki at first hand, has also treated the theme of nuclear holocaust in his poetry, as for example in his collection *A Coney Island of the Mind* (1958) in which he depicts with comic horror the consequences of that fatal, final hour:

> when some cool clown
> > pressed an inedible mushroom button
> and an inaudible Sunday bomb
> > > fell down
> catching the president at his prayers
> > > on the 19th green
>
> > O it was a spring
> > > of fur leaves and cobalt flowers
> > when cadillacs fell thru the trees like rain
> drowning the meadows with madness
> while out of every imitation cloud
> > > dropped myriad wingless crowds
> > > > of nutless nagasaki survivors
> > And lost teacups
> > full of our ashes
> > floated by.

> (No. 4, *Coney,* 14)

At the psychological level the crisis manifested itself as an insidious dehumanization and depersonalization of life. One enduring effect of the involvement of the United States in the Second World War was the growth of governmental bureaucracy and of corporate power. These factors, together with such phenomena as urbanism, mass communications, increased industrialization, and the triumph of technology, tended to create a leveling or a standardization of persons and places, a homogenized culture. Postwar prosperity permitted commercialism and acquisitiveness to flourish on an unprecedented scale, further reinforcing a climate of consensus, conformity, and complacency. Seduced by the prospects of affluence and prestige, large numbers of potentially dissident elements such as writers, artists, and intellectuals allowed themselves to be absorbed into universities, the communications industry, into government institutions or government-sponsored think tanks. Motivated perhaps by a deep unconscious longing for respite and security after the trials and upheavals of the depression era and the war, as well as by a desire for distraction from the anxieties of the cold war, Americans seemed content to retreat into a sort of womblike, sugarplum world that was safe and sanitized, placid, and bland.

The Beats were of the first and the few in the postwar period to express disenchantment with what was to them, in Henry Miller's phrase, an "air-conditioned nightmare," and to voice indignant disapproval of what they perceived as "dominant material mechanical militarist Mammon money America."[4] The Beats were appalled by what they saw as the diminishment of human potential and freedom, the constriction of consciousness, and the insipid systematization of life in the United States. In flight from the sedentary suburbs, from cultural orthodoxy, and the corporate way of life, they sought to find a more authentic mode of existence on the margins of society, among the dispossessed, the minorities, the rejects, and the outcasts of the American way of life.

Allen Ginsberg denounced in his writing "an America gone mad with materialism, a police-state America, a sexless and soulless America," contrasting its deplorable present state with "the wild and beautiful America of the comrades of Whitman . . . the historic America of Blake and Thoreau where the spiritual independence of each individual was an America, a universe, more huge and awesome than all the abstract bureaucracies and Authoritative Officialdoms of the World combined."[5] Somewhere among the abundance and the affluence, Ginsberg reminded us, among the automobiles, the televisions, the household appliances, the hi-fi sets, the fallout shelters, the SAC bombers, and the nuclear missiles, we had misplaced or displaced "the lost America of love" ("A Supermarket in California," *Howl,* 24).

Lawrence Ferlinghetti likewise bewailed an America "of the immigrant's dream come too true / and mislaid / among the sunbathers" (No. 3, *Coney,* 13) and deplored an America whose noble founding ideals were travestied by

> freeways fifty lanes wide
> on a concrete continent
> spaced with bland billboards
> illustrating imbecile illusions of happiness.
>
> (No. 1, *Coney,* 9)

Jack Kerouac lamented the passing of the wide-open, rowdy, irrepressible American spirit, the "wild, selfbelieving individuality" that he recalled from his depression mill-town boyhood,[6] and he expressed his dismay at its supersession by the eerie quiescence of postwar suburbia where

> you take a walk some night on a suburban street and pass house after house on both sides of the street each with the lamplight of the living room shining golden, and inside the little blue square of the television, each living family riveting its attention on probably one show; nobody talking; silence in the yards; dogs barking at you because you pass on human feet instead of on wheels . . . it begins to appear like everybody in the world is soon going to be thinking the same way . . . electrified to the Master Switch. (*Dharma,* 83)

The image of a central control, a "Master Switch," by which a dehumanized population would be totally ruled and regulated was also employed by Kerouac in his short story "CITYCitycity," a dystopian vision of the future of the world extrapolated from certain alarming tendencies the author observed in American society during the mid-1950s. In "CITYCitycity" Kerouac envisioned a grim future in which a three-tiered steel city encircles the entire earth. The inhabitants of this colossal, overpopulated, mechanistic megapolis are utterly regimented and manipulated by a ruling elite by means of computers, tranquillizing drugs, mass media (Multivision), and "Deactivation," which is a surgical process of general psychic pacification comparable to a prefrontal lobotomy.[7] A parallel vision of dehumanizing control through the collusion of technology and government may be seen in William S. Burroughs' *Naked Lunch,* in particular in the episode of the "The Complete All-American De-Anxietized Man" and in the "Interzone" sections.[8]

The third dimension of the crisis of postwar civilization in the West is that of spiritual consciousness: the alienation of humankind from the sacred energies of the spirit within and the corresponding desacralization of life and of the natural world. Of course, this aspect of the predicament of contemporary humankind is not peculiar to our age; the sacramental vision has been under assault in our culture for centuries by the forces of secularism, rationalism, and materialism. Since the time of John Locke and David Hume, the latter orientation has been preponderant, checked only momently in its relentless advance by the harassment and sabotage carried out by poets, artists, and other visionary irregulars. In the twentieth century the secularist-rationalist-materialist position has established unrestricted dominion, all the more absolutely in the atomic age.

The victory of the rationalist-materialist mind has left a ravaged and stricken landscape within and without. The devastation that it has wrought may be seen in the fragmentation of the psyche; in the estrangement of humans and nature, of humankind and the sacred; in the polluted and despoiled natural environment; in the blighted cities; in the sterility of mechano-technological civilization; and in the pervasive sense of exhaustion and ennui, the hysteria and the frivolous futility that characterize contemporary life. In the face of such waste and ruin the issue of spiritual consciousness has assumed a new urgency and pertinence.

Most particularly in this level of our cultural emergency—the metaphysical anguish caused by loss of contact with the sources of grace and vision—are the writings of the Beat Generation rooted and responsive.

The primitivism of Beat writing thus represents both a critique of urban-industrial civilization and a search to recover authentic human identity, to rediscover the nexus that joins individual human beings, the human community, nature, and divinity. The writers of the Beat Generation have pursued this common goal in various ways in their lives and their work, but each in his own manner recapitulates primitive processes of spiritual transmutation that consist of initiatory ordeals resulting ultimately in communion with vital and cosmic forces.

The theme of initiation is recurrent in the literature of the Beat Generation. It becomes the informing motif of Jack Kerouac's twelve-novel series *The Duluoz Legend,* of Richard Fariña's *Been Down So Long, It Looks Like Up to Me,* and of the novels of John Clellon Holmes. Initiation is also a dominant motif in Allen Ginsberg's "Howl" and in much of his subsequent poetry, in William S. Burroughs' novels *Junkie* and *Queer* and in *The Yage Letters,* in the prose and poetry of Lawrence Ferlinghetti, in the writings of Michael McClure, and in the autobiographical essays of Gregory Corso.[9]

The separate quests of the several Beat writers, as depicted in their works, share certain significant attributes from which a composite figure of the Beat hero may be derived. Such a synthesis of the characters of Jack Duluoz, Andy Raffine, Paul Hobbes, Ginsberg's "angelheaded hipsters," Gnossos Pappadopoulis, Burroughs' William Lee, Pete of McClure's *The Mad Cub,* and other protagonists of Beat literature illuminate the essential myth of the Beat movement: the quest for identity and vision.

According to such a composite construct, the Beat hero begins as one who feels estranged from the community and the world; the character bears a secret psychic wound and endures punishments and humiliations (often self-inflicted) because of this otherness, this apartness. The hero embarks upon a quest, only half-aware of his motives for so doing or of the goal or object of the search. In the course of the journey the Beat hero transgresses taboos, suffers torments, encounters helpmates, pursues fleeting ecstasies and visions, experiences both adversity and minor epiphanies. The quest culminates in a descent into the infernal depths of the hero's own psyche where in confrontation with the individual's own demons and own darkness, disintegration of the self begins. At the most extreme point of this distress and despair the individual suddenly discovers an image, experiences a vision that embodies the hero's particular power. This power redeems and renews the person who then returns to the human community and to the world with a consciousness transformed by vision, as a human being of insight and of power.

The process of psychic transformation undergone by the Beat hero, the development from a Beat to a beatific state, possesses significant affinities both with the rites of individual initiation as practiced in tribal societies and with the shamanistic enactment of redemptive rites for the tribe as a whole and for the world.

"Initiation represents one of the most significant spiritual phenomena in the history of humanity," writes Mircea Eliade. For, he tells us, "It is through initiation that, in primitive and archaic societies, man becomes what he is and what he should be—a being open to the life of the spirit, hence one who participates in the culture into which he was born."[10] The means of such initiation involves most frequently a series of ordeals which must be successfully undergone by the candidate. These almost invariably include a ritual death of the candidate and resurrection or rebirth into a new mode of being. Initiation also involves an imparting to the candidate of the sacred mysteries of the tribe, the nature of the mystical relations between the tribe and the supernatural powers, together with the myths and rituals by which the spiritual life of the tribe is sustained.

The Beats did not appropriate nor imitate primitive prototypes but sought rather to rediscover and revive the motivating essence of primitive magico-religious ritual within themselves. Their separate initiations have, therefore, the character of improvisation, intuited, re-created out of the unconscious mind according to the individual psychic needs of each quester. But it is precisely by means of this process, unselfconscious and unpremeditated in nature, that their art, as the record of their ordeals and their illumination, attains authenticity, efficacy, and universality. The Beat quest for identity and vision corresponds in its essential features to the basic pattern and purpose of primitive initiatory structures, that is: the experience of primal terror, of the demonic, and of contact with vital energies and generative powers.

Initiation was not regarded as an end in itself by the writers of the Beat Generation but as a means to a universal liberation and a reactivation of latent creative powers that would ultimately effect a transformation of human consciousness. In this regard and because of the particular character of their individual initiations, the Beat writers possess important similarities with the shaman in primitive cultures.

The shaman in tribal societies functions as a healer and a seer, the bearer of the mysteries and the myth giver—at once preserving the ancient connections between the human world and the realm of the supernatural and the sacred and at the same time giving expression to the necessary communal myths of the time. Those who are called to the shamanic vocation are frequently equivocal persons within the tribe—sufferers from mental disorders, psychological crises, or other types of symbolic deficiencies. Indeed, as Mircea Eliade has observed: "What separates a shaman from a psychopath is that he succeeds in curing himself and ends by possessing a stronger and more creative personality than the rest of the community."[11]

The psychic crisis or illness that afflicts the future shaman represents the sign of the individual's election or call, while the sufferings attendant upon the particular disorder constitute the special initiatory ordeals requisite to becoming a shaman. In effect, one becomes a shaman by resolving one's crisis or curing oneself of one's malady.[12] The parallel of the shaman's crisis and self-cure with the experiences of the Beat writers is striking and significant. In the case of each individual Beat writer we can see that his life is characterized by a prolonged psychic crisis that is finally resolved by means of a sudden vision or insight, whereby he is healed and discovers (or receives) his particular technique or tool, an embodiment of his own innate sacred power, to be employed in the maintenance and expression of his vision. The crises may, of course, recur, necessitating further suffering, new vision, the acquisition of new magical tools and powers and thus serving to promote the attainment of a higher degree of initiation, of self-knowledge, and of spiritual development.

The magical tools and techniques that I have alluded to above include Kerouac's spontaneous prose, Burroughs' cut-up method, Ginsberg's improvised poetics, Corso's automaticism, McClure's beast language, Ferlinghetti's voice of the fourth person singular, and so forth. The common denominator of such techniques is their goal of circumventing or of breaking through the rational, logical intelligence, the ego consciousness, to establish contact with the unconscious mind, with the deepest levels of being. Such techniques have their counterparts in the use of vision-inducing drugs and the cultivation of oneiric, ecstatic, and trance states by shamans. (The above-named shamanistic practices have also found wide usage among the writers of the Beat Generation.)

The fundamental, universal task of the shaman is to sustain and to defend the sacred, to expand insight and perception, and by means of personal rebirth and redemption, to regenerate the life of the community and of the world. The rite of initiation represents the very essence of this endeavor. Joseph Campbell has noted that "the effect of the successful adventure of the hero is the unlocking and release again of the flow of life into the body of the world."[13] Eliade observes that "through the repetition, the *reactualization* of the traditional rites, the entire community is regenerated."[14]

This enhancement and enrichment of the life of the world through the ritual acts of individuals is possible because of the essentially unitive nature of all created forms, the intimate, reciprocal relation of the microcosm to the macrocosm. In this regard the ultimate aim of shamanism is the complete and total renewal of the world, the final defeat of the powers of evil, and the re-creation of the cosmos according to its original perfection—an enterprise of which individual initiation is the microcosmic model.

At a more specific level, the role of the shaman is, as Eliade has described it, "the defense of the psychic integrity of the community. [Shamans] . . . are pre-eminently the antidemonic champions; they combat not only demons and disease, but also the black magicians . . . shamanism defends life, health, fertility, the world of 'light', against death, diseases, sterility, disaster, and the world of 'darkness.' "[15]

The affinities of the writers of the Beat Generation with tribal shamans are deep and essential in character. Indeed, it might almost be said that the Beats have unconsciously assumed the role of neo-shamans to the tribe of the postatomic, cold war, Vietnam War generation. Certainly, the major themes of Beat literature correspond in significant respects with the functions and tasks of shamans in primitive cultures.

The Beats share with the shamans both ultimate and immediate aims; that is, final universal regeneration and renewal and the day-to-day struggle against the demons and the black magicians, the powers of darkness.

A central motif in the writing of Lawrence Ferlinghetti is the goal of recovering original unity of being, of helping to establish "a new visionary society," and the bringing about of "a new pastoral era," while towards that end, he opposes and exposes the agencies of tyranny, nationalism, war, exploitation, and materialism, the powers of darkness. Similarly, Gregory Corso prophesies and strives to effect a return to Arcadia, to a paradisical condition of ultimate beauty and innocence. Corso, too, resists and denounces all the forces of violence and "unlife" in all their many guises.

Likewise Gary Snyder works through his poetry and his essays to aid in the achievement of a new golden age "of ecological balance, classless society, social and economic freedom . . . [a return to] The Garden of Eden."[16] Michael McClure envisions the final end of "bio-alchemical revolt" as an ecstatic and transfiguring return to absolute ontological unity, while Allen Ginsberg, resolute opponent of the demons of violence, intolerance, cruelty, and injustice, pronounces the following personal prophesy:

> the wanderer returns
> from the west with his Powers,
> the Shaman with his beard
> in full strength,
> the longhaired Crank with subtle humorous voice
> enters city after city
>
> to kiss the eyes of your high school sailors
> and make laughing Blessing
> for a new Age in America.
>
> ("Kansas City to Saint Louis," *Fall,* 34)

Ginsberg also struggles against the black magicians of our day: the evil conspiracy he divines among elements of the government, the military, the media, and advertising to distort and falsify reality through the abuse and perversion of language. In *Planet News* (1968) the poet denounces these "Warlocks, Black magicians burning and cursing the Love-Books . . . casting spells from the shores of America / on the inland cities, lacklove-curses on our Eyes";[17] he inveighs against their "Black Magic language" and their "formulas for reality" and endeavors to exorcise their blighting curse upon contemporary history and the human spirit ("Witchita Vortex Sutra," 119). William S. Burroughs also labors to lift the malediction upon language and human perception imposed by the pernicious wizards of big business, bureaucracy, organized religion, and the media. His cut-up technique represents a campaign of counter-magic directed against the deceptions and falsehoods of their fraudulent reality. "The word of course is one of the most powerful instruments of control as exercised by the newspaper and images as well, there are both words and images in newspapers. . . . Now if you start cutting these up and rearranging them you are breaking down the control system."[18]

Burroughs postulates that after all the interlocking control systems have been overthrown, when all the black magic preconceptions and formulas that direct and restrict our consciousness have been nullified, humankind would at last be in a position to challenge the biological limitations of existence, to transcend the body and time, and to achieve perfect freedom of consciousness in infinite space.

Jack Kerouac fought the demons and the powers of darkness with compassion and contemplation, prayer and meditation. He taught in his writings and in his life the fundamental and perennial virtues of kindness and of reverence for all life, perceiving that compassion is the essence of all spiritual wisdom, uniting the Tree of Buddha and the Cross of Christ. He prayed for the redemption of the world and for the salvation of all sentient beings, formulating a simple creed by which to live: "Make it your own way, hurt no one, mind your own business and make your compact with God" (*Desolation,* 329).

Kerouac also prophesied what he called "the Apocalypse of the Fellahin," the redemption and renewal of humankind by "the essential strain of the basic primitive, wailing humanity that stretches in a belt around the equatorial belly of the world from Malaya to India the great subcontinent to Arabia to Morocco to the selfsame deserts and jungles of Mexico and over the waves to Polynesia to mystic Siam of the Yellow Robe and on around . . . the source of mankind and the fathers of it. . . . As essential as rocks in the desert are they in the desert of 'history'" (*Road,* 229–30). Final universal regeneration would occur, Kerouac believed, in a Great Awakening of all things in God.

Notwithstanding the different figures in which they image their visions, it is clear that the writers of the Beat Generation are engaged in the same endeavor: the discovery (or recovery) of a new (or primordial) mode of being and of seeing. They are working to effect a revolution of consciousness and perception, striving to repossess the visionary faculties latent in the mind and the spirit of humans. Accordingly, the Beat enterprise is concentrated upon revival of the mythopoetic sensibility and the aspiration to sacramental vision.

The mythopoetic sensibility may be defined as a conceptual process founded upon metaphorical perception and mythic ideation; sacramental vision is a mode of apprehension whereby the natural world is seen as animate, sentient, sacred, and of one essence, one being.

The mythopoetic sensibility, as it is manifested in the literature of the Beat Generation, is inherent in the propensity of the individual Beat authors for the creation or reactivation of myth as a primary mode of expression. Occurrences of Beat mythopoeia or of the utilization of myth by Beat writers include Allen Ginsberg's use of Hebrew and Hindu myth; Gregory Corso's employment of Egyptian and Near Eastern myth; the creation of personal mythologies by Lawrence Ferlinghetti, Jack Kerouac, Michael McClure, Richard Fariña, and William S. Burroughs; Gary Snyder's adaption of figures and motifs from Amerindian and Oriental myth; and Diane DiPrima's exploration of the wolf-goddess archetype in her *Loba* poems. In addition, nearly all of the Beat writers have drawn extensively from popular culture—including films, comic strips, the pulps, and other sources—to forge a contemporary communal mythology that is accessible and pertinent to a postwar reading public and which is both American and international in character.

Textual evidence for the motif of the quest for sacramental vision in the work of the Beat writers is abundant. Lawrence Ferlinghetti has written of "the wish to pursue what lies beyond the mind / . . . to move beyond the senses" ("After the Cries of Birds," *Secret,* 3), and he has recorded in his poetry glimpses and glimmers of such transcendent visions, expressed in rhythm and image that direct mystical awareness of "the secret meaning of things," which is characterized by beauty, joy, light, and a sense of wholeness. Gregory Corso has affirmed in his poetry the unceasing manifestations of the transcendent infinite in the world: "Many many are the occurrences of Light!" ("Greece," *Man,* 25). Corso has distilled his perception of the essential unity and divinity of all that exists into a single phrase: "Spirit / is Life" ("Spirit," *Herald,* 41).

Instances of a like mode of visionary awareness occur in the work of Michael McClure who describes the experience of ravishing sensory delight and radiance when "the interwoven topologies of reality" reveal themselves as a single absolute ontological unity, and the universe manifests itself as "the messiah."[19] Epiphanies of a nature markedly similar to the foregoing may be read in the novels of John Clellon Holmes, for example: Stofsky's vision in *Go* of the Divine Presence immanent in the created world—"an impersonal, yet somehow natural love, cementing the very atoms" (*Go,* 83); the ecstatic affirmations of the jazz musicians in *The Horn,* summed up in Edgar Pool's imperative of "Celebrate!" (*Horn,* 237); and in *Get Home Free,* May's rhapsodic vision of the ultimate wholeness and the beauty of life, her sense of the essential and abiding sanity of the natural world.

Jack Kerouac has written too, both in his novels and in his poetry, of moments of sudden illumination, occurrences of beatific consciousness that are characterized by the experience of deep joy and of metaphysical insight. In *The Dharma Bums,* for example, he describes such an instance:

> After a while my meditations and studies began to bear fruit. It
> really started in January, one frosty night in the woods in the dead

silence it seemed I almost heard the words said: "Everything is allright forever and forever and forever." I let out a big Hoo, one o'clock in the morning, the dogs leaped up and exulted. I felt like yelling it to the stars. I clasped my hands and prayed, "O wise and serene spirit of Awakenerhood, everything's allright forever and forever and forever and thank you thank you thank you amen." What'd I care about the tower of ghouls and sperm and bones and dust, I felt free and therefore I *was* free. (109)

Perhaps the most rapturous rendering of a state of sacramental vision, of the experience of the world seen anew *sub specie aeternitatis* among the writers of the Beat Generation, is Allen Ginsberg's poem "Footnote to Howl."

Holy! Holy! Holy! Holy! Holy! Holy! Holy! Holy! Holy!
    Holy! Holy! Holy! Holy! Holy! Holy!
The world is holy! The soul is holy! The skin is holy!
. . . .
Holy the sea holy the desert holy the railroad holy the locomotive
    holy the visions holy the hallucinations holy the miracles
    holy the eyeball holy the abyss!
Holy forgiveness! mercy! charity! faith! Holy! Ours! bodies! suffer-
    ing! magnanimity!
Holy the supernatural extra brilliant intelligent kindness of the
    soul!

(Howl, 21–22)

The art of the Beat Generation represents, then, an endeavor to counter the negative energies of the age with positive energies, to counter fear and hatred with celebration, to counter impercipience with vision, to counter black magic with white magic. Reviving in their writing such primitive techniques as chant rhythm, improvisational composition, oneiric imagery, and extralexical sounds, adopting breath and voice as poetic measures, and restoring the word as magico-religious force, the Beats enact rituals of regeneration and liberation. The purpose of their rites is to resacralize a desacralized age, to remythicize and revitalize consciousness and perception, to redeem life from the repressive structures and destructive powers that constrain and constrict its free expression, to reestablish the primacy of the intuitive intelligence, and to reawaken the vital, life-affirming impulses of the senses and the psyche.

In this manner, the literature of the Beat Generation is a reassertion of the essential, archaic function of art as embodiment of the sacred and as vehicle of communal myth and vision.

"The Poets of the Kosmos," wrote Walt Whitman, "advance through all interpositions and coverings and turmoils and strategems to first principles."[20] Clearly, this is what the writers of the Beat Generation are and what they have done. Out of the despair, the rage, and the ruin of our age, the Beats have created a testament of new hope and belief. They have been and they continue to be an energizing, redemptive force in our literature and in our culture.

Notes

Selected Bibliography

Index

Notes

1 Introduction

1. John Clellon Holmes, Introduction to *Go* (Mamaroneck, N.Y.: Paul P. Appel, 1977), xiii. Further parenthetical references are to this edition; when necessary for clarity page references are preceded by *Go*.

2. Jack Kerouac, "The Origins of the Beat Generation," *Playboy*, June 1969, 42.

3. Kerouac, "Origins," 42.

4. Jack Kerouac, *On the Road* (New York: Signet Books, 1958), 161. Further parenthetical references are to this edition; when necessary for clarity page references are preceded by *Road*.

5. The phrase "Beat Generation" also occurs in John Clellon Holmes' *Go* (New York: Scribner's, 1952). The first draft of *Go* was begun in August 1949 and read by Kerouac in 1951. Thus it is difficult to say in whose work the phrase first occurs. Holmes' book was published five years before *On the Road*, so the first appearance in print of the appellation "Beat Generation" is his, though Holmes has always acknowledged Kerouac's invention of the phrase.

6. F. Scott Fitzgerald, "My Generation," *Esquire*, October 1928.

7. Paul Bowles, "Foreign Intelligence: No More Djinns," *The American Mercury* 72 (June 1951): 654.

8. Henry Miller, *The Books in My Life* (London: Icon Books, 1963), 100.

9. Thomas Mann, Introduction to *The Short Novels of Dostoyevsky* (New York: Dial, 1945), vii.

10. Malcolm Cowley, "Some Dangers to American Writing," *The New Republic*, 22 November 1954.

11. Kenneth Rexroth, "Disengagement: The Art of the Beat Generation," *New World Writing* 11 (1957): 37.

12. Samuel Beckett, *Waiting for Godot* (London: Faber and Faber, 1956), 94.

13. Liner notes to the LP *Readings by Jack Kerouac on the Beat Generation* (Verve Records, 1959). See also Ann Charters, *A Bibliography of Works by Jack Kerouac* (New York: Phoenix Bookshop, 1967), 60.

14. Donald Allen, ed., *The New American Poetry: 1945–60* (New York: Grove, 1960).

LeRoi Jones, ed., *The Moderns: An Anthology of New Writing in America* (New York: Cornith Books, 1963).

Richard Seaver, Terry Southern, and Alexander Trocchi, eds., *Writers in Revolt* (New York: Frederick Fell, 1963).

Paris Leary and Robert Kelly, eds., *A Controversy of Poets* (Garden City, N.Y.: Doubleday, 1965).

Donald Allen and Robert Creeley, eds., *New American Story* (New York: Grove, 1965).

Donald Allen and Robert Creeley, eds., *The New Writing in the USA* (London: Penguin, 1967).

Stephen Berg and Robert Mezey, eds., *The New Naked Poetry* (Indianapolis: Bobbs-Merrill Co., 1969).

Donald Allen and Warren Tallman, eds., *The Poetics of the New American Poetry* (New York: Grove, 1973).

2 Circular Journey: Jack Kerouac's Duluoz Legend

1. Jack Kerouac, *Travel Diary 1948–49,* quoted in *A Creative Century* (Austin: Humanities Research Center, University of Texas), 35.

2. Joseph Campbell, *The Hero with a Thousand Faces* (New York: Meridian Books, 1956), 30.

3. David H. Miles, "The Picaro's Journey to the Confessional," *PMLA* 89 (October 1974): 980.

4. Jack Kerouac, *The Town and the City* (New York: Harvest Books, n.d.), 3. Further parenthetical references are to this edition; when necessary for clarity page references are preceded by *Town.*

5. Jack Kerouac, Prefatory note to *Big Sur* (New York: Bantam Books, 1963). Further parenthetical references are to this edition; when necessary for clarity page references are preceded by *Sur.*

6. "I broke loose from all that and wrote picaresque narratives. That's what my books are." Quoted in Charters, *Bibliography,* 4.

7. For example: "At the age of 24 I was groomed for the Western idealistic concept of letters from reading Goethe's *Dichtung und Wahrheit.*" Quoted in "Biographical Note," in *The New American Poetry: 1945–60* (New York: Grove,

1960). And: "I went on writing because my hero was Goethe. . . ." Kerouac, "Origins," 42.

8. See Gustaf Van Croumphout, "Melville as Novelist: The German Example," *Studies in American Fiction* 13 (Spring 1985), 31–34.

9. Jack Kerouac, *Visions of Cody* (New York: McGraw-Hill, 1972), 318. Further parenthetical references are to this edition; when necessary for clarity page references are preceded by *Cody.*

10. Jack Kerouac, *Doctor Sax* (New York: Grove, 1959), 49. Further parenthetical references are to this edition; when necessary for clarity page references are preceded by *Doctor.*

11. I am indebted to Gerald Nicosia for calling my attention to Kerouac's wordplay with "ding dong," though our interpretations of the pun are at variance. Nicosia interprets the pun as conjoining "the joy of body and spirit." See Gerald Nicosia, *Memory Babe: A Critical Biography of Jack Kerouac* (New York: Grove, 1983), 409.

12. Jack Kerouac, *Maggie Cassidy* (London: Panther Books, 1960), 50. Further parenthetical references are to this edition; when necessary for clarity page references are preceded by *Maggie.*

13. Jack Kerouac, *The Subterraneans* (New York: Grove, Black Cat, 1971), 1, 3. Further parenthetical references are to this edition; when necessary for clarity page references are preceded by *Subterraneans.*

14. Jack Kerouac, *Tristessa* (New York: Avon Books, 1960), 8. Further parenthetical references are to this edition; when necessary for clarity page references are preceded by *Tristessa.*

15. Jack Kerouac, *Visions of Gerard* (London: Mayflower-Dell, 1966), 7, 11. Further parenthetical references are to this edition; when necessary for clarity page references are preceded by *Gerard.*

16. Jack Kerouac, *The Dharma Bums* (New York: Signet Books, 1959), 6. Further parenthetical references are to this edition; when necessary for clarity page references are preceded by *Dharma.*

17. Jack Kerouac, *Desolation Angels* (New York: Bantam Books, 1966), 27. Further parenthetical references are to this edition; when necessary for clarity page references are preceded by *Desolation.*

18. Jack Kerouac, *Vanity of Duluoz* (London: Andre Deutsch, 1969), 257, 274–75. Further parenthetical references are to this edition; when necessary for clarity page references are preceded by *Vanity.*

3 Allen Ginsberg's "Howl": A Reading

1. William Olcott, *Myths of the Sun* (New York: G. P. Putnam's Sons, 1914), 57.

2. J. E. Circlot, ed., *A Dictionary of Symbols* (New York: Philosophical

Society, 1962), 218.

3. Allen Ginsberg, *Howl and Other Poems* (San Francisco: City Lights Books, 1956), 9. Further parenthetical references are to this edition; when necessary for clarity page references are preceded by *Howl*.

4. Jane Kramer, *Allen Ginsberg in America* (New York: Random House, 1967), 101.

5. "The brilliant Spaniard" can be identified in a Ginsberg anecdote recounted in the *Journals*. He describes a fleeting glimpse of a Latin man in Houston in 1948: "Electricity seemed to flow from his powerful body. . . . I never in my life saw a more perfect being—expression of vigor and potency and natural rage on face—." Allen Ginsberg, *Journals: Early Fifties, Early Sixties,* ed. Gordon Ball (New York: Grove, 1977), 19.

6. For earlier elegiac treatments of the martyred visionaries of "Howl" by Ginsberg, see also Barry Gifford, ed., *As Ever: The Collected Correspondence of Allen Ginsberg and Neal Cassady* (Berkeley: Creative Arts, 1977), 115, 208–12.

7. Allen Ginsberg, *To Eberhart from Ginsberg* (Lincoln, Mass.: Penmaen, 1976), 12.

8. Ginsberg, *To Eberhart,* 11.

9. Jack Kerouac, "The Philosophy of the Beat Generation," *Esquire,* March 1958, 24.

10. Neeli Cherkovski, *Ferlinghetti: A Biography* (Garden City, N.Y.: Doubleday, 1979), 99–100.

11. Andrew Welch, *Roots of the Lyric: Primitive Poetry and Modern Poetics* (Princeton: Princeton University Press, 1978), 196.

4 *The Gnostic Vision of William S. Burroughs*

1. R. Mcl. Wilson, *The Gnostic Problem* (London: A. R. Mowbray, 1958), 69.

2. Hans Jones, *The Gnostic Religion* (Boston: Beacon, 1958), 44.

3. Jones, 45.

4. Elaine Pagels, *The Gnostic Gospels* (New York: Random House, 1979), 49.

5. William S. Burroughs, "Notes on These Pages," *Transatlantic Review* 11 (Winter 1962): 7.

6. William S. Burroughs, *The Soft Machine,* 3d rev. ed. (London: Calder & Boyars, 1968), 144. Further parenthetical references are to this edition; when necessary for clarity page references are preceded by *Soft*.

7. William S. Burroughs, *The Ticket That Exploded,* rev. ed. (New York: Grove, 1967), 142. Further parenthetical references are to this edition; when necessary for clarity page references are preceded by *Ticket*.

8. Colin Wilson, *Voyage to a Beginning* (London: Woolf, 1969), 156.

9. Aldous Huxley, *The Doors of Perception* (London: Chatto and Windus, 1954), 16.

10. William S. Burroughs and Brion Gysin, *The Third Mind* (New York: Viking, 1978), 32.

11. Arthur Rimbaud, *Oeuvres complètes* (Paris: Éditions Gallimard, 1972), 106–11.

12. "I is another." "True life is elsewhere." Arthur Rimbaud, *Lettres du Voyant* (Paris: Librairie Minard, 1975), 113.

13. "The goal is to arrive at the unknown by means of the derangement of all the senses." "The poet makes himself into a seer by means of a long, immense and systematic derangement of all the senses." Rimbaud, *Letters,* 113, 137.

14. William S. Burroughs and Allen Ginsberg, *The Yage Lettres* (San Francisco: City Lights Books, 1963), 60–62.

15. Jonas, 63.

16. William S. Burroughs, "The Art of Fiction XXXVI, Interview with William Burroughs," *Paris Review* 35 (Fall 1965): 22–23.

17. Michael B. Goodman, *William S. Burroughs: An Annotated Bibliography* (New York and London: Garland, 1975), 88.

18. Sinclair Beiles et al., *Minutes to Go* (Paris: Two Cities, 1960), 13. Further parenthetical references are to this edition; when necessary for clarity page references are preceded by *Minutes.*

19. William S. Burroughs, "Operation: Soft Machine," *Outsider* 1 (Fall 1961): 73.

20. Eric Mottram, *William Burroughs: The Algebra of Need* (London: Marion Boyars, 1977), 71.

21. William S. Burroughs, "The Beginning Is Also the End," *Transatlantic Review* 14 (Autumn 1963): 5–8.

22. Burroughs, "Notes," 7.

23. Pagels, 50.

24. Burroughs and Gysin, *Third Mind,* 44.

25. G. Van Groningen, *First Century Gnosticism: Its Origins and Motifs* (Leiden, Netherlands, 1967), 105.

26. J. Guitton, *Great Heresies and Church Councils* (New York: Harper & Row, 1965), 53.

27. Gary Snyder, *Earth House Hold* (New York: New Directions, 1969), 105. Further parenthetical references are to this edition; when necessary for clarity page references are preceded by *Earth.*

28. Géza Róheim, *The Origin and Function of Culture,* Nervous and Mental Disease Monographs, no. 69 (New York: n.p., 1943), 51.

29. Pagels, 152.

30. William S. Burroughs, "The Future of the Novel," *Transatlantic Review* 11 (Winter 1962): 6.

5 *"The Arcadian Map"*: Notes on the Poetry of Gregory Corso

1. Gregory Corso, "Power," in *The Happy Birthday of Death* (New York: New Directions, 1960), 75, 78. Further parenthetical references are to this edition; when necessary for clarity page references are preceded by *Birthday.*

2. Gregory Corso, "Biographical Note," in *The New American Poetry: 1945–60.* ed. Donald Allen (New York: Grove, 1960), 429–30.

3. Gregory Corso, *Gasoline* (San Francisco: City Lights Books, 1958). Further parenthetical references are to this edition; when necessary for clarity page references are preceded by *Gasoline.*

4. Samuel Taylor Coleridge, *Biographia Literaria,* vol. 1, ed. J. Shawcross (London: Oxford University Press, 1907), 202.

5. Percy Bysshe Shelley, *A Defense of Poetry,* in *The Complete Works of Percy Bysshe Shelley,* vol. 7, ed. Roger Ingpen and Walter E. Peck (London: Ernest Benn Ltd., 1965), 137.

6. Gavin Selerie, *The Riverside Interviews: 3, Gregory Corso* (London: Binnacle, 1982), 23.

7. James McKenzie, "An Interview with Gregory Corso," in *The Beat Diary,* ed. Arthur Knight and Kit Knight (California, Pa.: The Unspeakable Visions of the Individual, 1977), 24.

8. Gaston Bachelard, *On Poetic Imagination and Reverie,* trans. Colette Gaudin (Indianapolis: Bobbs-Merill Co., 1971), 19.

9. Selerie, 43.

10. Desmond King-Hele, *Shelley: His Thought and Work* (New York: Macmillan, 1971), 203.

11. King-Hele, 367.

12. King-Hele, 369.

13. John Fuller, "The Poetry of Gregory Corso," *The London Magazine,* n.s. 1 (April 1961), 74.

14. Gregory Corso, "Variations on a Generation," in *A Casebook on the Beat,* ed. Thomas Parkinson (New York: Thomas Y. Crowell, 1961), 95–96. Reprinted from *Gemini* 2 (Spring 1959): 47–51.

15. Fredric Jameson, *The Political Unconscious* (Ithaca, N.Y.: Cornell University Press, 1981), 183–84.

16. Gregory Corso, *The Vestal Lady on Brattle,* facsimile ed. (San Francisco: City Lights Books, 1969), 1. Further parenthetical references are to this edition; when necessary for clarity page references are preceded by *Lady.*

17. For a close reading of "In the Fleeting Hand of Time," see Carolyn Gaiser, "Gregory Corso: A Poet, the Beat Way," in *A Casebook on the Beat,* 266–75.

18. Shelley, 140.

19. See McKenzie, 9.

20. Eric Fromm, *Escape from Freedom,* (New York: Rinehart & Co., 1960), 157.

21. See Selerie, 30.

22. Gregory Corso, *Long Live Man* (New York: New Directions, 1962), 10. Further parnthetical references are to this edition; when necessary for clarity page references are preceded by *Man.*

23. Gregory Corso, *Elegiac Feelings American* (New York: New Directions, 1962), 37. Further parenthetical references are to this edition; when necessary for clarity page references are preceded by *Elegiac.*

24. Gregory Corso, *Herald of the Autochthonic Spirit* (New York: New Directions, 1981), 5. Further parenthetical references are to this edition; when necessary for clarity page references are preceded by *Herald.*

25. Gregory Corso, "Some of My Beginning . . . And What I Feel Right Now," in *Poets on Poetry,* ed. Howard Nemerov (New York, 1966), 175.

6 Homeward from Nowhere: Notes on the Novels of John Clellon Holmes

1. John Clellon Holmes, *The Horn* (London: Jazz Book Club, 1961), 15, 18, 21. Further parenthetical references are to this edition; when necessary for clarity page references are preceded by *Horn.*

2. John Clellon Holmes, *Get Home Free* (London: Corgi Books, 1966), 13. Further parenthetical references are to this edition; when necessary for clarity page references are preceded by *Home.*

7 From the Substrate: Notes on the Work of Michael McClure

1. Michael McClure, *The Mad Cub* (New York: Bantam Books, 1970), 3. Further parenthetical references are to this edition; when necessary for clarity page references are preceded by *Mad.*

2. Michael McClure, "2 for Theodore Roethke," *Poetry* 87 (January 1965): 218, 219.

3. Dante, *The Inferno,* trans. John Ciardi (New York: New American Library, 1964), 149–50.

4. Letter to the author from Michael McClure, 19 May 1986.

5. Michael McClure, "Mystery of the Hunt," in *Hymns to St. Geryon and Other Poems* (San Francisco: Auerhahn, 1959), 2. Further parenthetical references are to this edition; when necessary for clarity page references are preceded by *Hymns.*

6. Michael McClure, Untitled poem in *The New Book / A Book of Torture* (New York: Grove, 1961), 7. Further parenthetical references are to this edition; when necessary for clarity page references are preceded by *Torture.*

7. Michael McClure, *Dark Brown* (San Francisco: Auerhahn, 1961). Further parenthetical references to this unpaginated edition are cited in text as *Dark*.

8. McClure letter, 19 May 1986.

9. Michael McClure, Preface to *Hymns to St. Geryon & Dark Brown*, combined ed. (San Francisco: Grey Fox, 1979), ix. Printed also as "Statement on Poetics," in *The New American Poetry: 1945–60*, ed. Donald Allen (New York: Grove, 1960), 421–44.

10. Michael McClure, *Meat Science Essays*, 2d enl. ed. (San Francisco: City Lights Books, 1970), 77. Further parenthetical references are to this edition; when necessary for clarity page references are preceded by *Meat*.

11. Michael McClure, No. 50, in *Ghost Tantras* (San Francisco: Four Seasons Foundation, 1969), 57. Further parenthetical references are to this edition; when necessary for clarity page references are preceded by *Ghost*.

12. Michael McClure, "Program Notes for First Production of *The Blossom, or Billy the Kid*, in *The Mammals* (San Francisco: Cranium, 1972), 3. Further parenthetical references are to this edition; when necessary for clarity page references are preceded by *Mammals*.

13. Michael McClure, *The Blossom, or Billy the Kid*, in *The Mammals*, 13.

14. Michael McClure, *!The Feast!*, in *The Mammals*, 46.

15. Michael McClure, *The Beard* (San Francisco: Coyote, 1967), 12, 10. Further parenthetical references are to this edition; when necessary for clarity page references are preceded by *Beard*.

16. Michael McClure, *Poisoned Wheat* (San Francisco: Oyez, 1965), 17. Further parenthetical references are to this edition; when necessary for clarity page references are preceded by *Wheat*.

17. Michael McClure, Prefatory note to "The Surge," in *Selected Poems* (New York: New Directions, 1986), 22. Further parenthetical references are to this edition; when necessary for clarity page references are preceded by *Poems*.

18. Michael McClure, Foreword to *Rare Angel* (Los Angeles: Black Sparrow, 1974). Further parenthetical references are to this edition; when necessary for clarity page references are preceded by *Rare*.

19. Michael McClure, "Pieces of Being," in *Scratching the Beat Surface* (San Francisco: North Point, 1982), 125–27.

20. Michael McClure, "For James B. Rector," in *September Blackberries* (New York: New Directions, 1974), 7. Further parenthetical references are to this edition; when necessary for clarity page references are preceded by *September*.

21. Michael McClure, *Jaguar Skies* (New York: New Directions, 1975), 59. Further parenthetical references are to this edition; when necessary for clarity page references are preceded by *Jaguar*.

22. Michael McClure, *Gargoyle Cartoons* (New York: Delacorte, 1971).

23. Michael McClure, *Gorf* (New York: New Directions, 1976), 70. Further

parenthetical references are to this edition; when necessary for clarity page references are preceded by *Gorf.*

24. Michael McClure, *Antechamber and Other Poems* (New York: New Directions, 1978), 1. Further parenthetical references are to this edition; when necessary for clarity page references are preceded by *Antechamber.*

25. Michael McClure, *Fragments of Perseus* (New York: New Directions, 1983), 1. Further parenthetical references are to this edition; when necessary for clarity page references are preceded by *Fragments.*

26. Aniela Jaffé, "Symbolism in the Visual Arts," in *Man and His Symbols,* ed. Carl G. Jung (New York: Dell, 1968), 266.

27. William Wordsworth, Preface to *Lyrical Ballads* by Wordsworth and Samuel Taylor Coleridge, ed. R. L. Brett and A. R. Jones (London: Methuen, 1963), 254.

8 *Toward Organized Innocence: Richard Fariña's* Been Down So Long It Looks Like Up to Me

1. See, for example, such studies as R. W. B. Lewis, *The American Adam* (Chicago: University of Chicago Press, 1955); David W. Noble, *The Eternal Adam and the New World Garden* (New York: Braziller, 1968); and Ihab Hassan, *Radical Innocence* (Princeton: Princeton University Press, 1961).

2. Richard Fariña, *Been Down So Long It Looks Like Up to Me* (New York: Dell Books, 1967), 19. Further parenthetical references are to this edition; when necessary for clarity page references are preceded by *Down.*

3. For an extended treatment of the subject of Winnie the Pooh as heroic exemplar of innocent wisdom, the interested reader is referred to Benjamin Hoff, *The Tao of Pooh* (London: Methuen, 1982).

4. Concerning Richard Fariña's own preoccupation with the monkey demon and other demons, see Joan Baez, "Child of Darkness," in *Daybreak* (New York: Dial, 1968), 129–36.

9 *The "Spiritual Optics" of Lawrence Ferlinghetti*

1. Lawrence Ferlinghetti, *Her* (New York: New Directions, 1960), 9, 10. Further parenthetical references are to this edition; when necessary for clarity page references are preceded by *Her.*

2. Joseph L. Henderson, "Ancient Myths and Modern Man," in *Man and His Symbols,* ed. Carl G. Jung (New York: Dell, 1968), 110.

3. M. L. von Franz, "The Process of Individuation," in *Man and His Symbols,* 178.

4. Franz, 183.

5. Jolande Jacobi, *The Psychology of C. G. Jung,* rev. ed. (New Haven: Yale University Press, 1962), 111–12.

6. Franz, 196.

7. Lawrence Ferlinghetti, *Unfair Arguments with Existence* (New York: New Directions, 1963), 3. Further parenthetical references are to this edition; when necessary for clarity page references are preceded by *Unfair.*

8. Lawrence Ferlinghetti, *Routines* (New York: New Directions, 1964), 1. Further parenthetical references are to this edition; when necessary for clarity page references are preceded by *Routines.*

9. Lawrence Ferlinghetti, No. 2, in *Pictures of the Gone World* (San Francisco: City Lights Books, 1955). Further parenthetical references to this unpaginated edition are cited in text by poem number and when necessary for clarity followed by *Pictures.*

10. Lawrence Ferlinghetti, No. 3, in *A Coney Island of the Mind* (New York: New Directions, 1958), 13. Further parenthetical references are to this edition; when necessary for clarity page references are preceded by *Coney.*

11. Lawrence Ferlinghetti, *Starting from San Francisco* (New York: New Directions, 1961), 61–62. Further parenthetical references are to this edition; when necessary for clarity page references are preceded by *Starting.*

12. Lawrence Ferlinghetti, *The Secret Meaning of Things* (New York: New Directions, 1968), 18. Further parenthetical references are to this edition; when necessary for clarity page references are preceded by *Secret.*

13. Lawrence Ferlinghetti, *Open Eye, Open Heart* (New York: New Directions, 1973), 5. Further parenthetical references are to this edition; when necessary for clarity page references are preceded by *Open.*

14. Lawrence Ferlinghetti, *Who Are We Now?* (New York: New Directions, 1976), 4–5. Further parenthetical references are to this edition; when necessary for clarity page references are preceded by *Who.*

10 Friendly and Flowing Savage: The Literary Legend of Neal Cassady

1. Franz, 183.

2. Ann Charters, *Kerouac, A Biography* (San Francisco: Straight Arrow Books, 1973), 286–87.

3. W. H. Auden, "Today's Wonder-World Needs Alice," in *Aspects of Alice,* ed. Robert Phillips (London: Victor Gollancz, 1972), 8.

4. Norman Mailer, *The White Negro* (reprint, San Francisco: City Lights Books, 1957).

5. Allen Ginsberg, "The Art of Poetry VII," *The Paris Review* 10 (Spring 1966): 36.

6. Allen Ginsberg, *Reality Sandwiches: 1953–60* (San Francisco: City Lights Books, 1963), 11–16. Further parenthetical references are to this edition; when necessary for clarity page references are preceded by *Sandwiches.*

7. Walt Whitman, *Complete Poetry and Selected Prose and Letters* (London:

Nonesuch, 1971), 110.

8. Whitman, 710.

9. Allen Ginsberg, "Elegy for Neal Cassady," in *The Fall of America* (San Francisco: City Lights Books, 1972), 75. Further parenthetical references are to this edition; when necessary for clarity page references are preceded by *Fall.*

10. Tom Wolfe, *The Electric Kool-Aid Acid Test* (New York: Farrar, Straus & Giroux, 1968), 63. Further parenthetical references are to this edition; when necessary for clarity page references are preceded by *Electric.*

11. Henri Bergson, *Creative Evolution,* trans. Arthur Mitchell (New York: Modern Library, 1944), 218.

12. Leslie Fiedler, *Love and Death in the American Novel* (London: Palladin, 1970), 135.

13. Robert Stone, "Porque No Tiene, Porque La Falta," *New American Review* 6 (April 1969): 203. Further parenthetical references are to this edition; when necessary for clarity page references are preceded by "Porque."

14. Robert Stone, *Dog Soldiers* (Boston: Houghton Mifflin, 1974), 168. Further parenthetical references are to this edition; when necessary for clarity page references are preceded by *Dog.*

15. Ken Kesey, *Over the Border,* in *Kesey's Garage Sale* (New York: Viking, 1973), 151. Further parenthetical references are to this edition; when necessary for clarity page references are preceded by *Garage.*

16. Ken Kesey, "The Day after Superman Died," *Spit in the Ocean* 6 (1981), 147. Further parenthetical references are to this edition; when necessary for clarity page references are preceded by "Day."

11 Conclusion

1. See, for example, Norman Podhoretz, "The Know-Nothing Bohemians," *Partisan Review* 25 (Spring 1958): 305–11, 313–16, 318, and Robert Brustein, "The Cult of Unthink," *Horizon* 1 (September 1958): 38–44, 134–35.

2. William S. Burroughs, *Junkie* (New York: Ace Books, 1960), 40. Further parenthetical references are to this edition; when necessary for clarity page references are preceded by *Junkie.*

3. Allen Ginsberg, "Plutonian Ode," in *Plutonian Ode: Poems 1977–1980* (San Francisco: City Lights Books, 1982), 11–18. Further parenthetical references are to this edition; when necessary for clarity page references are preceded by *Plutonian.*

4. Lawrence Ferlinghetti, "Genesis of after the Cries of Birds," in *The Poetics of the New American Poetry,* ed. Donald Allen and Warren Tallman (New York: Grove, 1973), 447.

5. Allen Ginsberg, "Poetry, Violence and the Trembling Lambs," *The Village Voice,* 25 August 1959, 8.

6. Jack Kerouac, "Origins," 42.

7. Jack Kerouac, "CITYCitycity," in *The Moderns: An Anthology of New Writing in America,* ed. LeRoi Jones (New York: Corinth Books, 1963), 250–65; previously published as "The Electrocution," *Nugget* 4 (August 1959): 12–14, 57–60.

8. William S. Burroughs, *Naked Lunch* (New York: Grove, Black Cat, 1966).

9. Gregory Corso, "Moschops! You Are a Loser!" *Nugget* 7 (October 1962): 52–53, 66; "Notes from the Other Side of April," *Esquire,* July 1964, 86–87, 110; "The Times of the Watches," *Cavalier,* December 1964, 36–37, 92–94; "Between Childhood and Manhood," *Cavalier,* January 1965, 36–37; "When I Was Five I Saw a Dying Indian," *Evergreen Review* 48 (August 1967): 28–30, 83–87.

10. Mircea Eliade, *Myths, Rites and Symbols: A Mircea Eliade Reader,* vol. 1 and 2, ed. Wendell C. Beane and William G. Doty (New York: Harper & Row, 1976), 1; 169.

11. Mircea Eliade, *A History of Religious Ideas,* vol. 1 (Chicago: University of Chicago Press, 1982), 366.

12. See Mircea Eliade, Chapter 5, "Heroic and Shamanic Initiations," in *Rites and Symbols of Initiation* (New York: Harper & Row, 1975), 81–102.

13. Campbell, 40.

14. Eliade, *Myths, Rites and Symbols,* vol. 1, 170.

15. Eliade, *Myths, Rites and Symbols,* vol. 2, 280.

16. Snyder, 109–10.

17. Allen Ginsberg, "Television Was a Baby Crawling toward That Death-chamber," in *Planet News* (San Francisco: City Lights Books, 1968), 23.

18. William S. Burroughs, *The Job: Interviews with Daniel Odier* (New York: Grove, 1974), 33.

19. McClure, "Pieces of Being," 125–27.

20. Walt Whitman, Preface to 1855 *Leaves of Grass,* in *Prose Works 1892,* ed. Floyd Stovall (New York: New York University Press, 1964), 450.

Selected Bibliography

Allen, Donald, ed. *The New American Poetry: 1945–60.* New York: Grove, 1960.

Allen, Donald, and Robert Creeley, eds. *New American Story.* New York: Grove, 1965.

————. *The New Writing in the USA.* London: Penguin, 1967.

Allen, Donald, and Warren Tallman, eds. *The Poetics of the New American Poetry.* New York: Grove, 1973.

Auden, W. H. "Today's Wonder-World Needs Alice." In *Aspects of Alice,* edited by Robert Phillips, 3–12. London: Victor Gollancz, 1972.

Bachelard, Gaston. *On Poetic Imagination and Reverie.* Translated by Colette Gaudin. Indianapolis: Bobbs-Merrill Co., 1971.

Baez, Joan. "Child of Darkness." In *Daybreak,* 129–36. New York: Dial, 1968.

Beckett, Samuel. *Waiting for Godot.* New York: Faber and Faber, 1956.

Beiles, Sinclair, William S. Burroughs, Gregory Corso, and Brion Gysin. *Minutes to Go.* Paris: Two Cities, 1960.

Berg, Stephen, and Robert Mezey, eds. *The New Naked Poetry.* Indianapolis: Bobbs-Merrill Co., 1969.

Bergson, Henri. *Creative Evolution.* Translated by Arthur Mitchell. New York: Modern Library, 1944.

Bowles, Paul. "Foreign Intelligence: No More Djinns." *The American Mercury* 72 (June 1951): 650–58.

Brustein, Robert. "The Cult of Unthink." *Horizon* 1 (September 1958): 38–44, 134–35.

Burroughs, William S. "The Art of Fiction XXXVI, Interview with William Burroughs." *Paris Review* 35 (Fall 1965): 13–49.

————. "The Beginning Is Also the End." *Transatlantic Review* 14 (Autumn 1963): 5–8.

————. "The Future of the Novel." *Transatlantic Review* 11 (Winter 1962): 6–7.

————. *The Job: Interviews with Daniel Odier.* New York: Grove, 1974.

————. *Junkie.* New York: Ace Books, 1953. Reprint. New York: Ace Books, 1960.

————. *Naked Lunch.* Paris: Olympia, 1959. Reprint. New York: Grove, 1962.

————. "Notes On These Pages." *Transatlantic Review* 11 (Winter 1962): 7–8.

————. "Operation: Soft Machine." *Outsider* 1 (Fall 1961). 74–77.

————. *The Soft Machine.* Paris: Olympia, 1961. 3d rev. ed. London: Calder & Boyars, 1968.

————. *The Ticket That Exploded.* Paris: Olympia, 1962. rev. ed. New York: Grove, 1967.

Burroughs, William S., and Allen Ginsberg. *The Yage Letters.* San Francisco: City Lights Books, 1963.

Burroughs, William S., and Brion Gysin. *The Third Mind.* New York: Viking, 1978.

Campbell, Joseph. *The Hero with a Thousand Faces.* New York: Bollingen Foundation, 1949. Reprint. New York: Meridian Books, 1956.

Charters, Ann. *A Bibliography of Works by Jack Kerouac.* New York: Phoenix Bookshop, 1967.

————. *Kerouac: A Biography.* San Francisco: Straight Arrow Books, 1973.

Cherkovski, Neeli. *Ferlinghetti: A Biography.* Garden City, N.Y.: Doubleday, 1979.

Circlot, J. E., ed. *A Dictionary Of Symbols.* New York: Philosophical Society, 1962.

Coleridge, Samuel Taylor. *Biographia Literaria.* Vol. 1. Edited by J. Shawcross. London: Oxford University Press, 1907.

Corso, Gregory. "Between Childhood and Manhood." *Cavalier,* January 1965, 36–37.

————. "Biographical Note." In *The New American Poetry: 1945–60,* edited by Donald Allen, 429–30. New York: Grove, 1960.

————. *Elegiac Feelings American.* New York: New Directions, 1962.

————. *Gasoline.* San Francisco: City Lights Books, 1958.

————. *The Happy Birthday of Death.* New York: New Directions, 1960.

————. *Herald of the Autochthonic Spirit.* New York: New Directions, 1981.

————. *Long Live Man.* New York: New Directions, 1962.

————. "Moschops! You Are a Loser!" *Nugget* 7 (October 1962): 52–53, 66.

————. "Notes from the Other Side of April." *Esquire,* July 1964, 86–87, 110.

————. "Some of My Beginning . . . And What I Feel Right Now." In *Poets on Poetry,* edited by Howard Nemerov, 172–81. New York, 1966.

―――. "The Times of the Watches." *Cavalier,* December 1964, 36–37, 92–94.

―――. "Variations on a Generation." *Gemini* 2 (Spring 1959), 47–51. Reprinted in *A Casebook on the Beat,* edited by Thomas Parkinson, 88–97. New York: Thomas Y. Crowell, 1961.

―――. *The Vestal Lady on Brattle.* Cambridge, Mass.: Richard Brukenfeld, 1955. Reprint facsimile ed. San Francisco: City Lights Books, 1969.

―――. "When I Was Five I Saw a Dying Indian." *Evergreen Review* 48 (August 1967): 28–30, 83–87.

Cowley, Malcolm. "Some Dangers to American Writing." *The New Republic,* 22 November 1954.

Croumphout, Gustaf Van. "Melville as Novelist: The German Example." *Studies in American Fiction* 13 (Spring 1985): 31–44.

Dante. *The Inferno.* Translated by John Ciardi. New York: New American Library, 1964.

Eliade, Mircea. *A History of Religious Ideas.* Vol. 1. Chicago: University of Chicago Press, 1982.

―――. *Myths, Rites and Symbols: A Mircea Eliade Reader.* Vol. 1 and 2. Edited by Wendell C. Beane and William G. Doty. New York: Harper & Row, 1976.

―――. "Heroic and Shamanic Initiations." In *Rites and Symbols of Initiation,* 81–102. New York: Harper & Row, 1975.

Fariña, Richard. *Been Down So Long It Looks Like Up to Me.* New York: Random House, 1966. Reprint. New York: Dell Books, 1967.

Ferlinghetti, Lawrence. *A Coney Island of the Mind.* New York: New Directions, 1958.

―――. "Genesis of after the Cries of Birds." In *The Poetics of the New American Poetry,* edited by Donald Allen and Warren Tallman, 445–552. New York: Grove, 1973.

―――. *Her.* New York: New Directions, 1960.

―――. *Open Eye, Open Heart.* New York: New Directions, 1973.

―――. *Pictures of the Gone World.* San Francisco: City Lights Books, 1955.

―――. *Routines.* New York: New Directions, 1964.

―――. *The Secret Meaning of Things.* New York: New Directions, 1968.

―――. *Starting from San Francisco.* New York: New Directions, 1961.

―――. *Unfair Arguments with Existence.* New York: New Directions, 1963.

―――. *Who Are We Now?* New York: New Directions, 1976.

Fiedler, Leslie. *Love and Death in the American Novel.* New York: Criterion Books, 1960. Reprint. London: Palladin, 1970.

Fitzgerald, F. Scott. "My Generation." *Esquire,* October 1928.

Franz, M. L. von. "The Process of Individuation." In *Man and His Symbols,* edited by Carl G. Jung, 157–254. New York: Dell, 1968.

Fromm, Eric. *Escape from Freedom.* New York: Rinehart & Co., 1960.

Fuller, John. "The Poetry of Gregory Corso." *The London Magazine,* n.s. 1, April 1961: 74–77.

Gaiser, Carolyn. "Gregory Corso: A Poet, the Beat Way." In *A Casebook on the Beat,* edited by Thomas Parkinson, 266–75. New York: Thomas Y. Crowell, 1961.

Gifford, Barry, ed. *As Ever: The Collected Correspondence of Allen Ginsberg and Neal Cassady.* Berkeley: Creative Arts, 1977.

Ginsberg, Allen. "The Art of Poetry VII." *The Paris Review* 10 (Spring 1966).

———. *As Ever: The Collected Correspondence of Allen Ginsberg and Neal Cassady.* Edited by Barry Gifford. Berkeley: Creative Arts, 1977.

———. *The Fall of America.* San Francisco: City Lights Books, 1972.

———. *The Gates of Wrath: Rhymed Poems 1948–1952.* New York: Grey Fox, 1972.

———. *Howl and Other Poems.* San Francisco: City Lights Books, 1956.

———. *Journals: Early Fifties, Early Sixties.* Edited by Gordon Ball. New York: Grove, 1977.

———. *Planet News.* San Francisco: City Lights Books, 1968.

———. *Plutonian Ode: Poems 1977–1980.* San Francisco: City Lights Books, 1982.

———. "Poetry, Violence and the Trembling Lambs." *The Village Voice,* 25 August 1959. Reprinted in *The Poetics of the New American Poetry,* edited by Donald Allen and Warren Tallman, 331–33. New York: Grove, 1973.

———. *Reality Sandwiches: 1953–60.* San Francisco: City Lights Books, 1963.

———. *To Eberhart from Ginsberg.* Lincoln, Mass.: Penmaen, 1976.

Goodman, Michael B. *William S. Burroughs: An Annotated Bibliography.* New York and London: Garland, 1975.

Groningen, G. Van. *First Century Gnosticism: Its Origins and Motifs.* Leiden, Netherlands, 1967.

Guitton, J. *Great Heresies and Church Councils.* New York: Harper & Row, 1965.

Hassan, Ihab. *Radical Innocence.* Princeton: Princeton University Press, 1961.

Henderson, Joseph L. "Ancient Myths and Modern Man." In *Man and His Symbols,* edited by Carl G. Jung, 95–156. New York: Dell, 1968.

Hoff, Benjamin. *The Tao of Pooh.* London: Methuen, 1982.

Holmes, John Clellon. *Get Home Free.* New York: Dutton, 1964. Reprint. London: Corgi Books, 1966.

———. *Go.* New York: Scribners, 1952. Reprint. Mamaroneck, N.Y.: Paul P. Appel, 1977.

———. *The Horn.* New York: Random House, 1958. Reprint. London: Jazz Book Club, 1961.

Huxley, Aldous. *The Doors of Perception.* London: Chatto and Windus, 1954.

Jacobi, Jolande. *The Psychology of C. G. Jung.* rev. ed. New Haven: Yale University Press 1962.

Jaffé, Aniela. "Symbolism in the Visual Arts." In *Man and His Symbols,* edited by Carl G. Jung, 255–322. New York: Dell, 1968.

Jameson, Fredric. *The Political Unconscious.* Ithaca, N.Y.: Cornell University Press, 1981.

Jonas, Hans. *The Gnostic Religion.* Boston: Beacon, 1958.

Jones, LeRoi, ed. *The Moderns: An Anthology of New Writing in America.* New York: Corinth Books, 1963.

Jung, Carl G. *Contributions to Analytical Psychology.* New York, 1929.

Kerouac, Jack. *Big Sur.* New York: Farrar, Straus, and Cudahy, 1962. Reprint. New York: Bantam Books, 1963.

———. "Biographical Note." In *The New American Poetry: 1945–60,* edited by Donald Allen. New York: Grove, 1960.

———. "CITYCitycity." In *The Moderns: An Anthology of New Writing in America,* edited by LeRoi Jones, 250–65. New York: Corinth Books, 1963. Published as "The Electrocution." In *Nugget* 4 (August 1959): 12–14, 57–60.

———. *Desolation Angels.* New York: Coward-McCann, 1965. Reprint. New York: Bantam Books, 1966.

———. *The Dharma Bums.* New York: Viking, 1958. Reprint. New York: Signet Books, 1959.

———. *Doctor Sax.* New York: Grove, 1959.

———. *Maggie Cassidy.* New York: Avon Books, 1959. Reprint. London: Panther Books, 1960.

———. *On the Road.* New York: Viking, 1957. Reprint. New York: Signet Books, 1958.

———. "The Origins of the Beat Generation." *Playboy,* June 1959, 31–32, 42, 79.

———. "The Philosophy of the Beat Generation." *Esquire,* March 1958, 24, 26.

———. *Readings by Jack Kerouac on the Beat Generation.* Verve Records, 1959.

———. *The Subterraneans.* New York: Grove, 1958. Reprint. New York: Grove, Black Cat, 1971.

———. *The Town and the City.* New York: Harcourt Brace Jovanovich, 1950; Reprint. New York: Harvest Books, n.d.

———. *Travel Diary 1948–49.* Excerpted in *A Creative Century,* 35–36. Austin: Humanities Research Center, University of Texas, 1964.

———. *Tristessa.* New York: Avon Books, 1960.

———. *Vanity of Duluoz.* New York: Coward-McCann, 1968. Reprint. London: Andre Deutsch, 1969.

———. *Visions of Cody.* New York: McGraw-Hill, 1972.

———. *Visions of Gerard.* New York: Farrar, Straus, 1963. Reprint. London: Mayflower-Dell, 1966.

Kesey, Ken. "The Day after Superman Died." *Esquire* (Oct. 1979). Reprinted in *Spit in the Ocean* 6 (1981): 147–94.

———. *Kesey's Garage Sale.* New York: Viking 1973.

King-Hele, Desmond. *Shelley: His Thought and Work.* New York: Macmillan, 1971.

Kramer, Jane. *Allen Ginsberg in America.* New York: Random House, 1967.

Leary, Paris, and Robert Kelley, eds. *A Controversy of Poets.* Garden City, N.Y.: Doubleday, 1965.

Lewis, R. W. B. *The American Adam.* Chicago: University of Chicago Press, 1955.

McClure, Michael. *Antechamber and Other Poems.* New York: New Directions, 1978.

———. *The Beard.* Berkeley: Oyez, 1965. Reprint. San Francisco: Coyote, 1967.

———. *Dark Brown.* San Francisco: Auerhahn, 1961.

———. *Fragments of Perseus.* New York: New Directions, 1983.

———. *Gargoyle Cartoons.* New York: Delacorte, 1971.

———. *Ghost Tantras.* Privately printed, 1964. Reprint. San Francisco: Four Seasons Foundation, 1969.

———. *Gorf.* New York: New Directions, 1976.

———. *Hymns to St. Geryon & Dark Brown.* San Francisco: Grey Fox, 1979.

———. *Hymns to St. Geryon and Other Poems.* San Francisco: Auerhahn, 1959.

———. *Jaguar Skies.* New York: New Directions, 1975.

———. Letter to author, 19 May 1986.

———. *The Mad Cub.* New York: Bantam Books, 1970.

———. *The Mammals.* San Francisco: Cranium, 1972.

———. *Meat Science Essays.* 2d enl. ed. San Francisco: City Lights Books, 1970.

———. *The New Book / A Book of Torture.* New York: Grove, 1961.

———. "Pieces of Being." In *Scratching the Beat Surface,* 123–34. San Francisco: North Point, 1982.

———. *Poisoned Wheat.* San Francisco: Oyez, 1965.

———. *Rare Angel.* Los Angeles: Black Sparrow, 1974.

———. *Selected Poems.* New York: New Directions, 1986.

———. *September Blackberries.* New York: New Directions, 1974.

———. *Star.* New York: Grove, 1970.

———. "Statement on Poetics." In *The New American Poetry 1945–60,* edited by Donald Allen, 421–44. New York: Grove, 1960.

———. "2 for Theodore Roethke." *Poetry* 87 (January 1965): 218–19.

McKenzie, James. "An Interview with Gregory Corso." In *The Beat Diary,* edited by Arthur Knight and Kit Knight, 4–24. California, Pa.: The Unspeakable Visions of the Individual, 1977.

Mailer, Norman. *The White Negro.* Reprint. San Francisco: City Lights Books, 1957.

Mann, Thomas. Introduction to *The Short Novels of Dostoyevsky.* New York: Dial, 1945.

Miles, David H. "The Picaro's Journey to the Confessional." *PMLA* 89 (October 1974): 980–92.

Miller, Henry. *The Books in My Life.* New York: New Directions, 1951. Reprint. London: Icon Books, 1963.

Mottram, Eric. *William Burroughs: The Algebra of Need.* London: Marion Boyars, 1977.

Nicosia, Gerald. *Memory Babe: A Critical Biography of Jack Kerouac.* New York: Grove, 1983.

Noble, David W. *The Eternal Adam and the New World Garden.* New York: Braziller, 1968.

Olcott, William. *Myths of the Sun.* New York: G. P. Putnam's Sons, 1914.

Pagels, Elaine. *The Gnostic Gospels.* New York: Random House, 1979.

Podhoretz, Norman. "The Know-Nothing Bohemians." *Partisan Review* 25 (Spring 1958): 308–11, 313–16, 318.

Rexroth, Kenneth. "Disengagement: The Art of the Beat Generation." *New World Writing* 11 (1957): 28–41.

Rimbaud, Arthur. *Lettres du Voyant.* Paris: Librairie Minard, 1975.

———. *Oeuvres complètes.* Paris: Éditions Gallimard, 1972.

Róheim, Géza. *The Origin and Function of Culture.* Nervous and Mental Disease Monographs, no. 69. New York: n.p., 1943.

Seaver, Richard, Terry Southern, and Alexander Trocchi, eds. *Writers in Revolt.* New York: Frederick Fell, 1963.

Selerie, Gavin. *The Riverside Interviews: 3, Gregory Corso.* London: Binnacle, 1982.

Shelley, Percy Bysshe. *A Defense of Poetry.* In *The Complete Works of Percy Bysshe Shelley.* Vol. 7. Edited by Roger Ingpen and Walter E. Peck. London: Ernest Benn Ltd., 1965.

Snyder, Gary. *Earth House Hold.* New York: New Directions, 1969.

Stone, Robert. *Dog Soldiers.* Boston: Houghton Mifflin, 1974.

———. "Porque No Tiene, Porque La Falta." *New American Review* 6 (April 1969): 189–226.

Welch, Andrew. *Roots of the Lyric: Primitive Poetry and Modern Poetics.* Princeton: Princeton University Press, 1978.

Whitman, Walt. *Complete Poetry and Selected Prose and Letters.* London: Nonesuch, 1971.

———. *Prose Works 1892.* Edited by Floyd Stovall. New York: New York University Press, 1964.

Wilson, Colin. *Voyage to a Beginning.* London: Woolf, 1969.

Wilson, R. Mcl. *The Gnostic Problem.* London: A. R. Mowbray, 1958.

Wolfe, Tom. *The Electric Kool-Aid Acid Test.* New York: Farrar, Straus & Giroux, 1968.

Wordsworth, William, and Samuel Taylor Coleridge. *Lyrical Ballads.* Edited by R. L. Brett and A. R. Jones. London: Methuen, 1963.

Index